THE STREET SMART MBA

10 PROVEN STRATEGIES FOR DRIVING BUSINESS SUCCESS

Steve Babitsky
James J. Mangraviti, Jr.

The Street Smart MBA: 10 Proven Strategies for Driving Success

ISBN-13 (pbk): 978-1-4302-4767-8
ISBN-13 (electronic): 978-1-4302-4768-5

President and Publisher: Paul Manning
Acquisitions Editor: Morgan Ertel
Editorial Board: Steve Anglin, Mark Beckner, Ewan Buckingham, Gary Cornell, Louise Corrigan, Morgan Ertel, Jonathan Gennick, Jonathan Hassell, Robert Hutchinson, Michelle Lowman, James Markham, Matthew Moodie, Jeff Olson, Jeffrey Pepper, Douglas Pundick, Ben Renow-Clarke, Dominic Shakeshaft, Gwenan Spearing, Matt Wade, Tom Welsh
Coordinating Editor: Rita Fernando
Copy Editor: Judy Levine
Compositor: Bytheway Publishing Services
Indexer: SPi Global
Cover Designer: Anna Ischenko

Distributed to the book trade worldwide by Springer Science+Business Media New York, 233 Spring Street, 6th Floor, New York, NY 10013. Phone 1-800-SPRINGER, fax (201) 348-4505, e-mail orders-ny@springer-sbm.com, or visit www.springeronline.com. Apress Media, LLC is a California LLC and the sole member (owner) is Springer Science + Business Media Finance Inc (SSBM Finance Inc). SSBM Finance Inc is a Delaware corporation.

For information on translations, please e-mail rights@apress.com, or visit www.apress.com.

Apress and friends of ED books may be purchased in bulk for academic, corporate, or promotional use. eBook versions and licenses are also available for most titles. For more information, reference our Special Bulk Sales–eBook Licensing web page at www.apress.com/bulk-sales.

Any source code or other supplementary materials referenced by the author in this text is available to readers at www.apress.com. For detailed information about how to locate your book's source code, go to www.apress.com/source-code/.

Contents

About the Authors

Steve Babitsky is the Founder and President of SEAK, Inc., a professional education, training, consulting, and publishing company. Under Mr. Babitsky's leadership, SEAK has grown into a multi-million dollar national enterprise that caters to physicians, engineers, accountants, lawyers, and other professionals. Prior to his involvement with SEAK, Mr. Babitksy was a personal injury litigator and the managing partner of the law firm of Kistin, Babitsky, Latimer, and Beitman, which he grew into the most successful personal injury firm on Cape Cod. During this time, Mr. Babitsky also founded the National Organization for Social Security Claimants' Representatives, an association of over 4,000 attorneys and other advocates who represent Social Security and Supplemental Security Income claimants. Throughout his career, Mr. Babitsky has been a successful serial entrepreneur. He has co-authored over twenty books with James J. Mangraviti, Jr., including *Never Lose Again: Become a Top Negotiator by Asking the Right Questions.*

James J. Mangraviti, Jr., is Principal of SEAK, Inc., a professional education, training, consulting, and publishing company. In that capacity, he trains hundreds of expert witnesses each year through SEAK's scheduled programs for expert witnesses, invited presentations, and customized expert witness training programs presented to corporations, associations, and governmental agencies. A former litigator with experience in defense and plaintiff personal injury law and insurance law, Mr. Mangraviti is a prolific writer and has co-authored more than twenty books with Steve Babitsky, including *Never Lose Again: Become a Top Negotiator by Asking the Right Questions.*

Introduction

When I was eight years old, my family and I moved from a tenement that we shared with extended family members to a low-income housing project in the Lower East Side of New York City. To give you a sense of the place, every day I came home I had to make a potential life or death decision: how to get to my family's apartment on the twelfth floor. The problem with taking the elevator was that you never knew which drug addict, robber, or homicidal maniac was going to jump on at the last minute, giving you no chance of escape. I could take the stairs and have a better chance of escape, but I would still have to run the gauntlet of homeless people, cat-sized rats, heroin addicts, and assorted violent criminals to get home.

Let me give more of a flavor. One day when I was 11 or 12 years old, I was mugged at knifepoint. I handed over all my money and the muggers left. Being mugged was such a common occurrence in my neighborhood that I did not even bother to tell my parents.

I resolved early on in my life that I was going to work hard not only to escape the poverty of my childhood but later to be able to offer my own kids a better life than I had growing up. I wanted to control my own destiny and that of my family, so I left the projects and went to law school. After a few years spent working for other lawyers, I decided that the best way for me to succeed was to start and run my own law firm. Then, while I was still running my law firm, I resolved to diversify my income and do something different, so I started SEAK, Inc. (www.seak.com). SEAK is a continuing education, training, consulting, and publishing business that I founded in 1980 and continue to run with my family. Despite my lack of formal business training or business degrees, the two successful businesses I started and run have provided independence and financial security for me and my family for more than 30 years.

In 1992 I hired my business partner, Jim, and I quickly found that Jim and I saw eye to eye on the fundamentals of running a business—so much so that we are writing this book together. We both believe in executing the highest quality work, focusing on the customer like a laser beam, thinking long term, treating people fairly, having fun, not borrowing money freely, and not betting the farm or trying to defy the laws of gravity or common sense. Get-rich-quick schemes, living beyond our means, aggressive accounting, and creative financing are as repugnant to Jim as they are to me. We became a great team in no time.

* * *

The worldwide economic meltdown that started in 2008 happened in part because the leaders of the financial world and the top-ranking executives of big businesses in our country and others, many of whom have MBAs from top universities, seemed to have forgotten the basic tenets of good business. These well-intentioned, Ivy League trained geniuses were taught "sophisticated" business concepts that closely mirrored a sample curriculum from a leading business school's website, which claims that its MBA students will gain an in-depth understanding of their vision, values, motivations, and definitions of success; understand a framework for developing an integrated life plan; develop a language to communicate their life plan with those who are important to them; and reflect on entrepreneurial life. Remember, we do not have MBAs. What we have is a 30-plus-year track record of running successful businesses that are profitable year in and year out. We have little time for "reflecting," "developing languages," or worrying about our "vision." And in today's super-charged and high-speed business world, who really does? It is time to throw away your MBA—or save $150,000 and two years of your life by not getting one in the first place—and learn how to run a profitable business from experienced and successful businesspeople who pride themselves on their rock-solid ethics and practices.

Borrowing heavily, being financed by incomprehensible financial instruments, buying on margin, ignoring real profits and the needs of customers, being dependent on bankers, listening to economists who are no more accurate than fortune tellers and who have never run a business—these practices have failed dramatically and will, we hope, become things of the past. Businesspeople responsible for making critical business decisions can no longer afford to rely on business books with mice looking for cheese, fables with obscure lessons, hokey manifestos, lessons from businesses that have gone bankrupt, case studies from 30 years ago, feel-good bromides and general drivel. These so-called business innovators got us into the ongoing economic crisis in the first place. Sensible and time-proven, successful business strategies will get us out of it.

Businesspeople need a practical, down-to-earth, realistic, and easy-to-understand book that explicitly shows them how to seize control of their own financial futures—and our goal is that *The Street Smart MBA* will be that resource for you. Our over 50 combined years of in-the-trenches business experience have allowed us to organize and teach what we have learned about how to succeed in business into ten easy steps. They are:

- Step 1: Build a Superb Brand

  How do you develop a strong brand that will turn your customers into a highly motivated, no-cost sales force, allowing you to employ premium pricing, and building value in your brand and business?

- Step 2: Grow and Tap Your Network

  How do you obtain priceless assistance for your business without paying a dime for it?

- Step 3: Develop Products Customers Love

  How do you identify, evaluate, and develop ideas for new products and services?

- Step 4: Sell Your Products and Services Cost Effectively

  How do you maximize your sales revenue while keeping your marketing costs under control?

- Step 5: Control Your Costs and Increase Your Productivity

  How will spending less and running your business more efficiently help you improve your bottom line?

- Step 6: Take Charge

  How can you keep focused on making money and managing risk?

- Step 7: Recruit, Motivate, and Retain a Superior Workforce

  How do you get maximum productivity out of your staff while at the same time treat people well?

- Step 8: Deal With Customer Complaints Head-On

  How do you turn your critics into fans?

- Step 9: Manage Yourself

  How can you improve your business' bottom line by better managing yourself?

- Step 10: Become a Better Negotiator

  How can you improve your business' bottom line by refining your negotiating skills?

The Street Smart MBA teaches you how to be independent and self-reliant; carry little or no debt; develop and retain inexpensive and loyal labor; market your products in a cost effective and safe manner; build long-term relationships; mitigate risk; meet and exceed the needs, interests, desires, and passions of your customers; build a world-class brand; and make a profit each and every year. Why? Because the fact of the matter is that the vast majority of new businesses fail. Those that survive do so because their management is able to learn from its mistakes. In the more than 30 years we have spent running our business, Jim and I have made innumerable mistakes and have learned from each and every one of them. Our real-world experience from the school of hard knocks has been the best possible business education we could have hoped for, and we would not trade our experiences for an MBA from any school in the world. After all, a person's true business education only begins after one leaves college and graduate school, which is why we will only teach you business concepts that have been tested and proven in the field. Our techniques represent business reality, not academic theory.

Our goal is for *The Street Smart MBA* to help you avoid the mistakes we have made and teach you how to implement the techniques and insights that have helped make our business successful. Quite simply, we will teach you the practical, real-world lessons that it took us more than 30 years to learn. We have written *The Street Smart MBA* so that those who own or help manage a business or business unit will be able to immediately apply our numerous bottom-line suggestions to increase sales and decrease costs.

We have read many business books that focus on game theory, regression analysis, heavy quantitative analysis, and other supposedly high-level concepts. The problem we found with such abstract "approaches" is that they make many of these books torturously boring, often incomprehensible, and therefore ultimately useless. We were never trained to talk like an MBAer, and we have no desire to. You will not find any charts, graphs, or differential equations in this book. What you will find instead are practical, easy-to-understand, simply explained, and proven strategies for business success. Furthermore, we break each of the strategies we are discussing down into its own concise and easy-to-understand chapter. Each strategy is tangible and is reinforced with one or more real-world examples of how it works and why, and each chapter begins with a brief executive summary.

Jim and I also like to have fun. Trying things out, working through problems, and inventing new products are remarkably stimulating processes for us. We enjoy needling each other in our frequent, frank debates on to how to proceed with a variety of business matters. Humor is memorable, so we have decided to include our own experiences in this book to give you a flavor of the funny and memorable comments and occurrences that actually happened. We hope that you find *The Street Smart MBA* to be refreshingly easy to read, understand, and apply.

Summary of Summaries

Chapter 1. Build a Superb Brand

Build your brand through an intense focus on quality.

The most effective marketing tool your business will have is word-of-mouth marketing. Focus intensely on the quality of your products and you will reap great benefits from positive word of mouth. Think long term. When in doubt, do whatever it takes to protect the quality of your brand.

Turn down business that risks damaging your brand.

Knowing when and how to turn down work can substantially help you build your brand and your business. Be very careful about accepting work outside of your sandbox, work that you do not have the time to do properly, or work that would otherwise damage your brand. Do not get into lines of business that will likely dilute and possibly tarnish your brand.

Define and reinforce your brand with a well thought out tagline.

A tagline gives you the opportunity to define your brand. Choose it carefully, as your tagline will have an important effect on both your brand and your bottom line.

Treat your customers with respect and do not jerk them around.

An easy and feel-good way to help your business succeed is to build a rock-solid brand by treating your customers right. The nice thing about treating people right is that it is usually within your power to do so. So, how do we treat our customers right? By figuring out what we hate when we are customers and making sure that we do not repeat these mistakes. We also note how we like to be treated and attempt to emulate that wherever and whenever possible. You will build very effective and valuable word of mouth if you do not jerk your customers around.

Chapter 2. Grow and Tap Your Network

Give a heads up and do favors.

Giving colleagues a heads up is an effective way to foster and build long-term business relationships. It costs you nothing but a few moments of your time. The recipients will be happy to reciprocate and provide you with similar help.

Send a gift.

We have found that sending an unexpected gift can be extremely effective in building and solidifying relationships. To be most effective, the gift should be both thoughtfully selected and arrive unexpected (e.g., not in December). We also have found that targeted charitable donations can make a very favorable impression as well. In any event, there is little to lose from this technique, as giving gifts, even token ones, is a pleasure, and supporting charities is the right thing to do.

Mentor

Mentoring young people is an enjoyable way to pass along your experience and knowledge. It also can be—and often is—invaluable in their later success and your later success. The people that you mentor will never forget your help and guidance. When the opportunity presents itself, the people you have mentored will be more than happy to help you and your business with good will, referrals, and new business.

Don't be afraid to ask for help.

There are both right ways and wrong ways to ask for help. When done correctly, asking for help can cement relationships and provide you with tremendous benefits that may be impossible to obtain in other ways. On the other hand, asking for help in the wrong way is a surefire way to destroy relationships.

Chapter 3. Develop Products Customers Love

Listen to your customers.

It is extremely risky to develop new products without first researching what your customers want and how much they are willing to pay for what they want. If you want to pinpoint what new products you should develop and what new products you should avoid, listen to your customers. Use surveys and ask open-ended questions. Perhaps most important, pay particular attention to unsolicited suggestions that you might receive, as these are likely to be the most accurate predictors of what your customers want from you and what they would be willing to pay you to get it. If you want to succeed in business, listen to your customers.

Before you proceed with a new product, have a plan that covers all the necessary elements for success.

Of every 20 ideas you come up with for a new product, at best only 1 or 2 are likely to be viable. The way you find out what is most likely to be viable is to ask the hard questions and do your homework in advance. A new product will not be successful unless it meets certain conditions. If people don't want it, it will fail. If people are not willing to pay for it, it will fail. If you don't have a way to cost effectively sell it or distribute it, it will fail. Finally, if the product doesn't work or if it doesn't do what you claim it should do, it will fail. Be very critical of your own ideas and aggressively look for all potential fatal weaknesses before deciding to launch the product.

Read everything.

There is potential gold in reading as much as you can. Your reading list should include everything from financial news articles to your junk mail. Reading can inspire ideas for new products if you adapt what other people are doing or learn about new problems or opportunities. Reading can also show you how other people are selling and marketing their services and help you identify potential persons and organizations to do business with.

Turn problems into new opportunities by seeing the problem a little differently.

A great source of new product ideas are problems that you and others face on a regular basis. How do you make money from these problems? By viewing them differently than everyone else does. Instead of joining the chorus when other people are all complaining about the same problem, view the situation as an opportunity to create a product or service that provides a solution.

Develop and sell product extensions.

When looking for new ways to increase revenue and serve your customers, consider product extensions and sequels, which can be relatively easy to develop. After all, you may have a ready, targeted, and easy market for them, and you know the area well enough to be able to develop a first-class product. Product extensions can be very profitable and should be considered and anticipated as part of any business plan.

Chapter 4. Sell Your Products and Services Cost Effectively

Nobody (with something to sell) knows anything about marketing.

Throwing money at marketing experts and advertising is a very risky way to sell your products or services, and it is likely to result in failure. Even the best marketing experts operating in good faith have no guaranteed way of knowing exactly how to sell your product or service in a cost-effective manner. Similarly, even ads placed in the best media outlets have no guarantee of generating sales. The ideal way to structure a deal with any marketing partner is to set it up so that the partner shares in the risks and rewards. The simplest way to do this is by developing distributors for your products.

Test it out and see if it works.

When it comes to marketing, the absolute key to success is experimentation and trials. We have learned the hard way that nobody, no matter how bright or experienced they are, can accurately predict what will happen with a marketing plan. Furthermore, market research is never a guarantee of success. The best ideas flop. Crazy ideas are wildly successful. Use your data, follow your instincts, but always test your marketing method before you roll it out or bet the farm. You will never know with confidence what is going to happen until you test your idea by actually trying to sell something.

Track the results of your marketing efforts.

If you are going to market your products or services, you absolutely must devise a way to track each campaign's results. You will not be in a position to rationally evaluate the success of your various marketing efforts unless you are serious about tracking your results. Campaigns that do not have a positive return should be tweaked or discontinued. Campaigns that are proven to be working should be expanded.

It's the name, stupid.

How you name yourself and your products matters greatly. Think things out carefully before deciding on a name. We suggest testing various names and getting feedback before the name is finalized.

Image is everything.

Take stock of your image. It may well be worth the additional time and money to produce high-quality and polished websites, brochures, and business cards.

Understand how much a new client is worth.

It is only when you understand the true value of a new customer that you can accurately evaluate when your sales and marketing efforts are cost effective. To calculate the true value of a customer, you need to always keep in mind the potential for repeat business from this customer. You should also consider the potential and likelihood of the customer generating positive word of mouth for you and thus greatly increase the possibility that your new customer will lead to additional new customers.

Find yourself a niche.

There are tremendous advantages to operating in a narrow niche. When you do so, you will be able to define yourself as an expert in your field of choice and deliver superior products. Operating in a niche also may allow you to price your products and services at a premium rate. Finally, when you operate in a well-thought-out niche, you will be able to market your products and services in a more cost-effective manner.

Consider premium pricing.

In certain market niches, people will pay more for perceived quality. One way to increase the perceived quality of your product or service is to raise its price. The reason premium pricing works is that people will figure that they are getting a higher-quality product if they pay more. Consider finding a niche where you can use this technique.

Deadlines make things happen.

Deadlines are easy to implement and often boost sales. Customers tend to wait to make purchasing decisions until an offer deadline is near its expiration date, so you can expect a large spike in sales around that time.

Offer a money back guarantee—and honor it.

To boost sales, consider backing up your product or service with a money-back guarantee. Such a guarantee will help motivate you to produce the highest quality products and services. If you produce high-quality products and services, you will probably get very few returns. When you do receive a request for a refund, however, view the situation as an opportunity to build your brand as a stand-up organization by promptly issuing the refund without any hassles.

When someone tries to sell you something, sell them something.

Grabbing potential customers' attention is one of the biggest problems businesspeople face when they try to sell their products or services. Whenever someone from an allied field is trying to sell you something, look at the possible things you might be able to sell them or their company before you blow them off. Turn the potential problem or hassle of being sold something into a sales opportunity for your business. The person who contacted you will listen to you, because they initiated the original contact and need to be nice to you.

Pitch to your customers when their wallets are already open.

Make it easy for your customers to buy additional products and services from you when you are closing the sale. We have found that once your client has his or her wallet open for a sale, it is much easier to get that person to buy additional products and services from you. Design a protocol or a system for asking your customer if he or she would like to add additional products or services to their order. This is a very cost-effective way of increasing sales.

Capture and add to your database the names of potential customers.

Find ways to capture the contact information of leads who have expressed an interest in your products or services. Then add to your database this information and use it to solicit their business. Your payoff in additional sales can be quite dramatic.

Follow-up.

One of the most common sales mistakes that companies make is failing to follow up with their leads. Never quote a job and then fail to follow up with either an e-mail or a phone call. Following-up is a simple and effective technique to increase your sales. Develop a protocol and calendar system to follow-up with your leads so that nothing falls through the cracks.

Make it simple and easy for your customer to buy from you.

Make it as easy as possible for your customers to buy your products and services. Don't make them fill out complicated forms. Keep it simple. If you need to get further detailed information from your customer, do it after the sale. Simplifying an order form or ordering process can greatly enhance your sales.

Chapter 5. Control Your Costs and Increase Your Productivity

Do not fear technology; embrace it.

Using technology is a proven way to increase your company's efficiency and reduce its costs. If you are a technophobe, add a technophile to your team.

There are simply too many ways to reduce your costs and improve your efficiency through technology to forgo this technique for making more money.

Develop long-term relationships with vendors.

There are tremendous advantages to be gained from establishing long-term relationships with your vendors. Long-term vendors will know your business, your needs, and your quirks, and as a result, you can spend less time telling them what you need and more time running your business and making money. You also have tremendous leverage over long-term vendors and should be able to obtain and receive superior service, pricing, and concessions from them.

Keep a low overhead and avoid large, fixed expenses or commitments.

Try where possible to avoid long-term commitments/contracts and large, fixed expenses, such as mortgages, debt, and salaries. Such a policy can give you much-needed flexibility when faced with a crisis or changing business conditions. It will also give you greater leverage over your vendors and save you money.

Watch your vendors like a hawk.

Watch your vendors like a hawk. A responsible and compulsive person should be in charge of regularly reviewing the deal you are getting through research and competitive bidding. You will unfortunately find that these audits will often reveal that you are no longer getting the superior terms and pricing that you once enjoyed. If you have a competing bid in hand, you most likely will be able to get your vendor to quickly beat that bid. As a result, you will have instantly saved (i.e., made) money.

Consider buying over renting.

Do your homework and make an informed decision as to whether you are truly better off renting or buying. In some cases you can save (and thus make) tremendous amounts of money by buying as opposed to renting.

Read the fine print.

Carefully review each and every word in contracts before you sign them. Don't just focus on the price. Never assume that the fine print is not important and does not matter. The fine print can and will cost you a lot of money.

Chapter 6. Take Charge

Watch the little details.

You need to watch the little details. Little mistakes can and will create huge problems that will cost you a lot of money. Everybody makes mistakes. To minimize mistakes we suggest that you create and follow a protocol of checks that helps avoid these costly and easily preventable mistakes.

Answer your phone and return phone calls promptly.

Answer your phone and return your phone calls promptly: doing so will prevent you from missing fruitful business opportunities and will help you build your brand. Your customers will appreciate this rare courtesy. You should return calls promptly even when it looks as though the person you are responding to is not looking to buy something from you. This will help your reputation immensely and may give you an opportunity to turn the conversation into a closed sale.

Keep your eye on the ball.

Keep your eye on the ball. There's only so much time in a day, so spend it wisely on things that will make you money, not on what you like to do or what feels good. Don't have too many meetings; they can waste a tremendous amount of time. Also, resist the temptation to litigate or get in protracted disagreements with people. This is most often a losing proposition and will only cost you more time and money in the end.

Develop a protocol, along with a system of checklists to make sure you follow it.

Checklists, protocols, and procedure are very helpful ways to prevent mistakes. Develop protocols and procedures, and make sure that they are followed. Checklists and sign-offs help you avoid the need to rely on the memory and/or attention of the person you have tasked with a specific project. Following these simple steps will prevent myriad of problems and save you a good deal of time, money, and aggravation.

Weigh likely benefits against potential risks, and don't bet the farm.

It is absolutely critical to carefully weigh the likely possible upsides of a business decision against the potential risks. Unfortunately, predicting the future is more art than science, so you will always be making your decisions on imperfect and less-than-complete information. Regardless, remember to periodically review your protocols to see if they can be improved on. If you want to be in business on a long-term basis, always avoid making decisions that open your firm to the risk of serious failure. Don't ever bet the farm.

Keep in contact with the competition, and cooperate where you can.

Keep your competitors close. Build mutually beneficial relationships with them. There are many benefits to keeping the lines of communication open with your competition and staying on friendly terms.

Win the war, not the battle.

There's often very few profits to be made in proving you were right. Always keep your eye on your ultimate goal, which is the success of your business. Be very careful to only fight battles that move you closer to your goal. Concentrate on winning the war, not an individual battle.

Attack little problems aggressively and don't let them turn into BIG problems.

You are always going to be faced with problems in your business. Your goal should be to prevent little problems from turning into big problems. Doing so often requires active listening, awareness, and aggressive and immediate action once you have identified a little problem. It also requires carefully thinking through potential solutions to make sure that you won't just make the problem worse.

Recognize what is and what is not your problem.

The first question to ask yourself when confronted with a business problem should be, "Is this my problem or somebody else's problem?" You should not automatically ask yourself, "How do I solve this problem?" Just because you can solve a problem does not mean it is in your interest to do so. This ability to diagnose what is and what is not your problem will save you time and money. It may seem harsh, but you have enough problems of your own to deal with. You are not helping yourself by taking on additional problems.

Do not rely exclusively on e-mail; pick up the phone.

Don't be afraid to pick up the telephone. In many instances, using the phone is a better way to communicate than using e-mail. There are many advantages to phone communications. They help you and your business stand out, they are generally more efficient (depending on subject matter), they give you a chance to shine and bond with the person with whom you are communicating, they give you a read on the person you are talking to, and they ensure that your message isn't misunderstood or lost in a spam filter or overstuffed e-mail inbox. To make certain that people can easily call you, you include your telephone number in your e-mail signature.

Chapter 7. Recruit, Motivate, and Retain a Superior Workforce

Give interviewees a test assignment.

Testing can be a very effective technique when making hiring decisions. Requiring the completion of a pre-interview assignment can and will separate out those candidates who are hungry, resourceful, and motivated from those who are not. The testing process can also yield priceless evidence as to what the candidate is actually capable of doing—which is better than trusting the unsubstantiated claims they make on their resume. Another effective way to test a prospective employee is to try them out on a contract basis before you hire them as a full-time employee.

No employee is ever too old—or too young.

Be open-minded about hiring students, recent graduates, and retirees. The very young and retirees can provide your organization with tremendous value.

Mercilessly get rid of the bad apples on your staff.

One of the most unpleasant tasks that any manager must undertake is letting go of one of his or her employees. It's just not a fun thing to do. As such, some managers delay what needs to be done far too long. The problem with this approach is that one disruptive or unproductive employee can create jealousies within your organization. Other problems will inevitably cascade down from this individual and can poison the morale of your entire staff. Bad apples need to be terminated as soon as they are identified. Unpleasant as it may be, you must protect the business. You are responsible for feeding too many people to shirk this important responsibility.

Overpay your staff.

It may seem counterintuitive, but you may be able to improve your efficiency and increase your profitability by overpaying your staff, as doing so may allow you to decrease the total size of your staff, thus reducing your labor costs. You also will not suffer from turnover problems and are likely to have a well-motivated staff that you can count on when you need them. Overpaying your staff can also make you feel good about your business and the work that you are doing.

Treat people you terminate with compassion and respect.

Treat your employees with compassion and respect when you terminate them. Do not criticize them. Do not fight their unemployment benefits. Do not humiliate them. Provide a generous severance package, and don't screw them out of their bonuses. Treating people you have to fire with compassion and respect is the right thing to do. You will feel better about yourself, and you will also reduce the significant risks that former disgruntled employees can pose to you and your company. Your current employees will be watching you, and they will appreciate the compassionate way you dealt with a difficult situation.

Be flexible with your staff.

One of the absolute keys to profitability in business is being able to minimize staff turnover. One way to do this is to be flexible with your staff regarding their hours and their desire to work from home. Many employers are not flexible and cannot be so, but if you can be flexible with your staff, you can gain a competitive edge in the labor market. If you can find win–win flexible working solutions for you and your employees, they will be very unlikely to leave you. The reason for this is simple: your employees will be hard-pressed to find similarly flexible situations in any new job they might find.

Pay for performance.

There are many advantages to basing your employees' pay on their performance results. Each employee under the eat-what-you-kill model is paid exactly what they are worth to the company. As a result, they will be well-motivated to generate profits. In addition, you won't need to renegotiate their compensation every year. Finally, if you have multiple employees under your employ, they can each get the exact same deal, which will minimize jealousies and prevent the need for secrecy. To make pay-for-performance work, the formula it is based on must be fair and not subject to unfair manipulation by the employer.

Chapter 8. Deal with Customer Complaints Head-On

Talk directly with your customers as much as you can.

Talking with your customers is not a burden. Rather, it is a tremendous opportunity, so talk with your customers on the phone or in person as often as you can. Only by talking with them directly—and not through someone who is filtering their words—can you truly learn priceless information about what they like, what they dislike, what they want, and how much they are willing to pay for your products and/or services.

Talk with unhappy customers on the phone or in person, and get back to them right away.

Actually talking with your customers has become a lost art. Many companies purposefully refrain from listing a phone number on their webpage. This is unfortunate, because the best way to deal with unhappy customers is to actually talk with them. When you talk with your customers, you show them you care and are different than many other companies out there. You can also resolve miscommunication issues, problem solve, and often find out what is really happening.

Get rid of problem clients so you can focus on your good clients.

We have found that a large percentage of your problems will be caused by a small percentage of your customers. Problem customers will cost you money. Once we identify a troublemaker, we try to make that person happy, and then we do everything we can to avoid doing business with him or her in the future. We need to concentrate on making money and the vast majority of our good customers, not on dealing with troublemakers.

Realize that you can never make EVERYONE happy.

Just because someone is mad and complaining does not make them right. It is fact of life that the more people you deal with, the less likely it will be that you can make everyone happy. Listen to all the negative feedback you get. Where you are wrong, change your ways and make amends. If you are not wrong, however, and you can't meet a customer's request without taking an unacceptable cost, don't be afraid to stand by your beliefs. Trying to please everyone may mean you end up pleasing no one, and that's not the best way to run a business.

Don't say no. Focus on what you CAN do to help the unhappy customer.

Oftentimes a customer will complain, and you will not be able to say "yes" to them. In these situations, try to avoid saying "no" and instead focus on what you can do to help them with their problem. You will probably find that a helpful attitude is much more effective than telling your customer "no."

Let your customers off the hook.

Many times you may have the right to treat your customers in a certain manner, but just because you have this right does not mean that you should exercise it. If you and your business have not been severely damaged by a customer and his/her actions, consider waiving your right to respond in the way in which you are entitled to. What you give up might just come back to you many times over in the form of improved brand reputation, bolstered customer loyalty, and increased future business.

Chapter 9. Manage Yourself

Take care of yourself.

People who are not feeling well can and will make potentially costly decisions and statements that they may end up deeply regretting. To avoid this risk, you should prioritize taking care of yourself as a key business asset. Make sure that you get enough sleep, exercise, eat enough, and take the time to go to see your doctor when necessary.

Be persistent.

The nice thing about persistence is that it is completely within your control. You may or may not be born with extraordinary talent, but everyone can be persistent. Often times, persistence is actually more important than talent when it comes to achieving success. You can be as persistent as your willpower allows you to be. For this reason, persistence is a key element of success and often pays huge rewards.

Don't wait until the last minute.

Although it may sound pessimistic, you should always expect that something will go wrong in your business. Then, when something inevitably does go wrong, you will be in far better shape to deal with the problem than you would be if you had waited until the last minute to address it. Having extra time when you need it will make your life easier and your business more successful.

Sleep on important decisions.

An excellent way to make better decisions is to sleep on them. Sleeping on your decisions can help minimize the emotion involved in your decision-making process and lead to decisions that are more likely to be in your best long-term interest. We have found that the most beneficial times to sleep on your decisions is when someone has made you angry, when you are emotionally involved in a course of action, or when you are searching for a solution and sense that the answer lies somewhere in your own subconscious.

Have confidence in yourself.

Having confidence in yourself has many benefits and is an extremely valuable business asset. If you appear to have confidence in yourself, others will follow you and believe what you say. Confidence can also help you get through crises and rough patches. Finally, confidence can open many doors for you, because when you have confidence in yourself, you will be more likely to try something new.

Don't be afraid to fail.

Do not be afraid to fail. If you are afraid to fail, you will become paralyzed, and that paralysis will destroy your business. Understand that many things in business will not work out as you had hoped—and don't take it personally when they don't. That's just a part of being in business. If you learn from your failures and keep plugging away, you will find that the sum of your successes will far outweigh the sum of your failures.

Chapter 10. Become a Better Negotiator

In a win–win relationship, you win.

In many instances, you are better off negotiating a win–win solution rather than forcing the party you are negotiating with into a marginal deal. You win in win–win deals because they allow you to build long-term, stable, and mutually beneficial relationships. You lose in win–lose deals because they cause you to leave a sour taste in the other party's mouth and potentially poison the well, thus preventing you from engaging in future business deals with them.

Build negotiating power by emphasizing the possibility of long-term business.

A simple but remarkably effective way to obtain better terms in a negotiation is to emphasize that you have additional business that you would like to bring to the vendor in the future—if you are provided with superior terms and service. Emphasizing this point can, in effect, turn you into a very important client who commands premium pricing and treatment. Be wary of requests that lock you into long-term contracts, however. It is difficult to predict your needs many years out. Furthermore, once you are contractually locked in to an agreement, the quality of service you receive might nosedive, and prices may go down in the future.

You are best off dealing with the decision maker, not an underling.

You will obtain more advantageous negotiating results when you deal with the decision maker as opposed to an underling. Underlings want to look good in front of their superiors and may be reluctant to offer you fair terms because they are afraid that they will be perceived as giving away the store. In addition, underlings may not have the authority to give you what you are looking for and may be lazy, unresponsive, and/or uninformed.

Information is power, so do your homework.

The more information you have, the better the deals you will be able to negotiate. Finding out essential information, such as how much you can buy a given service for elsewhere or how much the potential buyer is willing to spend, is invaluable information.

Develop an alternative to improve your bargaining position.

When you are negotiating with a buyer, seller, or vendor, you will be much more effective and successful if you have alternatives in hand—especially if you can share these alternatives with the person with whom you are negotiating.

Beware of weak links in your negotiating team.

When negotiating as a team, it is critical that every team member is on the same page. Furthermore, one team member—and one team member alone—should be in charge of the negotiations. Anyone who has loose lips, is not a team player, or is a poor negotiator (in other words, a weak link) needs to be kept off the negotiating team and left at home.

Be prepared to walk away.

Make sure that the person with whom you are negotiating understands that you are prepared to walk away from the deal at any time. When the other party in a negotiation realizes that you can take or leave a deal, you will gain leverage over him or her, as it will appear as though you do not need the deal. This technique works effectively with both vendors and sales prospects.

Nothing should be agreed to until everything is agreed to.

Do not agree to any given term in a negotiation unless you know exactly what you are getting yourself into. Often times, you may need to negotiate many crucially important contractual details besides the price. Nothing should be agreed to until everything is agreed to.

Step 1: Build a Superb Brand

Neither Jim nor I went to business school or were business majors in undergraduate school. Everything we have learned about business, we have learned from our customers and the marketplace. We have made a tremendous number of mistakes over the years; indeed, a major purpose of this book is so that others can learn from our many mistakes. But we also hope to be able to emphasize one of the main reasons we believe that we have been able to survive despite all these mistakes: we have been intensely focused on our brand from Day 1. We take pride in who we are, how we do business, and what we sell. The fact that we have developed a positive brand reputation has allowed us to weather many, many storms, as people value our products and have a pleasant, respectful experience when dealing with us. It is for this reason that branding is the very first step for business success.

The nice thing about your business' brand is that it is pretty much within your control. We hope that the branding advice contained in this section can be emulated by you so that your businesses will benefit as much as ours has from establishing a superior brand.

1. Build your brand through an intense focus on quality.

EXECUTIVE SUMMARY: The most effective marketing tool your business will have is word-of-mouth marketing. Focus intensely on the quality of your products and you will reap great benefits from positive word of mouth. Think long term. When in doubt, do whatever it takes to protect the quality of your brand.

* * *

Recently, we received a call from the Federal Bureau of Investigation. No, we were not in trouble. They were exploring hiring us to train some of their special agents who frequently need to testify as expert witnesses. This is approximately how the conversation went:

FBI: Hi, I wanted to explore bringing you guys down here to train some of our special agents.

AUTHORS: That's great, we'd be delighted. How did you hear about us?

FBI: We have a file on you. No, just kidding. Three of our agents attended your conference last year and they spoke glowingly about it. I've been investigating potential trainers, and everyone we talk to says they same thing: You guys are very easy to deal with and do a fantastic job.

AUTHORS: Thank you for your kind words. Let's talk some more about what you need ...

We have conversations similar to this very often, where the person on the other end of the line mentions that he or she has heard great things about our work, and they generally end with a tangible monetary payoff for all the hard work we do to build and preserve our brand and reputation. Positive word of mouth is the reason why the FBI would even consider hiring a tiny, family-owned company based on Cape Cod, Massachusetts whose home office is above a sushi restaurant. It is also the reason we work so hard to build and retain the quality of our brand.

To be sure, positive word of mouth is the most valuable marketing tool you can possibly have. Positive word of mouth will help you reach people you normally would not reach, but who hear about you from their friends and colleagues. It also will help you close sales because clients who have been referred from a friend are much more likely to actually buy from you opposed to merely kicking the tires. There is a nonmonetary payoff to positive word of mouth, too, which is the feeling of pride that comes from your clients being extremely satisfied with their dealings with you. This can really give you juice. Our brand is that "We do high quality work on time and are easy to deal with," and we do whatever it takes to build and maintain that brand, even if doing so costs us money in the short term. What is your brand, and what would you do to protect it? Furthermore, how does protecting and furthering a high-quality brand pay off? Consider the following: Jim and I have put on the nation's finest expert witness conference since 1992. One of our attendees at the conference a few years ago was a forensic accountant. He was told by a colleague that he should really attend our course, as it was done at a very high level. He attended, and at the end of the four-day conference, came up to us and said, "You guys are a class act. You put on a great show. I am going to report this back to my boss."

A short time later we were called by the forensic accountant's boss, who asked us to put on a customized one-day training session for the entire company, so we prepared diligently and held yet another high-quality course. The company's president was involved in the role playing during the course and was suitably impressed. After the customized training program was completed, he declared that "all our experts will need to be trained one-on-one by these guys." This lucrative relationship has endured for years, and the accounting firm remains one of our best clients. However, none of this would have been possible were it not for positive word of mouth, which reflected our brand for excellence.

On the other hand, as you can imagine, negative word of mouth is as harmful to a business as positive word of mouth is helpful. Who has not decided against seeing a movie or going to a restaurant because of the negative recommendation of a friend? Recognize this fact and go to extreme lengths to avoid negative word of mouth, even if it monetarily benefits you in the short term to provide your clients with a lesser product or service.

A few years ago we developed a two-day conference and sought out trainers for a new, narrow, niche area. Lo and behold, we had trouble finding trainers, but we eventually settled on a husband and wife team. They came and were disorganized, unprepared, and spent most of the two-class days bickering with each other in front of the class. In sum, the course was simply terrible. The business problem we had now was that the course was very well attended and made us a good deal of money. We could have easily just put it on again with "The Bickermens" and made a quick buck, but that would have further damaged our brand, so we did things the hard way. We pursued a team of trainers from all over the country and brought them in at high expense and replaced 2 trainers with 14. This was tremendously time consuming and expensive, but it dramatically improved the course. Now more than 1,500 attendees have been through the new and improved course, and many of these alums tell their friends and colleagues about how great the course is. Even better, the course is so good that many of our attendees come back to retake it at again in the future. These are the powerful benefits of word-of-mouth branding. It's also why we are so particular about protecting our reputation.

How valuable can word-of-mouth marketing based on a quality brand be? We have found it to be the *only* effective marketing to sell certain types of services. For example, one of our services is providing private onsite training for corporations and government agencies. This can be a lucrative business opportunity, so we are always trying to successfully solicit more training gigs such as these. When we first started trying to spread the word about our private onsite training, we sent out every type of piece of direct mail imaginable. We placed ads. We sent out e-mails. We cold called. You name it, we tried it. But nothing worked. Instead, all of the work we have been able to land in this area has been the direct result of positive word of mouth. The story is always the same: someone goes to one of our conferences and sees us in action. They tell their boss about us and we are brought in to train the company. This type of in-house training represents about 15% of our annual profits. Simply put, without our positive brand, this entire product line would not exist. That is just another reason why we focus so much on building and preserving our brand identity and making it synonymous with high quality.

Once you develop powerful word-of-mouth recognition, you will be able to obtain and utilize testimonials from your customers that can be listed on your website to further help you build your brand for excellence. A look at one of the author's websites, testifyingtraining.com, provides prospective clients with testimonials from past clients who write about the quality of our work in their own words. At the top of the site is this letter of reference, which has helped us build our brand:

> In recognition of your outstanding assistance to the FBI in connection with its investigative efforts. Your cooperation was of immeasurable help to our representatives. I share their gratitude for your support, which assisted them in carrying out their responsibilities. You can take pride in the role you played in the success achieved, and my associates and I congratulate you on a job well done.
>
> —Robert S. Mueller, III, Director, Federal Bureau of Investigation

We are not kidding when we say that we are serious about protecting our brand. Recently we decided to develop a software program that will help our clients do their job. We spent over $30,000 on two different developers who were trying to get this software to work consistently and without bugs. After almost two years of development and much testing, beta versions still had quite a lot of repeated problems, and we lost faith in the ability of our developers, and we had a partners' meeting to discuss the situation. We all agreed that we were close to being able to sell this software. We agreed that we could sell it and generate a decent amount of revenue. The unanimous decision at the end of the meeting, however, was to terminate the project.

Why throw away a product that could generate money? Our thinking was simple, actually. We have been in business for over 30 years. We intend to be in business 30 years from now. As such, our most important asset is our brand. In other words, there was no question in our minds that we would rather throw away $30,000 in development money and large amounts of forgone revenue than risk selling a product that we feared would have undiscovered bugs and thus damage our brand. We also personally did not want to be associated with a product in which we did not have technical confidence. In addition, we did not want to spend more time on a project that we thought the developers would never be able to ever get up to our standards of quality.

Here is another example of how valuable a quality brand can be to a company. Jim is a boater. His family has been boaters for four generations. Since the 1960s, Jim and his family have always owned a particular brand of boat called Boston Whaler because Boston Whalers have developed the reputation (brand) for being the safest boat afloat and virtually unsinkable. Boston Whaler has been very clever in its marketing efforts. To show how safe its boats are, the company regularly videotapes one of its employees taking a chainsaw to one of its boats and cutting the boat into three chunks. They then show how each of the three pieces not only still floats but stays afloat while supporting the same number of people the boat is designed to hold when it's in one piece. Talk about a picture saying a million words and reinforcing a brand.

The results of Boston Whaler's positive brand reputation have been tangible. The company has a large and loyal customer base that sings its praises and provides the most valuable free advertising there is: positive word-of-mouth. Boston Whaler is also in the favorable position of being able to pitch high resale value as a selling point, thereby allowing the company to charge substantially more than its competitors for its boats because people are often willing to pay more for what they perceive to be a superior brand. Can you truly put a value on the well being of your children and loved ones? Boston Whaler is a perfect example of how quality can build brands and how brands can build success.

Consider this additional example. We have a friend who we will call Rob. Rob is a physician who does expert witness consulting on the side. In just five years he grew this "side" practice from nothing to a $200,000 per year business by working just one day per week. We were impressed with Rob's achievement, so we asked him what clever things he did to market himself. How did he network? Where did he advertise? Did he write a blog? Did he send out an electronic newsletter? Rob's response was that he did absolutely nothing to promote his consulting practice. Because he did a great job for his clients, his referrals were 100% based on word of mouth. Yes, that's right: Rob was able to build up a one day per week, $200,000 per year consulting practice on the sole basis of his brand. Rob's story is further proof of how tremendously valuable it is for businesses to build a strong brand based on the quality of their product or service.

Moreover, you can easily see the tangible benefits of a superior brand and customer loyalty when you look around the marketplace. Take Apple, Inc., for example; through the quality of its products, Apple has built a rabidly loyal customer base, which in turn has helped its profits and stock price soar. When Apple's iPad was launched in 2010, the company sold over 300,000 units on the first day alone. Many preordered and bought the iPad sight unseen. And that's not all; Apple's success with its iPods and iPads has spilled over and resulted in dramatic increases in sales of its laptops and other computer products. The brand value Apple has built up is probably best summed up by a quote from someone who waited in line to pick up their iPad on its launch date: "If Apple built a toilet seat I would probably buy it."

Apple's success is no mystery. Apple is instead a classic example of a business (and fortune) built not of trendy new paradigms but on proven, real-world, bedrock business principles, such as focusing on their brand and reputation.

2. Turn down business that risks damaging your brand.

EXECUTIVE SUMMARY: Knowing when and how to turn down work can substantially help you build your brand and your business. Be very careful about accepting work outside of your sandbox, work that you do not have the time to do properly, or work that would otherwise damage your brand. Do not get into lines of business that will likely dilute and possibly tarnish your brand.

* * *

Jim and I have found that another effective method of building and preserving your brand is to turn away business that risks damaging it. Too many businesses fall into the trap of taking any new work that comes in the door, but this can be a serious mistake and should be avoided at all costs. Accepting business that is not in your sandbox will dilute the quality of your products and services and damage your reputation and brand. These jobs may be winning you the battle, but they are almost assuredly losing you the war.

Jobs to decline on the basis of brand preservation generally fall into three categories:

1. You are unable to do a great job because the work is not within your true area of expertise.

2. You do not have the time to do a great job.

3. The type of work or the client you would be working for damages your brand.

Deciding which business opportunities to accept and which to decline is an ongoing battle. People call us all the time requesting that we assist them with projects that are not in our area of strength. The ability and willingness to turn down even potentially lucrative work that you know you cannot excel at is difficult for many businesses, but it is our philosophy that taking on business that we suspect we can only do a mediocre job on is a recipe for brand diminishment and long-term disaster.

Neither Jim nor I have practiced law since the 1990s, but regardless we are frequently asked to represent clients who find themselves in need of counsel for matters involving a wide array of legal issues. We take the attitude that to build a brand you must always deliver value to your clients and work as diligently as you can to help your clients succeed. As such, we turn down all of this potentially lucrative legal work. The reason is simple: we have not practiced law in many years, and each state's laws are different. If we took on this type of work, we would not do a superior job, which means that we would not be acting in our clients' best interests. We would much rather pass on a job than risk harming our clients and damaging our brand.

We are commonly asked to give presentations on topics that are outside of our comfort zone and area of expertise. For example, we recently got a call from someone looking to have us speak on a particular legal issue. Here is approximately how the conversation went:

EXECUTIVE DIRECTOR: We would like you to come out and do a two-day intensive training session on the fifth edition of the AMA guides for our lawyers. We know that you wrote the book *Understanding the AMA Guides* and that you were a Workers' Compensation trial attorney for twenty years. Name your price.

AUTHORS: We would love to name our price—and let me tell you, it would not be cheap—however, I have not practiced law since 1992. Although I could accept the assignment and do a decent job, you really need someone who deals with this on a day-by-day basis. Let me recommend a trial lawyer I know; he is current and knows ten times more than I do.

EXECUTIVE DIRECTOR: You didn't even ask how much we were willing to pay?

AUTHORS: We don't take on work unless we can do a world-class job. We would not do that here. It is not about the money.

EXECUTIVE DIRECTOR: Can you send me the contact information for this attorney? If you say he is that good, that is good enough for me.

AUTHORS: I am sending you his bio and contact information now and will e-mail him to give him a heads up.

A job you cannot handle is a tremendous opportunity to build your network by referring the job to someone else, which is why we referred this business to someone we thought was well qualified to handle it. When the referral is made, it is appropriate to shoot a note to the person you recommended to give them a heads up. For example:

> *Hey Charlie.*
>
> *Hope all is well. The Executive Director of State Bar Association wanted us to present for them. Since we are no longer in active law practice, we did not feel comfortable giving the presentation, so I referred him to you. You can expect his call shortly.*
>
> *Best regards,*
>
> *Steve*

Referring work out like this is a tremendously effective way to help build a loyal network. For more on networking, please see Chapter 2.

The marketplace is replete with examples of companies damaging their brand by moving away from their core business. Case in point: in the early 1970s the baby food manufacturer Gerber tried to get into the business of selling baby food to adults—Gerber Singles—which consisted of jars of food almost identical to what the company sold for babies. Not only did nobody want the product, but the name itself was depressing, as it was targeted toward people who lived alone. As a result, Gerber Singles were quickly scuttled by management after their launch, but the damage was already done. By deviating from their core area of expertise, Gerber damaged their brand and lost a good deal of money.

Harley Davidson provides yet another classic example of a company that damaged its brand by getting into a business it should not be in. Harley Davidson spent many years building a brand of macho. Its bikes were loud and powerful. The brand represented freedom. In the 1990s, however, Harley Davidson, which was making a fair amount of money from merchandising, went a little too far and developed, of all things, perfume. Even worse, it also developed wine coolers. Talk about how to damage a brand built on macho! Harley Davidson of course recognized its mistakes and pulled those products, and the company is now much more careful about what types of merchandise it will put its name on. But the lesson from Harley Davidson is clear: do not get involved in lines of business that can dilute and damage your hard-built brand.

Even if you have the skills to do a particular job right, keep in mind that you must also evaluate whether you have the *time* to do the job right. Taking on work when you do not have the time to do a superior job can have far-reaching consequences, as evidenced by the following example, which hits close to home—literally: one fall, I called in a bunch of contractors to get a quote for putting a brick walkway in front of my house, and I eventually found one that I liked—we will call him Mickey—who gave me a good price. I told Mickey that the walkway obviously needed to be done before the ground froze here in New England and it started snowing. No problem, I was told, he would start around November 1st and the job would take two days.

Around November 1, I gave Mickey a call. He explained that he was busy and would start in a couple of weeks. I called again in two weeks and he explained that he was still busy and would start at the beginning of December. December 1st came around and Mickey never showed up. I did not bother to call him again to ask why. I did not want to deal with Mickey anymore. He did not keep his word. His brand was irrevocably shattered in my mind. In the spring I found another contractor—and I tell this story to anybody who is interested in or looking for a contractor referral. I tell them to avoid Mickey, who left me hanging, and I recommend the new contractor I found. In a nutshell, this is the branding risk you take by agreeing to take on work that you are too busy to handle.

So, if you do not have the time to do a job right, what do you do? Here's what: a few years ago we were asked by an allied organization to host a joint seminar as part of the organization's big trade show. The seminar would be on a Monday, but unfortunately, it was set to start in California the day after a huge four-day conference of ours had just finished. For us to even get to the trade show we would have to rush from Cape Cod to Boston in the late afternoon, hop on a plane to California, and wake up exhausted to teach the course.

We talked internally about this project at great length. We knew a lot about the subject of the seminar and theoretically could do a great job with the assignment. We had major concerns, however. What if our flight was cancelled and we could not appear? What if the plane was delayed and we got no sleep? Even if the planets aligned and we arrived on schedule, we would be wiped out while teaching the seminar. We considered the possibility of having one of us leave early from the Cape Cod based conference, but we decided against this approach because we did not want to damage our brand. In the end, we decided to pass on the California seminar. Our reason was simple: the scheduling of the assignment presented more brand risk than we were willing to accept.

Now, let's say that you have the skills *and* the time to do a bang-up job on a given project. Should you take it? Not if the type of work or the client you would be working for risks damaging your brand. A big part of our business involves training expert witnesses on how to deal with attorneys, cross-examination, trial tactics, and so forth. The experts trust us. They know that we are looking out for their best interests, and we have developed a tremendous brand that experts recognize and respect. Recently, however, we were approached by a professional association for lawyers to do some training *on how to destroy experts*. Here is approximately how the conversation went:

EXECUTIVE DIRECTOR OF BAR ASSOCIATION: We see you have written ten textbooks on expert witnessing. We would like to invite you to come out and teach our young lawyers the most effective ways to cross-examine and destroy experts. You guys know all the tricks of the trade. The young lawyers are not getting enough trial experience and need to know how to rip apart the experts. How much will this cost us?

AUTHORS: I appreciate the offer and your kind words, but we will have to turn this down. We just do not feel comfortable training lawyers on how to cross-examine with the intent of "destroying" expert witnesses, who in many cases will be our own clients and customers. I do know some excellent lawyers that I can recommend, however.

The decision to turn down the bar association's work was an easy one. We were being asked to take an assignment that might work against the interests of our current clients. We knew what we were doing—and we could have done a superb job. We turned the assignment down without even a discussion, however, because working against the interest of our current client base could have proven to be a public relations and branding disaster of the first order.

There is a right way, by the way, to turn down work: be gracious, be polite, thank them for the offer, and say you are flattered. Ending the conversation on good terms will increase the chances that the other party will call on you for future assignments you can accept. In addition, always be responsive. The person calling is usually under some time pressure to get the assignment locked down. If you know you will not accept the assignment, tell the other person this during the first call. Do not drag it out or make the other party wait an extended period of time while you mull it over. Your prompt reply will help the person move on and not lose any more time.

It is also a good idea to explain why you are not accepting the assignment. When you explain that you do not accept work when you cannot do a world-class job, or you are already very busy with work due to your reputation, or that you do not accept work you even suspect you cannot complete on time, you are helping to build your brand. The potential client will respect your honesty and integrity and may very well contact you in the future because of it. And do not forget to try to be helpful. When you cannot accept an assignment, new work, and so forth, you are probably in a good position to recommend someone who can. A prompt, solid recommendation helps build your goodwill and your brand with both the person looking for help and the person you recommend. The person recommended will often reciprocate by referring work to you when he can.

3. Define and reinforce your brand with a well thought out tagline

EXECUTIVE SUMMARY: A tagline gives you the opportunity to define your brand. Choose it carefully, as your tagline will have an important effect on both your brand and your bottom line.

* * *

We struggled for many years to increase the attendance at our programs for expert witnesses. We poured money into different marketing campaigns. We brought in celebrity speakers. Still, we struggled with attendance. At the same time this was happening, we would frequently receive calls from potential attendees, who would all ask the same question: "Your stuff is mainly for physicians. I am not a physician. Would your expert witness course help me?" The answer to this question was always an emphatic, "Yes!"

A little aside here: when a customer calls with a complaint, comment, or compliment, he or she is giving you a tremendous opportunity for feedback. We assume that for every customer who calls with an issue, there are many others who feel the same way but did not bother to contact us. That is one of the reasons why, if multiple customers call us with the same concern, we take that as a sign of the highest significance. For more on the importance of talking to your customers, please see Chapter 8.

Back to taglines: if you were to look at the agenda of our expert witness conference, you would be able to see that it is applicable to all types of experts, but we were still being asked if and how the event applies to nonphysicians. As a result, we made the conscious decision to not use any physicians on our faculty. It did not matter, and it did not work. We were still getting the calls about being "only for doctors," and our attendance still was not growing as much as we would have liked.

After much internal discussion, we concluded that we had to do whatever we could to change the perception that our products and services were "just for doctors." We recognized that part of our problem was self-created and could not be fixed overnight, and we were able to pinpoint the reason: for twenty years, each piece of letterhead, each envelope, and each brochure we had mailed out had our logo with the following tagline on it: "Legal and Medical Information Systems." At the time this tagline was created, we served mainly doctors and lawyers. But 20 years later, we had outgrown our tagline, and it was now obviously a part of our problem.

One day I was reading a piece of my junk mail.[1] On it, the company had a tagline that read, "Excellence in [Their Industry] Since 1962," or something similar. I immediately got an inspiration. What if we adapted that tagline to fit our business? I proposed to my partners that we immediately change our tagline from "Legal and Medical Information Systems" to "Excellence in Education Since 1980." After a very brief discussion, they wholeheartedly endorsed my idea. But changing our tagline was not easy; in fact, it involved a good amount of work. We had to hire a graphic artist to design a new logo. We had to change all our web pages. We had to reprint envelopes and letterheads. In the end, however, the results from this simplest of simple changes were astounding. Within two years of launching the new tagline, we never again received another call or comment about our being "just for doctors." Furthermore, the proof was in the pudding: the attendance of nonphysicians at our expert witness conferencing significantly increased.

When brainstorming your tagline, remember that some of the most effective taglines are the simplest. For example, the Reebok walking shoe, EasyTone, had the tag line, "Better legs and a better butt with every step." The shoe was selling so fast with this tagline that Reebok was hard pressed to keep up with the orders. Of course, if you make a claim in your tagline, you had better be able to back it up. The FTC was of the opinion that Reebok was not able to

---

[1] See Chapter 11 on the importance of reading everything.

substantiate with scientific proof its advertising claim regarding its EasyTone shoes, and Reebok subsequently settled for $25,000,000.

If you are skeptical about the power of taglines, consider whether you have ever been influenced by a tagline in one of your buying or business decisions. We certainly have been. When possible, we prefer to deal with privately held businesses as opposed to publicly traded corporations. Large corporations can be inflexible, overly bureaucratic, and slow to make decisions. Privately held businesses like our own, however, tend to be more flexible and responsive. Furthermore, you can often cut quickly to the chase and gain the best possible concessions by talking directly to the owners of the business.

A large part of our business involves contracting with hotels to hold the continuing education seminars and conferences our firm produces. When contracting with hotels, we prefer privately held properties, for the reasons mentioned previously. As part of our search for a new property a few years ago, one hotel in particular caught our eye when we saw their tagline, which read, "Where hospitality is a family tradition." The fact that the hotel was family owned made it stand out, and we put it on the list of hotels we would visit and possibly do business with. The hotel eventually earned our business, and our relationship has now grown to the point where we have put on multiple programs at this property, which have been worth hundreds of thousands of dollars in business to the hotel. The business we will do in the future will likely total in the millions of dollars. And to think, all of this business was largely related to their simple but effective tagline.

Several businesses in the marketplace use taglines, as we did, to change a deeply ingrained perception. Take the pork industry, for example; pork has the reputation, developed over many millennia, of being an unhealthy food to eat. Overcoming this perception in an increasingly health-conscious population is crucially important for those who make their living from selling pork. Their answer, of course, was to use a tagline to change perceptions, and hence the National Pork Board coined the tagline, "Pork, the Other White Meat," in 1986. This tagline was a simple and effective way to address a serious branding problem.

The marketplace is also filled with great examples of taglines being used to define a brand to the business's huge advantage. In our minds, the best taglines explain in a very few short and powerful words the critical essence of the brand. As a result, some taglines that we consider to be particularly effective are Federal Express ("When it absolutely, positively has to be there overnight"), BMW ("The Ultimate Driving Machine"), and Energizer Batteries ("It keeps going, and going, and going …"). These taglines are memorable and send powerful messages to potential customers.

The power of effective and memorable taglines cannot be overestimated. How many of these can you quickly identify?

1. We try harder.[2]

2. Have it your way.[3]

3. Does she or doesn't she?[4]

4. The silver bullet.[5]

5. Fair and balanced.[6]

6. Nothing runs like a Deere.[7]

7. Just do it.[8]

8. Get a piece of the rock.[9]

9. The few, the proud.[10]

4. Treat your customers with respect and do not jerk them around.

EXECUTIVE SUMMARY: An easy and feel-good way to help your business succeed is to build a rock-solid brand by treating your customers right. The nice thing about treating people right is that it is usually within your power to do so. So, how do we treat our customers right? By figuring out what we hate when we are customers and making sure that we do not repeat these mistakes. We also note how we like to be treated and attempt to emulate that wherever and whenever possible. You will build very effective and valuable word of mouth if you do not jerk your customers around.

* * *

We have found that an easy way to greatly assist your business and increase your chances of succeeding is to simply treat your customers with respect. There are two pillars of our brand. First, as discussed earlier, we produce

---

[2] Avis

[3] Burger King

[4] Clairol

[5] Coors

[6] Fox News

[7] John Deere

[8] Nike

[9] Prudential

[10] US Marines

high-quality work. Second, we are a pleasure to deal with. We treat our customers with respect and do not jerk them around. By treating our customers as we ourselves would want to be treated, we have been able to build up very positive word of mouth while at the same time taking pride in our service.

Here's an example of what we mean. Every once in a while, we conduct a marketing campaign whereby we offer a special bonus or premium to any customer that buys a product or service by a certain time. For example, we might offer to review and critique a new client's resume if they sign up for one of our directories by a certain date. The problem arises, of course, when, through the inevitable computer error, an existing client who is already in the directory receives that offer. When this occurs, we invariably get a request from the existing client for us to review their resume. Although the offer was for new clients, we do not hesitate to tell them that we would be glad to promptly review their resume. We will never jerk our clients around and treat them worse than people who are not yet our customers. Nothing infuriates a long-term, loyal customer more than learning that a new customer is being treated better than he is.

Here is another typical example. Every year we run a seminar for which we offer the registrant a free book that our company publishes—a book that we normally sell for $135—if he or she signs up by a certain date. At the seminar, after we already had his money, one of our clients came up to me and said that he had previously purchased the book that we had sent him for free. He was wondering if he could have a different book instead. We were standing in front of the book table at the time. I did not even hesitate and responded, "Of course, which one would you like?" He picked out a book and asked where he should mail the returned book. I told him not to bother, and he responded to me that we were "a class act and a pleasure to deal with." In the years since this incident, this client has spent thousands of additional dollars with us for training and consulting. Such is the power of treating your customers the way you would like to be treated yourself.

We do not just treat our customers well when we have little to lose monetarily. We offer money-back guarantees if any one of our customers has to cancel for up to two weeks before the start of a conference, and in one particular case, a blizzard swept through the country right at the start of a Florida-based conference. Many attendees were unable to attend because of the blizzard, so we went above and beyond what we had promised in our brochure and sent full refunds to any attendee who could not make the conference due to the blizzard. Contractually, we were not required to do so. Nevertheless, not only did we provide refunds, but we sent out checks promptly with a personal letter. Our customers greatly appreciated this gesture. It cost us over $25,000, but the value to our brand and reputation was immeasurable.

On the flip side, let me give you an example of how to damage your brand by jerking your customers around. Recently we received a special promotional flyer from a hotel we had been doing business with for a few years. The hotel was obviously hurting, and it offered a 10% credit for any business booked by such-and-such a date. We called the hotel to book an annual conference that we had held at their location on the same weekend for the previous three years. We talked about what we needed. At the end of the conversation, I stated to the sales rep, "And, of course, we'd like to take advantage of the 10% offer you sent us." Her reply was ill considered and infuriating: "Well," she said, "that's only for new business."

I promptly gave the sales person a piece of my mind. First, nowhere on the flyer she had sent out did it say that the promotion was limited to new business. Second, was it their policy to treat strangers better than loyal, annual customers? Third, I was getting calls every day from competing properties, would she like us to go there? Fourth, why in heaven's name would she send me this offer if she would not honor it? Was she intentionally trying to make me angry? She said that there was nothing she could do, but she said that her boss would call me shortly.

In about five minutes I got a call from her boss. He apologized profusely and told me, "Of course we will honor this special offer." He had recognized it made no business sense to jerk around a good existing client and treat that customer worse than new customers. This is the kind of mistake we try to avoid. On a related note, do not screw people with crazy rebates. We have all had the experience of locking onto an advertised price that includes a rebate only to later discover that the seller is committed to doing everything possible to discourage you from actually getting the rebate by making the process complicated and time consuming. If we want to lower the price on one of our products or services, we actually lower the price. We do not jerk people around.

We put great stock in working with professionals and companies that are easy to deal with. In fact, this is one of the major criteria we use when deciding who we should work with. Some of the speakers and trainers we try to hire to teach at our conferences are challenging. They require numerous e-mails, phone calls, hand holding, and convincing. There is delay after delay to check their calendars, check with their employers, check with their spouses and/or significant others, and so forth. One simple request to speak can drag on for weeks, even months, and consume many wasted hours. Other trainers and speakers are easy and a pleasure to deal with. Here is a recent exchange with one of our easy-to-deal-with faculty members:

AUTHORS: Tom, we are putting together a two day conference in Seattle on October 2nd and 3rd, and I am wondering if you would like to teach the course with me?

TOM: Sounds like fun. Let me check my calendar. ... Yes, I am free.

AUTHORS: We can pay an honorarium of $4,000 plus expenses. What do you think?

TOM: Count me in. I will put it on my calendar. Send me the additional details when you have them.

AUTHORS: Will do. Thank you and all the best to the family.

The entire transaction took less than five minutes. We use Tom whenever we can because he is an excellent trainer, *and he is so easy to deal with*. But how important, really, is "being easy to work with" for potential customers and businesspeople? Our internal research indicates that being "easy to work with" is consistently in the top ten attributes customers and businesspeople look for.

Jim and I are businesspeople. We are also consumers. The way that we work on our brand of being easy to deal with is to take note of everything we detest about companies that provide lousy and infuriating service and everything we love about companies who provide us with great service. We take note of all the good and bad experiences we have when we are the customer and try to emulate what we liked and avoid what we did not like. Simply put, we strive to treat people the way we wish we were treated. There are many variables in business that are beyond your control. The beautiful thing about treating your customers right, however, is that doing so is entirely within your control.

One of the things we hate is when companies hit you with hidden charges and surprises on your final bill. Who has not been angered and felt betrayed when they examine a bill and see a hidden charge, basically a rip-off that they were not told about and were not expecting? We avoid surprising our customers with extra charges by employing a policy of transparent fixed-cost pricing. We charge a premium for our training, but the service we offer is excellent, and we do *not* nickel and dime our clients. Our clients do not have to worry about any nasty surprises when they get their final bill from us, and they very much appreciate our no-surprises pricing model. Here is how a conversation with a prospective client who is looking to hire us to do some training typically goes.

NEW CLIENT: We would like to hire you to do one day of corporate training on negotiating. What is your typical fee?

AUTHORS: Excellent. When is the date, where is the location, how many attendees are you expecting, and will they be charged to attend?

NEW CLIENT: It is April of this year, the 17th, and it is in Chicago at an airport hotel. We will have fifty to sixty employees, and as they are employees, they will not be charged. In fact, we have to bribe them with dinners out and a reception.

AUTHORS: The fee is $12,500 flat fee.

NEW CLIENT: What about travel?

AUTHORS: Included.

NEW CLIENT: Meals?

AUTHORS: Included.

NEW CLIENT: Handbooks? Do you provide handbooks?

AUTHORS: We do. We have a 237 page handbook and will provide copies at no additional charge. When we say flat fee, we mean it. We are training professionals and understand that knowing exactly how much something is going to cost is important.

NEW CLIENT: Excellent. Would you like us to have legal draft up a contract so we can get you a check for …?

AUTHORS: All we need is an e-mail confirming the details. We do not ask for advance payment, but we would appreciate it if you could have the check available on the date of the training.

NEW CLIENT: That was easy.

AUTHORS: Exactly.

Another thing we detest as customers is impersonal and unhelpful telephone support. Who has not been aggravated by pressing 1 and 2 endlessly and waiting on the line for heaven knows how long? When someone finally picks up, the customer service representative generally sounds like he or she is somewhere far away and can be hard to understand. The connection is often poor, and sometimes you can even hear other customer service representatives talking in the background, making it difficult to communicate. To make matters worse, it takes a good five minutes to even *find* a customer support telephone number because the company wants to discourage calls.

We take other companies' telephone support missteps as an opportunity to do things better and different. Instead of outsourcing our customer support services, we have one of our long-time employees answering our phones. She is competent, friendly, and articulate. There is no "call center" noise in background. Our telephone number is prominently displayed on our websites and in our promotional material. You cannot imagine the number of compliments we get on how nice, helpful, and responsive our staff is on the phone, which just goes to show that you can build your brand and help your business succeed by taking simple yet powerful steps to serve your customers.

Speaking of serving your customers, get back to people promptly. Another one of our pet peeves is nonresponsive people. Who has not been frustrated when someone you are doing business with does not call back when they said they would? We make a point to call people back. This helps build our brand of being easy to deal with. Many new clients are very pleasantly surprised when we call them back precisely when we say we would.

Do not take yourselves too seriously. If someone is fun, you are more likely to want to be in business with him or her. On the other hand, if someone is arrogant, you will not ever want to do business with him or her again. We like to believe that not only are we easy to deal with, but we are also fun and a pleasure to work with. Many companies forget to have some fun while getting the job done, which is too bad, because fun is contagious, is appreciated by your clients, and results in great word-of-mouth brand building. Jim and I commonly take our clients out to dinner, make jokes at each other's expense, and let them have some fun as well. For example, Jim and I took a group of our clients out to dinner recently with their wives and spent a few hours trading stories, insults, jokes, and just having fun. Here is some ribbing that was typical of the evening:

STEVE: Yes, I attended Jim's wedding. He married a beautiful, intelligent, highly paid corporate lawyer, with a killer smile. All through the room there was only one question being asked: Why Jim?

For several hours we refrained from talking shop and enjoyed ourselves. The clients had fun, and we got a thank you e-mail from them a few days later. It ended with the following sentiment: "You guys are a blast to work with!"

Deliver on time. Who has not been annoyed when something they were promised has not arrived on time? We have never been late with any product, service, conference, or training in 30 years. We hear all the time that our satisfied customers tell others, "They are not the cheapest, but they are the best, and they always deliver on time." Can there be better word-of-mouth branding? For 20 years we published a workers' compensation newsletter that was double columned, typeset, and 36 pages in length. In total, we released 240 issues of that newsletter, and not one was ever delivered late. When we discontinued the newsletter, we received dozens of nice letters about how much our subscribers loved it and looked forward to receiving it each month. Contrast the experience of our subscribers with my experience with a newsletter that I occasionally received. The editor and publisher were chronically late about the newsletter's publication until the situation was just hopeless. One day I received one of the funniest letters saying that because they were *two years late,* the editor and the publisher had decided to start all over again and forget about their missing issues.

Here is another example: Jim and I agreed to write a book for a major publisher, and we were given by contract eight months to complete it. We finished the manuscript, which was in excellent shape, in six months and sent it along to the publisher. A few days later, we received a phone call from our publisher:

PUBLISHER: We received a package from you with what looks like a manuscript.

AUTHORS: Yes. We finished the book a bit early and figured we would send it in.

PUBLISHER: But nobody ever finishes on time, let alone early.

AUTHORS: We do.

PUBLISHER: Well, I just don't know how we are going to deal with this. . . . We figured you would be three to six months late, but early? I will have to get back to you.

The book was put on hold for a month until our editor was ready to work on it. Despite the surprise, this publisher greatly appreciated that we delivered our work on time. At the present time, the book is in its fifth edition, and we have made hundreds of thousands of dollars from our relationship with this publisher.

Pay your bills and refund requests immediately and do not drag them out, no matter what. For example, we hire trainers to teach preconferences for us. The trainer's fee is negotiated, and then he shows up at the preconference to do his teaching. On his arrival, he is met by a SEAK partner and presented with his check. No need to wait until after the training has been completed;

no need to draft and submit an invoice; and wait 30, 60, or 90 days for it to be paid. We dole out cash on the barrelhead to demonstrate to our trainers that we have confidence that they will do a good job and respect them as professionals.

Stand by your work. We offer a 30-day money-back guarantee on almost all of our products.[11] Despite the fact that our products are premium priced and can easily be copied and returned, we receive less than 1% in returns each year. In those rare instances when someone does ask for a refund, however, we do not argue with them. Instead, we process their return and give them their money back promptly. How serious are we about standing by our work? Recently we were halfway through a consult with a client, but we felt as though the consult was not going as well as we had hoped. We called the client.

AUTHORS: We are not happy with the results you are getting from our consult.

CUSTOMER: I was a little disappointed but I know you were working hard at it.

AUTHORS: Working hard is good, but you need results. I am mailing back your entire consulting fee. We hope this helps.

CUSTOMER: Wow. I really appreciate it. Thank you.

We would like to close this chapter by leaving you with two positive examples from industries that have otherwise gained a reputation for jerking their customers around with poor service. First, think about taking a typical trip to your physician. We have all experienced the classic problems: the doctor disrespects your time by overbooking his schedule, which results in very long wait times. When you are sick, it's hard to get an appointment. The doctor is not open on weekends or at night. You cannot reach the doctor on the phone, and he is not likely to call you back. Contrast this with the experience my daughter Karen had with a local chiropractor a few years back; we will call him Dr. Mack. Karen threw her back out on a Friday afternoon and called Dr. Mack's office for an appointment. To our great shock, Dr. Mack said he would see her on Saturday. Not only that, Dr. Mack talked to Karen on the phone and gave her advice on how to stay comfortable before her appointment. Karen went in for her appointment on Saturday. She was seen precisely on time. Later that evening we were all having dinner at home and the phone

---

[11] See Chapter 4 as well.

rang. Karen answered and almost fell off her chair when she discovered who was calling. It was Dr. Mack checking in on how she was doing.

Dr. Mack very shrewdly decided to do things differently in his avoidance to act in a way that is consistent with what people hate most about visiting the doctor's office. His strategy has been extremely effective. We recommend him to everyone we can. Similar experiences by many other "wowed" patients have helped him build an extremely successful practice. Treating people right is a simple technique, but it has worked very well for him.

Next up, think about taking a trip to the airport. Most people cringe at the thought, as there is another location where customers feel more disenfranchised or disrespected. But if you are a Southwest Airlines (SWA) customer, you might have a different reaction. What SWA has done very effectively is to simply avoid doing many of the things that the big carriers do to anger their customers. In the process, the company has built itself a great brand and a very loyal customer base.

The instances of SWA doing things in a more customer-sensitive manner are numerous. For example, in the days when a Saturday night stay was a prerequisite if you wanted to snag the best airfares, SWA was the only major player that refrained from this practice. More recently, other airlines have begun to charge extra for checked bags. SWA does not. Most other airlines charge for snacks. SWA does not. We just took a flight with one major carrier who was charging for *nonalcoholic* drinks in-flight. SWA would never do this.

The results speak for themselves. SWA has become the most consistently profitable airline in the country. A large part of their business model is quite simple and remarkably effective: figure out what the competition does to anger travelers and do things differently. Treat a customer right and they will become loyal, sing your praises, and help you build a great brand.

As this chapter has made clear, there is no more effective and satisfying way help your business make money than to build a positive brand. Never underestimate the importance of doing a quality job and generating word of mouth, turning down work that risks your brand, using a well thought out and effective tagline, and treating your customers the way you yourself would want to be treated. Next we will focus on networking, which is another feel-good tool to help your business succeed.

Step 2: Grow and Tap Your Network

One of the most fulfilling ways to turn straw into gold is to build a solid network of contacts that can help your businesses. Building a network is both personally rewarding and professionally profitable. This chapter provides techniques for building a rock solid network and properly tapping into that network when needed.

1. Give a heads up and do favors.

EXECUTIVE SUMMARY: Giving colleagues a heads up is an effective way to foster and build long-term business relationships. It costs you nothing but a few moments of your time. The recipients will be happy to reciprocate and provide you with similar help.

* * *

An easy, effective, and satisfying technique for networking and building long-term relationships is giving colleagues and people you work with a heads up and doing favors for them. As such, you should liberally share information, leads, opportunities, and connections that you are privy to and that can help the people in your network. Giving a heads up and sharing information costs you little or nothing. What you receive in return, however, can be invaluable. First, you can feel good about helping out someone in your network. Second, the fact that you have helped someone out means that he or she probably won't soon forget what you have done, which can be very valuable. Let me give you some examples of what I mean.

Recently I received an e-mail from an occupational health nurse who was working as a case manager for one of the nation's largest fast food chains. She said that she would love to speak at one of our conferences. I called and spoke with her and told her I was happy to take her resume and put her in our speakers file. In passing, she mentioned that she was in the process of replacing her workers' compensation lawyers, and I immediately recognized that this information would be very helpful to one of my contacts, I'll call him Rob. So I called Rob and mentioned this development, which took me all of five minutes. To say the least, Rob was very appreciative. He asked if I would make the introduction, which I was happy to do. Bottom line: Rob landed part of this national account, and as far as he is concerned, I walk on water.

Fast forward a year. I was struggling to do some research concerning a new product we were developing in an area in which Rob had expertise, so I called Rob up and politely asked for help. Rob proceeded to spend the next hour on the phone with me, telling me everything I needed to know about my problem. When the conversation ended, Rob said one more thing. "If you need *anything* else, call me. Anytime." The sharing of helpful information had clearly cemented our mutually beneficial relationship.

Here is another quick example. A couple of years ago, Jim and I were asked to give a presentation to a large international organization at its annual conference. There was no honorarium provided, so it did not make sense for us to accept the work. That is not the end of the story, however. Instead of just forgetting about the presentation, we realized that one of our consulting clients would very much appreciate the opportunity to speak at the conference because it would give him tremendous exposure. Therefore, we called up our client—we'll call him Sam—and asked if it would be okay if we recommended him to speak in our place. Sam was extremely appreciative of the offer, and the organization ended up enlisting Sam to give the presentation, which gave Sam's firm tremendous exposure. We have been doing increasing amounts of work for Sam's firm ever since giving him this heads up.

In another example, Jim received an e-mail from a friend of his, we'll call her Laura, whom he had not seen or spoken to in a good number of years. The e-mail stated that Laura was starting a self-publishing business. Instead of just ignoring the e-mail or sending back a simple "that's great" response, Jim recognized that he was in a good position to help his friend out with her new venture. Jim called Laura and explained that our company runs a large writing seminar for physicians and lawyers and then offered her a free exhibiting booth at this seminar. Laura was ecstatic. She exhibited and made several great contacts, and three of these contacts turned into her very first paying customers. The booth cost us nothing. The whole thing took a few minutes to arrange. Laura was extremely appreciative, however, and we were able to build and strengthen our network and help a nice person out.

Not all heads ups are referrals or business opportunities. One of the trainers we work with, we'll call him Tony, had just started doing some extremely lucrative consulting work with law firms that defend a major industry. One day Tony shot me an e-mail that mentioned in passing that he was just about to expand his work to plaintiff law firms. I immediately picked up the phone and called him, and during that call I advised Tony that he was about to make a potentially fatal mistake. I explained that as a former trial lawyer, I knew that once an attorney started to work for plaintiff firms, the defense firms will never, ever use that attorney again. This advice saved Tony from making a disastrous mistake and losing a very substantial and lucrative long-term client. Tony is now a rock solid member of our network.

Here's one final example. When Jim graduated law school in the early '90s, the labor market was atrocious, and he had a lot of trouble finding a good entry-level legal job. The way he broke into the industry was when a friend of his, we'll call her Donna, left her job at a law firm. Donna gave Jim a heads up and recommended him to the firm's senior partner as her replacement, and Jim ended up getting the job. It was his big break, and he could not have done it without the help Donna had graciously and selflessly provided. To this day, Jim goes out of his way to proactively help Donna in anything that she does. He is extremely grateful and will never forget what she did for him. In our opinion, Jim's reaction is typical of what people feel when they have been helped out by someone.

2. Send a gift.

EXECUTIVE SUMMARY: We have found that sending an unexpected gift can be extremely effective in building and solidifying relationships. To be most effective, the gift should be both thoughtfully selected and arrive unexpected (e.g., not in December). We also have found that targeted charitable donations can make a very favorable impression as well. In any event, there is little to lose from this technique, as giving gifts, even token ones, is a pleasure, and supporting charities is the right thing to do.

* * *

One of the best ways we have found to build relationships is to send your contacts small, meaningful gifts. The gifts need not be expensive. In fact, it is best if they are not. What the gift should be, however, is personal and thoughtful. The correctly selected gift shows that you truly care, that you listened, and that you took the time to do something special.

Here's what we mean and what we do not mean when we talk about selecting a gift. We have all received over the holidays many mass-mailed gifts from vendors—usually sweets and other edible gift baskets. We also have received many holiday cards. The problem is that these gifts do not leave an extraordinary impression. Instead, they leave the impression that the sender is just like everybody else. If you want to make a superior impression on someone, we suggest thinking carefully about the gift and refraining from sending it during the holidays. This will really make your small gesture stand out.

We had a very high-powered, and very nice, attorney—we'll call her Sally—speak for us one year. Sally mentioned in passing at one point during our July conference that her favorite oldies song was "Under the Boardwalk." We decided to try to cement our relationship with Sally and have some fun at the same time, so we located a CD featuring the "Best of the Drifters" that prominently featured her song. We sent it along to her with a personal handwritten note. The cost of the CD was only $12.95, and the whole thing took me and my admin about 30 minutes total. A few days later I received a call from Sally. She was extremely appreciative. She could not believe that we had remembered what she had mentioned in passing and was quite impressed that we had been thoughtful enough to give her this small gift, which she very much valued. Sally has been a very strong member of our network ever since, and she has helped greatly in our efforts to find talented and knowledgeable speakers—which is critically important for a company like ours involved in the business of putting on conferences. Our experience with Sally is a perfect example of how a simple, thoughtfully selected gift can help you succeed in business.

Here's a second good example of this concept. I am socially acquainted with a corporate attorney, we'll call her Nancy, who is extremely well qualified and has many years of experience in her field. She is an Ivy League law school graduate. She has represented Fortune 500 companies. She is the type of person who would be charging over $500 plus an hour for her time if she were in a law firm. Nancy also happens to be Jim's wife. One evening I was out to dinner with Jim and Nancy, and I of course immediately turned to my favorite part of these social events—busting Jim's chops. I started to explain to Nancy how Jim sees everything through this great big prism of how it affects him personally. For example, I kidded, "If someone dies, his first thought would not be, 'Oh, that's terrible,' but, 'How does this affect me? When's the funeral? Can I still go boating this weekend?'" I continued to bust Jim's chops in this manner while Nancy kept laughing and heartily nodding.

A few weeks later Nancy comes home from work and finds a small package from me. I had sent her a small prism. She called me up howling with laughter and told me how much she loved it. But wait, this story gets better. About a month after the prism arrived, Nancy found and fell in love with a house that she wanted to buy. Jim resisted because he did not want to move during the short boating season we have in Massachusetts, and Nancy was pretty dejected. The next day, Nancy got a call from Jim, who said, "OK, we can buy the house." Nancy asked why he changed his mind, and Jim stated that he saw the prism on Nancy's desk. The epilogue of this story is simple and powerful. Whenever I need any quick, behind-the-scenes legal advice on a corporate matter, Nancy is *more* than willing to help me. This has saved us tens of thousands of dollars over the years in legal fees. I also get the satisfaction of retelling this story and continuing to bust Jim's chops.

We would like to conclude this section on gift giving by mentioning another variation of this technique that we have found to be effective—namely, determining a charitable cause that is of particular interest to someone and making a donation to that cause. Doing so will not only help you cement the bonds of a relationship but also will allow you to advance a passion for philanthropy. Here are a couple of examples.

One of our annual conferences features the same keynote speaker each year, we'll call him Marty. Marty is a famous person, and his presence is critical to the success of this conference. When we learned that Marty had a son with Asperger's syndrome, we sent, without being asked, a donation in Marty's name toward a foundation whose goal it is to find a cure for Asperger's. The donation was acknowledged by Marty and was very much appreciated, and it helped further cement our relationship. Not only has Marty continued teaching for us for over ten years, but we felt genuinely good about the gesture, because one of our missions is supporting charity.

Here is one final example: When we learned that the son of a long-term SEAK employee was deployed to Iraq, we made a donation to our town's military support group and sent him and his unit a care package. Our simple gesture was very much appreciated by the employee, and we felt good about doing our small part to support the troops as well. Making a personal, well thought out, charitable donation in the name of someone who will appreciate it feels good and helps cement relationships and builds loyalty.

3. Mentor

EXECUTIVE SUMMARY: Mentoring young people is an enjoyable way to pass along your experience and knowledge. It also can be—and often is—invaluable in their later success and *your* later success. The people that you mentor will never forget your help and guidance. When the opportunity presents itself, the people you have mentored will be more than happy to help you and your business with good will, referrals, and new business.

* * *

A simple and easy way to help your business succeed is to mentor young people. The people you mentor will become rock solid members of your network. Just look at Jim and I. Many years ago, when Jim was a young lawyer, he began working for me at my business. Jim helped with many projects and really complimented my own skills and experience. As he said he would do all along, however, Jim left me when he was able to secure a job at the type of law firm he had been targeting. He practiced law for a few years, and during this period I continued to mentor him. I would proactively check in with him every so often. I referred cases to him. I answered any questions he might have. When he was faced with crisis, I offered my advice. In the meantime, though, I really missed having Jim be a part of my business. I wished I had him back working for me.

One day I got a call from Jim, who said that he was fed up with the law firm environment and wanted to come back to work for me. My reaction was immediate. "Yes!" I exclaimed into the phone. Jim has been with me ever since. We have been through good and bad times together. We have grown the business to 10 plus times the size it was when he first joined me. He has repaid the mentoring favor by helping to mentor my two children, both of whom work in the business. And all of this happened because my mentoring of him helped build a solid, mutually beneficial relationship. And you know what? Even if Jim had never helped me in my business again, the mentoring still would have been worthwhile because it was the right thing to do and felt good.

Here's another example of how mentoring can benefit your business in the long run. Several years ago a family friend asked me for help with their precocious son, we will call him Zed, who was in high school and was very bright. He was, however, having trouble with authority and studying and seemed to utterly lack direction. Honoring the request of Zed's parents, I began a dialogue with this young man and found him to be very well read, extremely intelligent, and very mature and sophisticated in the ways of business. He was truly remarkable for a teenager. Despite his failing grades, Zed was actually giving investment advice to some of his high school teachers and was managing a few of their portfolios. I agreed with his parents that his high school record could undermine his chances to do what he was so good at in the future, so I began a mentoring process with this extraordinary young person. I helped him by relating how I myself had had similar issues during high school and talked him through a stock market implosion and several business ideas.

Unfortunately, Zed's problems at school intensified. Despite the fact that he was a business savant, he was still flunking out of high school. As you might expect, his parents were very agitated and considered various forms of discipline to get this teenager to live up to his potential. Nevertheless—and despite his parents' protests—Zed quit high school without graduating. At this point in time, I was again consulted and continued mentoring the young man. After spending even more time with Zed, my advice to his parents was completely different from the advice they had received from friends and professionals. Simply put, I advised them to let him be, let him work it out for himself, and let him decide what he was going to do. I also recommended that they be nice to him, as he was going to be rich in short order and they would be probably working for him someday soon.[1]

Zed eventually found his own way, obtained a GED, and decided on his own to go to college. Despite the fact that he was in his teens, he obtained several high-powered positions writing financial stories and news and began earning a six-figure salary while attending college. He was even able, while still a teenager, to land a six-figure literary contract to write some business books.

Jim and I were so inspired by Zed's success that we decided to write our own business book and proposal. When we hit a brick wall while trying to obtain a high-powered New York literary agent, we sent Zed our book proposal to look over. He liked it and agreed to send it to his agent—but he did not just send it along. Instead, he included a very nice recommendation and some kind words about the authors. To make a long story short, his agent agreed to represent us, and our book was sold at auction to the highest bidder. None of this would have likely happened without the help that Zed provided us. Mentoring a high school dropout was our key to breaking into writing business books.

4. Don't be afraid to ask for help.

EXECUTIVE SUMMARY: There are both right ways and wrong ways to ask for help. When done correctly, asking for help can cement relationships and provide you with tremendous benefits that may be impossible to obtain in other ways. On the other hand, asking for help in the wrong way is a surefire way to destroy relationships.

---

[1] Postscript: Zed's mother is already working for him and enjoying every minute of it.

* * *

One of the key advantages to building a solid and wide network is being able to tap into that network when you occasionally need help—and do not be afraid to ask for help when you need it. Asking for help cements relationships due to the subtext of your request. That is, by asking for help from one of your contacts, you strongly imply that you trust and value his or her insight, experience, knowledge, and judgment. Such implied trust is flattering to many professionals, including us!

But be careful when asking for help, as there are both good and bad ways to do so. The key to using this technique effectively is to ask for help the good way. To that end, the following are several guidelines that we follow when asking for help:

- Make it simple and easy for the recipient to comply.

- Only ask the person to do something that is likely to be within his or her comfort zone.

- Do not let the only time you call or write to be when you are asking for something.

- ALWAYS say thank you afterwards.

We occasionally ask our colleagues and customers for their help when we are developing our products and courses. We are always mindful of the time it will take them to respond to our request, and we try to make the process as easy and efficient as possible. Letting the recipients know that your request for help will be simple, quick, and easy to respond to is important. The recipients are more likely to reply and less likely to resent the request. So, what is the best way to ask for help? Here's a sample request.

> Dear Mary,
>
> I have one quick question I am hoping you can help with.
> How much do you think is appropriate to charge for one day of training for psychologists like yourself?
>
> Thank you for your insight and help.
>
> All the best,
> Steve

For these simple "one question e-mails" we receive an 80 to 90% response rate, as it only takes a few seconds for our recipients to read and respond to our request. It is not a burden to them, and the information we receive back may be priceless. Sometimes, however, we have to ask our recipients for more detailed information or have more than one question. To make these types of requests easier on the recipients, we have found that it is helpful to structure the request in bullet-point fashion. As an added bonus, working with bulleted lists also makes it easier for us to collate and use their responses. Here's a sample e-mail of this technique in action.

> *Dear Fred,*
>
> *I am doing research on the biggest problems consultants have when they are trying to get paid and would appreciate your insight.*
>
> *Could you send me, in bullet points, what you see as their five biggest problems?*
>
> *As always, thank you for your help.*
> *Steve*

Another tool that we use when asking for help is the short, open-ended question, which is easy for the recipient to respond to and quick to read. Because this type of question is simple by nature, the recipient can respond in a brief manner if that is all the time he or she has. The fact that the question is open ended also helps us gather information without prejudicing the answers. For example, recently we were working on a new course that is targeted to occupational health professionals. We selected 14 trusted colleagues and sent them this simple and easy-to-respond-to e-mail, which generated valuable feedback and helped us modify and develop a course that ended up making us a large amount of money.

> *Dear Mary,*
>
> *We are developing a new occupational medicine course. I have attached a one-page outline for the proposed course. Please give me your frank opinion on whether this course will appeal to occupational health professionals.*
>
> *Thank you so much for your help and insight.*
>
> *All the best,*
> *Steve*

While asking for help can positively impact your business, it is important not to go too far and ask for too much. You do not want people in your network to think that they are being put upon or taken advantage of. To ensure that your recipients will not be put off by your request, only ask for assistance for that which is likely to be within their comfort zone.

Our lifeblood as a conference business is getting effective and knowledgeable presenters to agree to speak for us. One technique we have used very effectively in this regard is to tap our network for help. More specifically, we routinely ask for referrals/introductions for new speakers from our network of past speakers. Take the following e-mail request for assistance, for example.

> *Dear John,*
>
> *As you know, we rotate our speakers each year, and we rely on this year's faculty to nominate speakers for next year's conference. Can you nominate two well-spoken and accomplished speakers like yourself for next year's program?*
>
> *As always, I truly appreciate your help.*
>
> *All the best,*
> *Steve*

We recruit many extraordinary speakers in this fashion, and this practice has helped us greatly in maintaining the high quality of our conferences and therefore our brand.

Life is so hectic nowadays that one of the most difficult things to do is to reach busy people, but we have used our network to help in this regard. We have found that people in our network are usually more than happy to provide us with an introduction when they can, and that shortcut saves us valuable time. We use this technique successfully all the time. For example, recently we were trying to get in touch with a famous author. We had no luck after repeated attempts, so we decided to tap into our network for a little assistance. We shot over the following e-mail:

> *Dear Fred,*
>
> *We have been trying unsuccessfully to get in touch with bestselling author, _____. As you know, he is a bit reclusive. I know that you work with him. Would you be willing to make the introduction? I have attached a short bio of myself with my contact information.*
>
> *Thank you so much for your help.*
>
> *All the best,*
> *Steve*

The introduction worked. We got through to this A-list author, who ended up speaking at our writing conferences for many years and helped us make a good deal of money. If we had never tapped into our network to ask for an introduction, we probably would have never formed this lucrative relationship.

Always remember that it is important that you not only call or write to your contacts when you need help. Networking will not work for you if you treat it as a one-way street. Instead, try not to ask for anything during most of your conversations with members of your network. One good way we do this is to send an occasional e-mail saying hello and asking about your contact's health, business, family, and life. We also always offer our assistance in anything our contact may need, a practice that is always much appreciated. Here are a couple of quick examples of this.

A few years ago, a speaker that had spoken for us many times had a severe heart attack. When we heard about it, we sent him a get-well card and let him know that we were thinking of him and if there was anything he needed from us. We followed up with a call three months later to see how he was doing. He appreciated our thoughtfulness, made a full recovery, and continues to speak for us. Another time, one of our trainers cancelled a few days before a training assignment due to a cancer diagnosis. We called and were supportive. We spoke to him a few more times, offering him encouragement, and we offered to do anything we could to assist. He greatly appreciated the calls, is on the mend, and will be speaking for us again shortly.

It is also crucially important to always thank the people who help you. Thanking those who offer you assistance is both polite and necessary, and you can extend your gratitude by phone, e-mail, or even by letter. For example, one colleague we deal with, we'll call her Terri, always sends a nice handwritten thank you note after being the recipient of our help. It is so unusual nowadays to get a letter in the mail, let alone a handwritten one, and her kind notes really make her stand out in our mind as a special, exceptionally thoughtful person. Whenever Terri needs anything, we bend over backwards to help such a classy, thoughtful, and exceptionally nice person.

Now that we have covered some of the right ways to ask for help, what are some of the wrong ways to do so? The *wrong* way to ask for help is to remind people of past favors and overtly call in IOUs. Such an approach is crass, boorish, ineffective, and unnecessary. Let me give you an example.

Recently I received a call from someone who wanted to cash in on a past favor he had done for me, and I was suitably offended. Keep in mind that it is pretty hard to offend a former trial lawyer who grew up in New York City. Here is how the call went:

CALLER: Hi, Steve and Jim, remember me? We did some "business" a while ago.

AUTHORS: Vaguely. What "business" did we do again, and when was that?

CALLER: Eight years ago. You asked me to speak at a conference and I spoke for you.

AUTHORS: That explains it. In the past eight years we have had about 1,000 speakers. What can we do for you?

CALLER: I am calling in my favor. I have a flyer for a new directory you are publishing and would like a free $495 listing.

AUTHORS: We are sorry, but we cannot do that.

CALLER (Taken aback and insulted): I am shocked you will not do this after what I did for you. Let me tell you, I will never speak for you again, and will have nothing good to say about you or your company.

AUTHORS: We are sorry you feel that way.

Why did we refuse to do anything for the caller? Well, frankly, we were offended by the rude way in which he demanded something from us. He would have had much better luck if he had kept in touch over the last eight years and asked in a different way, such as, "I am interested in expanding my business and was wondering if your directory was right for me?" Maybe then we would have offered to do something for him.

Here's another example of how *not* to ask for help. Namely, do not make your first contact in many years one in which you are asking for something. The following happened just the other day, when I received an e-mail from an attorney who I had not heard from in 24 years.

> *Dear Steve,*
>
> *I am just writing to see how you and Ellen and the kids are doing. I know it has been some time since we talked. How is the practice of law going? Are you still kicking butt?*
>
> *I recently started a business where I promote _____, and I am wondering if you could help me?*
>
> *Thank you,*
> *Serena*

Here is the truthful response I could have sent, but did not.

Dear Serena,

Yes it has been a while … about twenty-four years. My kids are now in their mid-thirties, have families, and are doing well.

My wife passed away five years ago from cancer.

I have not practiced law since 1992 and am well into my second career …

The lesson is clear. Trying to ask for a favor from someone you have never kept in touch with is awkward and usually not successful.

We get requests for help all the time, and we truly try to be as helpful as possible, but one category of requests that we can't help with is when we are asked to do too much. These types of requests are easy to refuse and sometimes even mind-boggling. Here is an example:

PAST ATTENDEE: Remember me? I attended your writing course on Cape Cod four years ago?

AUTHORS: Hi! How is your writing going?

PAST ATTENDEE: Great. That is why I am calling. I finished my novel and have self-published it. It looks really good. Could you read it, write a favorable review, and e-mail the favorable review to your (extensive) e-mail list?

AUTHORS: We're sorry, we cannot e-mail promotional material to our list due to privacy regulations.

Although we should not and do not "keep score," colleagues who ask for enormous favors or continually ask for help quickly become overbearing and resented. Eventually, they wear out their welcome, destroy their relationship with you, and are all too easy to refuse.

Networking, as you probably agree by now, is a force multiplier. Helping your network out by giving your contacts a heads up, sharing information with them, sending them gifts, mentoring them, and the like will make it easier for you to obtain priceless assistance when you need it most. Not only is networking helpful to your business' bottom line, but it can be fun and rewarding, so network as much as you can. Of course, networking and branding can only help you if your business develops products that people want to buy. Our next chapter explains what we have learned over the years regarding product development.

Step 3: Develop Products Customers Love

New product development is an important part of any successful business, and the development process can be a lot of fun: you get to be creative. You get to try something new. If the product takes off, you make money. But new product development can also be fraught with danger. If you build something that no one ends up buying, you will have wasted much time and money. This chapter provides the painful but valuable lessons we have learned regarding new product development.

1. Listen to your customers.

EXECUTIVE SUMMARY: It is extremely risky to develop new products without first researching what your customers want and how much they are willing to pay for what they want. If you want to pinpoint what new products you should develop and what new products you should avoid, listen to your customers. Use surveys and ask open-ended questions. Perhaps most important, pay particular attention to unsolicited suggestions that you might receive, as these are likely to be the most accurate predictors of what your customers want from you and what they would be willing to pay you to get it. If you want to succeed in business, listen to your customers.

* * *

One of the biggest challenges you will face when running a business is how and where to find good information. For many important questions, you can't just go and Google the answer. Moreover, no amount of traditional research can help you. And when the question you are asking is what new product or service your customers want and would actually be willing to buy, there is only one resource that will give you the answer you are looking for: your customers.

We are intelligent. We're experienced. What we have learned the hard way over the years of running our business, however, is that no amount of intelligence or experience will enable you to accurately determine what your customers want or will buy. Put another way, it is basically impossible for the two of us to just sit around the room and declare with any real confidence what our customers will and will not want to buy. Instead, we have learned that the way to determine what products and services your customers would purchase from you is to listen to what your customers have to say.

Prior to learning this invaluable lesson, we created too many products and services that our customers had little to no interest in buying. Here is a typical example. The main source of our business revenue is from the continuing education seminars that we put on each year. We put on the seminar and people pay us tuition to attend. Generally speaking, our seminars are very well received, and we all make a good living from putting on these seminars. So one day, I presented Jim with a brilliant idea for a new product.

STEVE: I have an idea for a new seminar.

JIM: I'm almost afraid to ask, but go ahead.

STEVE: We know a lot about seminars, right?

JIM: That I will agree with.

STEVE: Let's put on a seminar that shows other people how to put on seminars. I already have a name for it: I'll call it the "Seminar on Seminars." What do you think?

JIM: I think you have no way to sell it and we have no idea if anybody wants it or would be willing to pay for it. Other than that, it's pretty good.

STEVE: This idea isn't pretty good, it's really good. We know a lot about seminars.

JIM: But who are we going to sell this to? Did you do a needs assessment, you know, send out a survey to potential customers to gauge how much potential interest there is in this? Has anyone asked for this?

STEVE: That's the beauty of this. This idea is so good and so valuable that everyone will want it and we'll be able to dramatically grow our company. It's transformational.

JIM: Let's do some more research on this and see if anybody wants it.

STEVE: I have news for you. I've already developed the course. I wanted to surprise you. It is really, really good, and I don't want to wait. Give me a plan for selling it, and let's schedule it for some time in the next few months. Any questions?

JIM: Yeah, do you know the name of a good bankruptcy lawyer? I think we might need one after this.

Despite Jim's protestations, I insisted that we move forward. The reason was simple: *I had fallen in love with my own idea.* And yes, we put on the seminar. We should have named the seminar *Titanic* or *Hindenburg* for the results that came back. We spent $25,000 promoting it, but only three people registered, paying $295 each. We lost our shirt because we had developed a very helpful, very informative product *that no one wanted to buy.* This mistake could have been avoided if we had actually *asked* our customers what they might want and *listened* to what they had to say.

Having learned our lesson all too well, our standard procedure now is to survey our customers on what products we should develop. We have three main, formal ways that we do this. First, when we see our customers in person at one of our seminars, we ask them to fill out forms or respond to written surveys about potential new product ideas. Second, we send out e-mails to our customers and ask them to fill out a brief survey using *Survey Monkey*, a commonly used and inexpensive online tool for gathering information. In each of these two cases we usually raffle off a prize to respondents to encourage participation. Finally, we send an e-mail off to select customers and ask them an open-ended question so as not to preordain the results. These emails are simple, brief, and to the point:

Dear Fred:

I was wondering if I could ask you a quick question. We are thinking of developing product X, which we would sell for $Y. I would very much appreciate your frank thoughts.

All the best,

Steve

Listening to our customers has saved us large amounts of money. The vast majority of what we thought was our best and brightest ideas that we have run by our customers have turned out to either have tepid or nonexistent demand. Although it never feels good when your customers tell you that one of your product ideas is of little interest to them, it is much, much better to find this out *before* you spend large amounts of money developing and marketing that new product.

Unfortunately, however, a positive needs assessment result regarding a potential product is certainly no guarantee that that product will wind up being successful. There are many reasons for this. The results from your needs assessment may have been biased, as the respondents may have been trying to be nice. Alternatively, the product you promised in the needs assessment might not be as good as what you actually end up producing. Sometimes the marketplace even changes between needs assessment and launch. There are all types of variables. There is one guarantee, however: developing a product without first getting input as to what your market actually wants and would actually pay for is a very risky way of doing business and should be assiduously avoided.

One final point: we have often found that the best ideas our customers gives us come unsolicited, so when your customers talk to you about what they really want, *listen to them.* Let me give you a couple of quick examples.

Jim and I are experts on negotiating. We have written three books on negotiating, and for many years we have taught seminars on the topic. A few years ago, we were teaching some high-powered professionals a two-day course on negotiating. Toward the end of the course, we included a brief list of some questions to ask during a negotiation to help improve your results. One of the attendees came up to us after the class and said to us, "Is there any way you could develop a list of more such questions. The few you gave me were in and of themselves worth the $1,200 price of the course." A light bulb went off in our heads after hearing this important feedback. What if we were to write a book containing questions to use during negotiating? To make a long story short, we ended up writing such a book called *Never Lose Again* and then submitted it for publication, at which time a bidding war broke out among the publishers who wanted to buy the book. We were on to something because we had listened to our customer. It is fair to say that we probably never would have come up with this idea on our own.

Here is one final example. For many years we have published a professional directory of physicians who perform examinations for insurance companies. Very recently a nonphysician (a physical therapist) sent us an e-mail pretty much begging us to list him in the directory even though he is not a physician. It turned out that he also performed services for insurance companies, and, again, a light bulb went off. After a process of further research, we ended up opening up the directory to nonphysicians and increasing our profitability. Logistically, this was easy for us to do; all we needed to do was to add a new section to our directory. But we had never done this before because we had never realized there was this demand. Our simple and successful product expansion was possible only because we had listened to our customers, the source from which our best new product ideas often come.

Here is one final example to show just how valuable can it be to listen to your customers. One of our best friends used to work as a senior executive at one of the largest privately held investment houses in the country. Back in the mid-1990s, this particular company, we'll call them Acme Investments, was very small—a tiny fish in a large ocean. Acme's core business consisted of providing financial advisors with financial advice that they would pass along to their individual investors. These advisors were paid on commission based on sales of investment products.

One day the company held a conference for its financial advisors and solicited ideas from them as to how to make more money. One of the financial advisors stood up and stated, "I'm getting a lot of pushback from my investor clients for our sales charge for putting these people into mutual funds. They hate it. They don't trust our advice and think we're just trying to sell them stuff and churn their account for our own benefit. Several clients have suggested that we instead charge for our advice by collecting a small annual percentage of each investor's assets. That way, our interests are aligned with the customer's interests. The more we make for them, the more we get paid. Is this model something we can consider?"

We don't need to get into the messy details of the investment industry, but suffice it to say that at that time, nobody else was charging the way the customers had suggested. Acme soon thereafter instituted this new pricing structure, and the results were phenomenal. Based almost exclusively on this newly structured product born from the suggestions of clients, Acme grew very rapidly to become the top firm of its type in the entire country. When *the head of the firm cashed out in the early 2000s, his shares were worth $1.6* *billion dollars.* Such is the real-world value of listening to your customers for ideas and advice on product development.

2. Before you proceed with a new product, have a plan that covers *all* the necessary elements for success.

EXECUTIVE SUMMARY: Of every 20 ideas you come up with for a new product, at best only 1 or 2 are likely to be viable. The way you find out what is most likely to be viable is to ask the hard questions and do your homework in advance. A new product will not be successful unless it meets certain conditions. If people don't want it, it will fail. If people are not willing to pay for it, it will fail. If you don't have a way to cost effectively sell it or distribute it, it will fail. Finally, if the product doesn't work or if it doesn't do what you claim it should do, it will fail. Be very critical of your own ideas and aggressively look for all potential fatal weaknesses before deciding to launch the product.

* * *

A chain is only as strong as its weakest link. So it is with product development. A new product will not succeed unless *every last element* of the following chain is satisfied:

1.   People want the product.

2.   People are willing to pay a workable price for the product.

3.   There is a cost-effective way to market, sell, or distribute the product.

4.   There is a cost-effective way to produce and deliver the working product.

Product development is neither horseshoes nor hand grenades. We have learned the hard way that "close enough" will not do. You need to be able to satisfy each of the four conditions if you want to be able to expect to have a profitable new product. Doing so will also help you weed out the impractical ideas and concentrate on the ones that can make you money. As for Jim and I, we have made many, many costly mistakes in this area and hope that you can learn from these. For example, many years ago we developed a video and workbook program, entitled *Help Your Child Achieve*, that was targeted to the parents of underachieving children. This product was the single biggest financial calamity that our business ever suffered. The reason for this was simple: we developed the product without thinking through and researching whether anybody would be willing to pay for it and how we would be able to sell it. The product won awards, but no one wanted to buy it and we did not have a viable plan to sell it. Through this experience, we learned that quality alone is not enough. People must want to buy your products for a workable amount, and you need to have a way to sell what you create.

Here's another example. Several years ago, Jim called me up to discuss a new idea he had come up with. Here's approximately how the conversation went:

JIM: Are you sitting down?

STEVE: Don't tell me … You have another idea.

JIM: Hear me out. You know how we're big on listening to our customers?

STEVE: Yes.

JIM: Well, I get three to four requests a year from physician clients of ours asking for my advice on which lawyer they should hire when they have a legal problem specific to physicians.

STEVE: I get those calls too; go on.

JIM: We know how to publish directories, right?

STEVE: Yes, we've been doing that for many years.

JIM: What if we created a *National Directory of Physician's Counsel*. We'll sell listings to lawyers that specialize in representing physicians. We could make a fortune.

STEVE: Interesting. How do you think we should proceed?

JIM: Let's send out some needs assessments to doctors and lawyers and see what they think.

STEVE: I don't want to do that. Let me tell you why. *This idea is so good, I don't want the secret to get out in advance, as someone could steal it from us.*

JIM: You're right.

We eventually launched this new product. At substantial cost we marketed it to attorneys and convinced hundreds of law firms to sign up for a free first year. At great cost we printed and mailed to physicians tens of thousands of copies of the directory. We developed a custom database and website. Then, after a year, the moment of truth arrived: we asked the listed firms to pay to renew their listings. Of the 300 plus law firms in the directory, only 12 renewed. We refunded their money and folded up our latest Edsel. Our hubris and corner cutting had cost us dearly.

What had gone wrong? The law firms didn't get cases from the listing, so they didn't renew. The question, then, was: *why* didn't the law firms get cases? We are always getting calls from clients looking for advice on which lawyer to hire. How could this be? We did some research on the back end to find out, and what we discovered was very revealing. We asked our physician customers *why* they hadn't used the directory, and the answer was clear: they would never hire a lawyer out of what looked to be a yellow pages type product. These were serious legal matters they had, and we expected them to hire a lawyer blind, out of a directory. Were we nuts?

We had grossly miscalculated. Just because clients had asked our advice regarding who to hire as a lawyer did not in any way mean they were willing to pick a lawyer out of a list in a directory. We should have asked this question *before* we developed our product. We should have more carefully thought about the four elements of a successful product launch before spending (and losing) the large amount of money we did launching this directory that (almost) no one used.[1] Because we didn't, we paid a severe price, as well we should have.

Once the proponent of an idea falls in love with his own idea or concept for a new product, a poor result should not come as a surprise. Love can be blind. The temptation to rush the product to market is often irresistible. Because we have four partners, however, we now use a checks and balance system. If we can't convince all four partners to proceed with a product, we scrap it. Sometimes the "discussion" is heated and protracted, going on for weeks, but the process works and has saved us untold amounts of money and time. The lesson here is that the proponent of the idea should never be the one to make the sole decision about proceeding with it. He or she is too much in love with the idea. Use checks and balances before proceeding.

In the early years of our business, we probably developed over 50% of the ideas that we had. About 75% of our new products in those years flopped. Products that flop do little for your brand or your bottom line. We were batting .250. We now probably develop only about 5% of the ideas we have. It was a long maturation process. Our current procedure is to thoroughly vet

---

[1] We only heard of one person actually using the directory. Jim's wife, who is also a lawyer, was able to reconnect with a friend from law school who was listed in the directory and with whom she had lost touch. This was the only instance we know of the directory actually being used. Not a record to be proud of. There was nobody to blame for this debacle but ourselves. We had failed to do our homework and ask the hard questions before launching the product.

our ideas. We make sure that we have good answers to all our questions about our ideas. We don't let ourselves fall in love with our own ideas. We verify that we have strong and credible evidence that can meet all four of the elements of successful new product launching. And, what do you know the turnaround in results has been astounding. In recent years, less than 10% of our new products and services have lost money. Now we're batting .900.

Here are some additional instructive examples. One of our good friends, we'll call him Irving, is a very talented investment manager. Irving graduated from two top business schools and spent many years working as a portfolio manager for one of the best performing investment firms in New York. He is very good at picking stocks. But eventually, Irving decided that he no longer wanted to work for someone else, and he figured that because he was such a superb money manager, he would start his own one-person hedge fund. He has been at it for four years now, and he has indeed established a very good track record for picking stocks . The problem, however, is that he has had a difficult time attracting investors and, consequently, he is not doing nearly as well as he would like.

What happened is perfectly clear to us, because we have made similar mistakes so many times ourselves. Irving jumped into business without a solid and viable plan for element number 3 on our list above. He had no idea how to cost effectively market, sell, and distribute his money management services. Now, let's not forget: Irving has great things going for him. His investment performance has been superb. The prices he charges his clients are lower than his competition's. His business is struggling, however, because this is just not enough. He also needs a way to sell his services in a cost-effective manner. The bottom line is that he would have had an exponentially greater chance of success if he had figured out in advance of his fund's launch how he was going to sell his services.

Consider this final example, which is probably the poster child for the consequences that can befall you when you don't have your key ducks in a row prior to launching a new product or venture. Toward the end of the dot-com boom, one of our friends, we'll call him Barry, decided to resign from his position as the CEO of a prestigious investment firm to launch a dot-com company based on a catchy URL he had acquired the rights to. Barry left a lot of money from his former job on the table in terms of unvested stock options and the like to make this switch, but he did not want to miss out on the dot-com gold rush that he saw going on all around him.

At the time, we asked Barry what his business model would be, and he stated that he and his partners had many ideas and that they were sure they'd find one that worked. We didn't have an Ivy League MBA like Barry. We were just two self-taught guys running a boring brick-and-mortar business. Keeping in mind the hard lessons we had learned about needing a solid product plan, we sensed disaster, but we still wished Barry all the best. To make a long story short, in less than a year, the dot-com venture was no more and Barry was out of work. Barry and the talented and accomplished team he had put together had burned through all of their seed capital, hadn't launched one product, and hadn't raised one cent in revenue.

Usually, problems arise because businesspeople are strong on three of the four components but are missing one—and then they gloss that last one over. In this dot-com example, however, Barry and his team had a grand slam of wishful but unrealistic planning. They had no well-thought-out plans for any products that somebody would pay for. They had no idea how to sell whatever they came up with. They had no idea if they could even make the product they would eventually develop work from a technological standpoint. What they had was a talented team of traditionally educated business executives, a great sounding URL, and a lot of ambition and guts. It wasn't enough.

Countless highly intelligent and successful people fell into the same problem during the dot-com boom, and they did this for the same reason that many people in the 2000s believed that real estate prices would always increase at a double-digit rate. That is, they believed in new, revolutionary methods that were pushed by all kinds of the best and brightest experts. Meanwhile, we made a profit in the years 2000 and 2001. Our business was also profitable in 2008, 2009, 2010, 2011, and 2012. A large part of our success is that, whenever we have to choose between revolutionary new business theories that few understand (and even fewer can explain) and the real-world business lessons we have learned over the years, we go with the real-world lessons. They may not be sexy or cutting edge, but they are profitable year in and year out.

3. Read everything.

EXECUTIVE SUMMARY: There is potential gold in reading as much as you can. Your reading list should include everything from financial news articles to your junk mail. Reading can inspire ideas for new products if you adapt what other people are doing or learn about new problems or opportunities. Reading can also show you how other people are selling and marketing their services and help you identify potential persons and organizations to do business with.

* * *

One of the most productive ways to come up with new product ideas is to try to read as much as you can. We personally read the *Wall Street Journal* (especially the Marketplace and the Personal Journal sections of the paper), business and trade magazines, newsletters, posts from discussion groups, and even every piece of "junk mail" that we get. We feel that reading is so important that we have even designated one of our partners to be our "official reader" and keep us all updated with summaries of all critical articles and materials.

Why would a small company like ours spend the time and resources to read so much? It is exactly because of our size that we do it. We do not have millions of dollars to spend in product development, so why not utilize, adapt, and modify many of the excellent new ideas, products, and services that are being written about on an almost daily basis?

We suggest that you select and read key materials and process the information you glean from them through your own prism. Questions you want to be asked while reading are:

- Does this or can this affect/impact us directly or indirectly?

- Is there an idea/concept/product/service that we can adapt, modify, or improve on?

- Does coming at an analogous problem a different way from the perspective of a different industry suggest or open our minds to something new or better we can do?

There are four main benefits of reading everything:

1. Ideas for new products and services—not to mention ideas for how to market and sell these products and services—may present themselves or help crystallize your thinking.

2. You are presented with trends in the marketplace that you can capitalize on.

3. Companies may be mentioned that you may want to work for or with.

4. Information will be made available that you can utilize in your research.

Let's look at a few examples of how reading everything has helped us develop new products and make money. A number of years ago we read an article in a medical journal that described physicians' growing dissatisfaction with the practice of medicine. Selling to physicians is one of our niches.[2] As a result, the article immediately inspired us to come up with the idea for one of our now annual conferences, Non-Clinical Careers for Physicians, which is

---

[2] For more on niches, please see Chapter 4.

designed to help physicians explore the numerous nonclinical opportunities available to them. The conference includes inspirational presentations, talks on making a career transition, and presentations on the opportunities available in specific industries (i.e. Pharma, insurance, finance, etc.) and is very highly rated. Once we started running these conferences, we quickly noticed that the physicians attending were anxious about actually getting a job once they decided to leave clinical medicine. We had another idea: what if we tapped into the Great Recession and offered free attendance to recruiters and employers who were specifically hiring physicians for nonclinical positions? Where did this inspiration come from? It came from yet another article that we had read, this time an article in the *Wall Street Journal*: "As Layoffs Rise, Jobless Throw Career Fairs," by Dana Mattioli. So we modified our conference to include recruiters and employers and thus add a job fair component to it. The result was a 15% increase in attendance.

Here's another example: We read an article in the *American Bar Association Journal* titled "Law Firm Websites That Work" that analyzed many law firm websites and reviewed what made them successful. This article helped unlock our idea that, for a fee, we could offer a service to our clients whereby we would review their websites and tell them where they were going wrong. This website review idea had already been lurking somewhere in our subconscious, but the article we read helped to bring it to the forefront. Our dedication to reading had once again helped us find a new idea and help our business succeed.

One of the biggest mistakes companies make is that they do not read their junk mail. Some businesspeople take pride in never even opening any junk mail or promotional material, but we have learned over the years that, to the contrary, there can be valuable lessons in junk mail.

Let me explain what I mean through a few examples. Because we are both lawyers, we receive letters and junk mail all the time from people trying to sell us business and professional books. We received one several years ago for a book titled *The Biggest Missteps [certain type of professional] Make and How to Avoid Them*—and it's a good thing we opened that flyer. The product we saw gave us an idea: why not create some "biggest mistakes" books of our own? In the end, that's exactly what we did. We took the concept, put it through our prism, and started our own line of "biggest mistakes" books that put our own spin on our own areas of expertise. This one piece of junk mail directly resulted in three profitable new products that we adapted for our niches. The first of these was *The Biggest Legal Mistakes Physicians Make and How to Avoid Them*. When this book worked well, we decided to write another, *The Biggest Mistakes Expert Witnesses Make and How to Avoid Them*. We also created a seminar on the same topic. All three of these profitable products were the direct result of actually opening and reading our junk mail, and we are likely going to continue this theme and create additional "biggest mistake" products in the future.

There are additional advantages to reading everything that is not directly related to this chapter on product development, but they are important, so I would like to mention them here anyway. To start with, reading everything may enable you to identify people or companies that you might want to do business with. One thing that we find particularly helpful is using publications to find presenters for our conferences. For example, a number of years ago I came across a medical journal article on disability in the workplace that was written by a young doctor. As it turned out, the young doctor was a rising star in her field, forensic psychiatry, a clinical professor at a prestigious university, and the author of several recent landmark books in her field. She had not yet really been discovered when I read her article and signed her on to start speaking for us, but I had caught this rising star due to reading everything.

You can and should also use your junk mail to identify companies you might want to do business with as well. We receive solicitations all the time that we use to identify potential business opportunities. The fact that they are mass mailed does not deter us. In fact, it makes us even more willing to investigate the opportunities further. Why?

- Because mass mailings are targeted, many of the companies are aligned to our business either directly or indirectly.
- These companies are looking for new business opportunities.
- These "junk mailers" have money to spend.

For example, when a junk mail piece comes from a specialized publisher, we contact them to see if they would like to distribute our books. They've already spent the money to identify their synergy with us, so why not turn the tables? In effect, we turn the piece of junk mail that they were using to try to sell *us* something into an opportunity for us to sell something to *them*.[3] We have found several important distributors this way.

Companies that you may want to do business with may also be mentioned in an article. For example, an article in the *Wall Street Journal*, "Lilly Taps Contractors to Revive Pipeline," by Jonathan D. Rockoff, discusses how Pharma outsources by some of the tests it conducts on its drug candidates. How could an article like this help us as a conference and training company? A close reading of the article reveals that Pharma is using contract research organizations (CROs), a $20 billion industry with 1,000 CROs, to conduct its

---

[3] See also Chapter 4.

testing. We were shamefully unaware of these companies, but after we put this new information through the SEAK prism, several potential new ideas came to light. Perhaps we could:

- Have the companies recruit at our nonclinical career conference for physicians.

- Sell these companies expert witness or other training or consulting products.

- See if they are interested in advertising in our three national directories.

- Research if these CROs have potential speakers for some of our conferences.

The lesson is clear. Many good leads and potentially viable ideas were presented by one simple article. We still needed to thoroughly evaluate each idea the article generated, but the short article was eye-opening nonetheless.

You can also use your junk mail to see how other people are selling their products and services. A few years ago we received a junk mail solicitation for a conference that contained small thumbnail headshots of each of the presenters on its cover. It looked great. A light bulb went off in our heads: what if we used this technique on our conference brochures? We did, and we then saw an upward bump in attendance. This was all possible because we had gotten a good brochure design idea through reading our junk mail.

4. Turn problems into new opportunities by seeing the problem a little differently.

EXECUTIVE SUMMARY: A great source of new product ideas are problems that you and others face on a regular basis. How do you make money from these problems? By viewing them differently than everyone else does. Instead of joining the chorus when other people are all complaining about the same problem, view the situation as an opportunity to create a product or service that provides a solution.

* * *

One of the most satisfying aspects of running a business is being able to solve your customers' problems. Products that solve a problem can be immensely successful and profitable. The key is to see things a little differently than everyone else does. How do you do that? By both recognizing the problem and seeing it as an opportunity to create a new product or service that offers a solution. As for Jim and I, we use our own training, experience, insight, imagination, intuition, and creativity to turn problems into opportunities. Our experience has been that you can train/teach yourself to see things in this way. As such, when Jim or I see a problem arise, we look for the opportunity lying below. When we search for a product/service we need that does not exist, we immediately ask, "Why not? How many other businesspeople need the same thing? How can we fill this vacuum?" When we are frustrated with an existing product/service, our thought is not to waste our time by writing a scathing e-mail to the manufacturer. Instead, we start to think about how it should be done or how it should work, and then we see if *we* can do it better. We treat every problem we run into as a potential business opportunity.

Let me give you a couple of examples of where this approach has been wildly successful. Early on in my career I was a workers' compensation lawyer and started working on Social Security disability cases. Under Federal Law, covered employees can get monthly benefits if they can prove they were disabled. After a few cases I knew I needed help, so I tracked down a lawyer in Georgia. Here is how our conversation went:

STEVE: Attorney Peterson, I just started doing these Social Security cases and they are tough, with tons of regulations.

PETERSON: Very complex. I have been doing these for years and still have not figured them out.

STEVE: What is the best group or association I can contact for research and support?

PETERSON: As far as I know, there is none.

STEVE: You mean to tell me that with thousands of lawyers in the United States working on these cases, there is no association or group at all?

PETERSON: Precisely.

STEVE: If I tried to start a group like this, would you want to be ...

PETERSON: Absolutely, and I know at least fifty other lawyers that would join in a heartbeat.

So I started the National Organization of Social Security Claimants' Representatives (NOSSCR), which was a runaway success from day one. Hundreds of lawyers joined, and we exchanged research, materials, and briefs. An 800 number was started so that sick and injured workers could get immediate access to lawyers who specialize in this area. We ran national conferences, over 2,500 lawyers joined the organization during my time there, and NOSSCR is still running strong over 30 years later. The organization may well be my single most important professional accomplishment as a lawyer. Thousands of lawyers had faced the same problem, but I was the only one who saw that problem as an opportunity and took advantage of it.

Here is a second example. Back when I was a worker's compensation lawyer, I used to attend conferences for workers' compensation lawyers. The conferences were disappointing. Much of the information presented was stuff that either I already knew or didn't apply to the state in which I practiced. Much of the information that I needed, such as medical information, was not provided. I saw these problems as an opportunity.

What if I created a workers' compensation conference that was much different than those that I had attended? At the time, the lawyers doing workers' compensation had their own conference and the occupational health physicians and nurses who treated compensation claimants each had their own conference. What if I created a conference by and for all three groups? The doctors could learn from the lawyers and nurses. The nurses could learn from the lawyers and doctors. The lawyers could learn from the nurses and doctors. It wouldn't be the same old, same old, and it could solve the problem of attending lousy conferences where repetitive, narrow information was presented.

My idea was a result of my seeing this problem differently than others did. I created the first *interdisciplinary* (doctors, lawyers, and nurses) workers' compensation and occupational medicine conference in the country, and it has been running for over 30 years now. The vast majority of attendees come back in future years, as they are so satisfied with the product. What is more, we have made millions of dollars in profits over the years from the conference. All this was possible because I was able to recast the problem. I didn't come home from my legal conference and write a letter to the organizer telling him how his program was disappointing. What I did do was view this situation as an opportunity for a competitor to step in with a superior product. Then I created that superior product and cashed in. Turn a bad experience as a customer into a multimillion dollar product. Practice and develop the skill of being able to look at problems and see simple and elegant solutions that you can turn into successful products and services.

5. Develop and sell product extensions.

EXECUTIVE SUMMARY: When looking for new ways to increase revenue and serve your customers, consider product extensions and sequels, which can be relatively easy to develop. After all, you may have a ready, targeted, and easy market for them, and you know the area well enough to be able to develop a first-class product. Product extensions can be very profitable and should be considered and anticipated as part of any business plan.

* * *

Businesspeople can learn many valuable lessons from Hollywood. One such lesson that we learned the hard way is that there is potentially a large amount of money in product extensions, such as sequels. If you have a product that people like, consider creating another or a similar product that is designed in large measure for those who already own your first product.

The best example of product extensions is Hollywood's love affair with sequels. Over 20 James Bond movies have been successfully made, and more are on the drawing board. Other examples include novels written in a series (such as Tom Clancy's Jack Ryan series) and many video games, such as the *Call of Duty* series of video games, which have focused on various theaters of World War II and skirmishes in the current era. Instead of reinventing the wheel, the product developer is tapping into his brand and what he knows people have wanted to buy in the past in an attempt to recreate the magic and cash in.

As an added bonus, product extensions are less risky propositions than other products due to your built-in customer base and their brand loyalty, both of which will make it much easier to sell your second product. Furthermore, product extensions enable you to easily gather market research. Here is what we mean. Let's say you have a certain number of people who have bought a product from you. If you are considering developing an extension of this product, the customers who bought the first product are a great resource to query to see what they would like or not like in the product extension. Finally, product extensions can be much easier to produce than the original product that they are based on. As the product developer, you have already developed subject matter expertise regarding the product, so the amount of time and money you must spend to create an extension is usually less than what you spent to create the first product from scratch.

In our business, Jim and I are always looking for ways to extend our successful products. For example, we have created product extensions for many of the successful books that we have published. Our first book for expert witnesses was *How to Excel During Cross Examination: Techniques for Experts That Work*, which was published in 1997. Over the first five years that the book was in print, we sold almost 4,000 copies of this book, which is a very large number for a small independent publisher. In 2002 we started kicking around a product extension for this book. Here is how the conversation went:

JIM: I think we should do a new cross-examination book.

STEVE: Why? The old book is still selling well, and in fact it is one of our top sellers. If it's not broken, why fix it?

JIM: Three reasons: First, sales are starting to fall off. Second, with our built-in following among expert witnesses, we can raise the price of the new book. Instead of charging $59.95, we can charge $99.95. Third, we know a lot more now and can make a new book much, much better than the original.

STEVE: Let's do it.

In 2003 we published the product extension to our first cross-examination book, *Cross Examination: The Comprehensive Guide for Experts,* and sold it for $99.95. It sold very well, and continues to sell well all these years later. For this reason, we followed up this book product extension with many others, all of which followed the same formula: take a hot book product, update and improve it, raise the price, and sell it successfully to our built-in, loyal customers. We have made money on all of these product extensions. We also have successfully developed product extensions for our conferences as well. For example, we followed up on our basic expert witness conference courses with a more advanced course we called "The Master's Program."

The Master's Program turned out to be highly successful, and no wonder. First, we had a large pool of satisfied customers that was interested in expert witnessing to market it to. This helped make our marketing efforts cost-effective because we were only trying to reach our existing customers. Second, we knew a lot about expert witnessing, so we didn't have to reinvent the wheel to produce the product. Third, we were able to solicit the input and feedback of our customers as to whether they would be interested in this product extension through focus groups and surveys. When the feedback informed us that our customers had a strong interest in the product extension, the risk of failure with the new product decreased.

The Master's Program further confirmed for us how profitable and well-received product extensions can be. As with most good business principles, the extensions could be applied to many different lines of our business (or, more important, yours). For example, after running successful writing conferences for both doctors and lawyers, Jim proposed a more advanced writing course. I fought him tooth and nail, but finally I relented and reluctantly let him draft and send out a needs assessment. (This is our way of placating each other when we think the other partner has a stupid and potentially expensive "great idea.") As it turned out, our customers were indeed very interested in attending a small advanced writing conference.

After gaining invaluable feedback, we developed a course with a strictly limited number of attendees (36) to ensure that each participant received significant personal attention. We also were able to charge more for this two-day course, and because we were only targeting alumni of our previous writing courses, our marketing costs were very low. In the first three years that we ran our advanced writing course, we sold it out by sending only two e-mail blasts to our alumni. Our profits were huge and the course was extremely well received.

We have found that our product extensions contribute a disproportionately high percentage of our organization's total profits. Because of this fact, we are constantly exploring how we can create extensions to our successful products or product lines. Indeed, whenever we consider new product lines, we also consider the chances of being able to develop extensions to those lines down the road.

The truth of the matter is, no business will be successful unless it develops products that customers are willing to pay for. As discussed in this chapter, we recommend that you listen to your customers to get ideas for new products, think things through very carefully before committing to a new product, read as much as you can for ideas, see problems as opportunities, and consider developing product extensions to your successful products. We focus next on how to market and sell the products that you develop.

Step 4: Sell Your Products and Services Cost Effectively

The best product or service in the world will do you little good if you can't market it successfully and cost-effectively. We have learned through the school of hard knocks the three fundamental rules of marketing, which are detailed in this chapter. First, you can't rely on anyone else to sell your product for you—no matter how much money you throw at them. Second, nobody knows for sure how a marketing campaign will turn out. The only way to know for sure is to try it out and see what happens. Third, it's no use spending money on marketing unless you also have a plan to track your results and see what's working and what's not working. We have discovered many easy-to-implement techniques that can greatly affect your sales and marketing success. These techniques are described in the following pages.

1. Nobody (with something to sell) knows anything about marketing.

EXECUTIVE SUMMARY: Throwing money at marketing experts and advertising is a very risky way to sell your products or services, and it is likely to result in failure. Even the best marketing experts operating in good faith have no guaranteed way of knowing exactly how to sell your product or service in a cost-effective manner. Similarly, even ads placed in the best media outlets have no guarantee of generating sales. The ideal way to structure a deal with any marketing partner is to set it up so that the partner shares in the risks and rewards. The simplest way to do this is by developing distributors for your products.

* * *

One of the most expensive lessons we learned is that you need to be responsible for marketing your own product or service. Throwing money at the problem can be a recipe for disaster. Here's our sorry tale.

I am the proud father of two wonderful, underachieving children. My children are bright and capable, but they never performed as well as they could have in school. I was extremely frustrated by this situation and figured that there were millions of parents who felt the same way. I also had seen Hooked on Phonics and other similar products on TV for years. Companies were obviously making millions from their efforts to help parents help their kids, so I came up with what I thought was a brilliant idea. I spent $75,000, plus a year of my time, and produced a video and workbook program titled, *Help Your Child Achieve*. I hired the world's leading experts to create the content of the program, and I retained graphic design firms to design the custom-made case. The product looked beautiful, was very warmly received, and even won an award from a national parenting organization.

Then it came time to sell our award-winning program. I knew the product was very good and very helpful, so I decided to hire a high-priced boutique marketing company located in fancy offices in downtown Boston. When I went in to hire them, I met with the owner, who explained to me in exhaustive detail how good they were at selling things, how wonderful my program was, and how much money I was going to make. With all the money I was going to make, I started to think that I should pick out a nice condo on the water in Boca! So I forked over a check for $125,000 (in 1994 dollars) to this marketing company for a marketing campaign. They produced a 30-second TV commercial featuring *Help Your Child Achieve* and set up an 800-number for ordering, a warehouse, and a fulfillment center. Then they bought airtime for the spot on TV.

The day of the launch came. I was working out in my basement at 4:30 a.m. and was half-watching TV when on came my ad. I started to get calls from early-rising friends, who asked, "Was that you on TV at 4:30 a.m.?" As it turned out, the times that the marketing company had purchased for the advertisement turned out to be the very cheap ones, when very few people were watching. This concerned me, but I figured, hey, we paid these Boston guys six figures, so they *must* know what they are doing.

After a week had passed, I called up to check on how sales were going of our $100 award-winning product—of which we had produced an initial inventory of 3,000 sets. The answer came back: "Our records show five to date." So I responded, "Five hundred isn't that bad. Do you expect the numbers to pick up?" "Well, ahh, that's five, not five hundred." Apparently, the marketing company had bought cheap airtime so they could keep as much of the $125,000 we had paid them as possible. What did they care if our product sold or not? They were *getting paid the same amount regardless of results* and cashed in on our mistake.

The initial campaign ended after three weeks, and in that time, we sold twelve units. The project to date had taken in $1,200, and I had paid out over $200,000. This was obviously not going to be made up in volume, so I made an appointment to go back and see my blue-chip marketing company. I made sure to take my blood pressure medication before the meeting, too. But when I got to the meeting the owner of the marketing company was conveniently unavailable. He instead sent out his 25-year-old assistant to take my fury. Predictably, his assistant suggested that if we just threw some more money at the situation, we'd be able to turn things around.

Here was my verbatim response: "Under no circumstances am I giving you *any* more money. You couldn't sell insulin to a diabetic. I could have sold more units hiring homeless people to hand out flyers in front of the Park Street subway station."[1] The assistant's jaw dropped. When he recovered, he once again tried, per his boss's instructions, to try to get some more easy money out of us. My response was curt, "Are you confident you can sell this?" "Yes," was the reply. "OK," I responded, "then *you* put up the money for another ad and I'd be happy to split the sales with you fifty-fifty." "Ahhh, ahh, we can't do that, I'm sorry."

I had made a serious mistake and lost $200,000, but I had also learned two very valuable real-world lessons. First, you can't just throw money at a marketing problem. Two, no so-called expert or anyone else can definitively tell you what will work with regards to marketing your product or service. The only way to definitively see what will and will not work when marketing your product or service is to conduct a test campaign, try it out, and see what happens. We'll talk more about this later. I learned another hard marketing lesson a long time ago that I'll share you with now: you can blow a lot of money for little to no return in advertising. The issue is the same. When you're buying the ad, the seller will tell you how wonderful and effective it will

---

[1] This was most likely true.

be, but the truth is, it usually isn't. The only way to tell is to try it out and track your results. We'll talk more about that later as well.

There is an epilogue to *Help Your Child Achieve*. We were, in fact, ultimately able to generate additional revenue from this product, but it wasn't quite the way we had planned. After the disaster with the marketing company, we closed our warehouse account and moved the remaining stock to our home office basement. Later that year, the basement flooded and damaged some of our inventory. We were able to collect a small amount of insurance on the ruined programs.

You can see ample evidence in the marketplace that even the so-called best and brightest organizations, those who have huge marketing budgets and hire experienced marketing pros, agencies, and consultants, create and launch marketing campaigns that are massive failures. In the 1960s, Xerox aired a commercial showing a monkey operating a copier. The point was that its machine was easy to operate. The ad, however, offended the secretaries who used Xerox's products and was ultimately deemed a failure. The worst-selling Beatles album of all time was *Yesterday and Today* released in 1966. When it was launched, the album cover featured the Beatles in butchers' clothes with a hacked-up and bloody baby doll. Burger King recently ended its campaign of ads featuring a creepy-looking King character. In one infamous ad, a man wakes up next to this character. The bottom line is that no so-called expert, no matter what their track record is or how much they charge, can tell you with certainty what will and will not work to sell your product or service.

In terms of marketing partners, we have learned our lesson: the payment needs to be based on performance, and the partner needs to be willing to accept at least part of the risk of failure. When you structure the deal such that your partners will only get paid if their marketing efforts succeed, they will be more motivated to market your product and *will only agree to participate if they truly believe they can sell the product.* This is what we should have done with Help Your Child Achieve. If we had approached numerous companies and nobody would share the risk with us, maybe we would have been smart enough to realize that Help Your Child Achieve was a "New Coke" that nobody wanted. Then we could have limited our losses. Shame on us, but we learned our lesson. Ever since the Help Your Child Achieve debacle, our focus has been on using distributors, because distributors' interests are aligned with our own. They only get paid if they actually sell our products. The more they sell, the more the distributor gets paid. If they don't think they can sell our product, they won't take it on.

The marketing advice we have shared with you in this section is similar to the guidance we give people when they ask us how good of a legal case they have as a potential plaintiff. Our standard advice is as follows: if you want to find out what a lawyer *really* thinks of your case, ask him to take it on a contingency basis. If he thinks your case is a winner, he will. If he doesn't, he won't. Don't agree to an hourly basis unless, of course, you just want to enrich the lawyers.

2. Test it out and see if it works.

EXECUTIVE SUMMARY: When it comes to marketing, the absolute key to success is experimentation and trials. We have learned the hard way that nobody, no matter how bright or experienced they are, can accurately predict what will happen with a marketing plan. Furthermore, market research is never a guarantee of success. The best ideas flop. Crazy ideas are wildly successful. Use your data, follow your instincts, but always test your marketing method before you roll it out or bet the farm. You will never know with confidence what is going to happen until you test your idea by actually trying to sell something.

* * *

Our business is run by eight very bright, talented, dedicated, and experienced individuals. Our staff is also very creative, so we are always coming up with clever ideas to market our products and services. The overriding lesson that we have learned the hard way over the years is that nobody, no matter how bright or experienced they are, no matter how much data they have, can accurately predict how well a given marketing campaign will do. As such, it is best practice to test your marketing idea first with an actual offer. Once the results of this test show that your strategy is indeed profitable, the method can be rolled out to a larger audience.

Here's a good example of what we mean. Many years ago we were trying to market our first book on negotiating via direct mail. Our marketing piece was in a standard-sized business envelope that had our company's logo and return address on it. The sales of the book weren't as high as we would have liked, so we had a meeting to discuss how to improve sales. Here's about how it went:

STEVE: I think the big problem is that people don't know who we are and don't open the envelope.

JIM: Sounds reasonable.

STEVE: What we need to do is get them to open the envelope. Then they'll see how good our book is.

JIM: Logical.

STEVE: I have an idea.

JIM: Your last idea cost us $200,000.

STEVE: People love dogs. Instead of using our logo as a return address, let's address the envelope from me and my wife, and I'll put a picture of my black lab, Gus, on the envelope. Look how successful Martha's Vineyard's Black Dog has been!

JIM: That's really unorthodox, but you might be onto something. We could make a lot of money if this works.

We agreed to try it out on a very small scale and sent out 5,000 brochures in the "Gus" envelopes. The results proved that all our "logic" wasn't worth a hill of beans: We sold *zero* books with this new strategy. Had we just gone with our logic and experience and rolled this idea out without testing it first, we would have lost a fortune.[2]

A few years later we were looking to develop a new course for some of our clients. We surveyed our clients and found that there was very strong support for a course on entrepreneurial skills. We had an internal debate as to how to jump into this market because the survey results were some of the most positive we have ever seen. Finally we decided to test the idea out on a very small scale and in a low-risk way—and it's a good thing we did! When we actually rolled out the test product, the response was tepid. The lesson here was clear: even needs assessment data and research do not guarantee that your marketing campaign will generate positive results. The only way to really see what is going to happen is to actually try to sell something on a small scale and see if it works.

Here's another example. Recently we had another meeting to figure out a way to generate more revenue during our slow season. Here's approximately how that conversation went:

STEVE: I am thinking we should send out a letter to some of our clients to see if we can drum up consulting work, where they'd hire us as consultants.

ALEX: What would the letter say?

---

[2] In fact, we continued to test various marketing pieces for this book until we were finally able to find one that worked. It was the thirteenth piece that worked, and we successfully rolled it out nationally. Often, you may need both persistence and patience to find an effective marketing technique.

STEVE: One sentence. If you are interested in dramatically expanding your expert witness practice, please call me.

JIM: OK, then what?

STEVE: When they call, I tell them that for $7,500, paid in advance, I will consult with them and work with them to dramatically expand their practice.

ALEX: They are going to be pissed when they call and you ask for $7,500.

JIM: This is the stupidest thing I've heard from you in a long while, and that's saying a lot.

ALEX: I think you're losing it.

STEVE: Let me try it out with 300 clients.

My partners ultimately agreed to the small 300-person test, mainly, I think, to shut me up. We sent out 300 letters, and as a result, I received about 20 calls. Of those that called me, 7 ended up hiring me for $7,500. So, we spent $150 on a letter and took in over $50,000 in consulting fees. It was the highest margin we had ever made on a direct mail piece. The bottom line again was that *nobody* could accurately predict how well the letter would do. An unorthodox approach can certainly work, but the only way to truly know is to try it out on a small scale and see what happens.

Here's one more example. Many years ago, I became interested in writing fiction. I signed up for a local fiction writing course and an idea dawned on me. Medical thrillers were selling well. We have many physician clients. They have money. Why not create a fiction course especially for physicians? So Jim and I had another one of our frank discussions.

STEVE: I think we could make money on a fiction writing course tailored to physicians.

JIM: Are you nuts?

STEVE: No, I'm serious. Just hear me out and don't interrupt me.

JIM: You have two minutes.

STEVE: I bet many doctors would love to write fiction. They want to be the next Robin Cook or Michael Palmer. I checked extensively and there is not and has never been a course on writing for physicians.

JIM: I'm sure there's a good reason for that. Sorry, can I speak now?

STEVE: Sure.

JIM: Look, fiction courses are a dime a dozen. You can take them almost anywhere for, like, ten dollars an hour. How are we gonna make money like that?

STEVE: Doctors will pay more for higher quality and for something at a high level that is specifically tailored to them.

JIM: You're guessing.

STEVE: I sent out a needs assessment to ask our customers if they are interested.

JIM: Let me see the results ... Steve, it says here that only ten percent of those surveyed were interested in this.

STEVE: Read more closely, though. Of those ten percent, almost every one of them was extremely enthusiastic.

JIM: OK, fine. But the needs assessment also says that in order to come, they'd want the course to be taught by a New York Times bestselling physician author. Those don't grow on trees and don't come cheap.

STEVE: I think I can get one who used to live here in Falmouth.

JIM: You think some surgeon making hundreds of thousands of dollars is going to take several days off of work and fly around the country to learn how to become a novelist? The chances of becoming a big-time writer are astronomically small. The doctors will lose tons of money by shutting down their practice.

STEVE: Jim, except for your expense reports, you're not a fiction writer. You don't see the passion others feel for fiction writing.

JIM: OK, I'll tell you what. If you insist on this crazy idea, here's what needs to happen. We need to test the seminar in a low-risk, low-cost way to see what will happen. We will only market it to our customers. We will hold it locally. We won't sign a hotel contract with cancellation provisions. Oh, and you need to get a famous *New York Times* bestselling author to teach the whole thing.

STEVE: You're on.

I was able to meet all of Jim's conditions (I actually got **two** *New York Times* bestselling authors to agree to teach the course), and we tried out the course under the low-risk test conditions that he had specified. We put on the course, and a crazy thing happened: It worked. Against all odds, it worked.

The doctors wanted it. They traveled to Cape Cod from as far away as Alaska and Hawaii. The course ran for 13 years and generated hundreds of thousands of dollars in profits, and eventually we expanded this business line into three other writing conferences. None of this would have happened if we hadn't tried out this seemingly crazy idea. The bottom line is that crazy ideas sometimes work, so don't be afraid to try them. The "Snuggie," a blanket with sleeves that started out as a punch line on late-night TV, has had sales over 25 million to date. Over 500,000 Chia Pets, clay figures coated with seeds that, when watered, sprout green "fur," have been sold each year since the craze started in 1977. Ernö Rubik invented the Rubik's cube in 1974, and over 350 million cubes have been sold worldwide to date.

Here's one final example that proves that needs assessment data cannot be fully trusted when it comes to predicting how well a product will sell in a marketing campaign. Many years ago, a huge nonprofit with hundreds of thousands of members was trying to get us to agree to start an expert witness directory for them. They had an extremely bright, award-winning PhD scientist running this project, but he was new to the business side of things. Our PhD contact was very gung ho about the project because he had sent out a needs assessment and determined that 17.9% of the nonprofit's 100,000 members would join this new expert witness directory. We were highly suspicious of this high number, and we told the nonprofit so. They couldn't figure out what our problem was. We'd all make a fortune! There would be almost 18,000 experts paying us hundreds of dollars each to be listed in a directory. They had the numbers to prove it! Can't we see the simple facts? We couldn't lose!

After much negotiating, we agreed to only *try out* the directory on a very small scale and in such a way that we could walk away if what we thought would happen actually did. We did a test mailing, the results were horrible, and we walked away. Our losses were limited because we resisted the urge to rely heavily on the oh-so-tempting needs assessment data, insisted on conducting a marketing test, and developed an exit plan in case sales did not pan out as hoped. Our prudence and skepticism saved us and our client hundreds of thousands of dollars in losses.

Remember that making decisions without trying them out first can be problematic. For example, Tropicana decided to update its orange juice cartons without adequate testing and then rolled out its new, different-looking cartons in 2009. The customer backlash was immediate. The corporate parent company, PepsiCo, was hit with e-mails, phone calls, letters, and social media comments claiming that the new packaging made the orange juice look ugly, stupid, bargain brand, and so forth. After less than 30 days, PepsiCo retreated and went back to the traditional Tropicana carton that customers had grown to expect and love.

3. Track the results of your marketing efforts.

EXECUTIVE SUMMARY: If you are going to market your products or services, you absolutely must devise a way to track each campaign's results. You will not be in a position to rationally evaluate the success of your various marketing efforts unless you are serious about tracking your results. Campaigns that do not have a positive return should be tweaked or discontinued. Campaigns that are proven to be working should be expanded.

* * *

We publish a directory for expert witnesses. Experts pay to list themselves in our directory, and then we send the directory to law firms all over the country and try to get cases for the listed experts. It's a simple business model, similar to the Yellow Pages. Three or four times a year, however, I have the following conversation with one of the expert clients who is listed in our directory:

EXPERT: Steve, I'm sorry to say your Expert directory is not working for me.

STEVE: How many new cases did you get this year?

EXPERT: About ten to twelve.

STEVE: Did you ask the ten to twelve lawyers if they found you in the directory?

EXPERT: No, was I supposed to?

STEVE: How else can you know it's not working for you?

EXPERT: I never thought of that. Good point.

The point, of course, is that to determine whether a marketing campaign is working or not, you need to develop a procedure that tracks the results of the campaign. There are many ways to do this. For an expert witness or a professional in any other businesses, a simple way to track the results of your marketing campaigns is to simply ask in the initial conversation with a new client, "How did you hear about us?"

In our business, marketing expenses are our biggest budget busters. We simply don't have dollars to waste on marketing campaigns that do not generate a positive return on our investment. We also like to test out many new products and marketing campaigns. As a result, we are very, very serious about tracking the results of our campaigns. As with everything else in business, we learned to track our results in the school of hard knocks and by making dumb mistakes.

For thirty-plus years we have run a very successful National Workers' Compensation and Occupational Medicine Seminar in July of each year. Many years ago, when I hired Jim as my protégé, one of the first tasks I gave him was marketing this conference, which at the time was responsible for about 90 percent of our business's profits. Here's about how the conversation went:

STEVE: Jim, I would like you to take over the marketing of the July conference.

JIM: Sure, but as you know, I'm a lawyer, not an MBA. This is brand new to me. What am I supposed to do, exactly?

STEVE: Here are ten mailing lists that we rent every year. You call up the organization with the list and ask them to send you mailing labels. Then I hire this lady down the street, and she works in her garage, addressing over 100,000 brochures by hand. When they are ready, we rent a truck and we haul them to the post office.

JIM: How much does all of this cost?

STEVE: Well, each brochure costs around 40 cents to mail out when you include the costs of renting the mailing label, printing, postage, and paying the lady down the street to address them all.

JIM: That really adds up. How do you know if each list is worth the money you spend on it?

STEVE: We don't.

JIM (looking at me in disbelief): So, you could have been mailing from a list for years and years *that loses money?*

STEVE: That's a good point. Let's figure something out.

What we agreed to do was place a different code on the brochures that were sent from each of the mailing lists that we had rented. When people sent in their registration forms, we could see which code was on the form and which list was most profitable. It turned out that three of the ten lists were losing money. In addition, two of the ten lists were working so well that we could increase our profitability by mailing to that list multiple times. The knowledge gained by this simple tracking procedure allowed us to decrease our costs and dramatically increase our revenues and profitability.

There are different simple ways even a small business can track results. For example:

- When a new prospect contacts you, ask them how they found out about you. Train your staff to do this.[3]

- Place a special phone number, P.O. Box number, or e-mail address on the marketing materials that you use to get a good idea of how much response you get from that particular offer.

- Offer a discount or free premium if the customer mentions a particular brochure, ad, or other marketing material.

- Use priority codes on marketing materials, as discussed earlier.

- Include coupons that can be tracked in your marketing.

- Send your customers a simple thank you e-mail and ask them how they found out about you.

- Use common online tracking features to determine whether an online order was the result of a particular e-mail you sent. Use Google Analytics or a similar service, which provide free, detailed reports on your website traffic. These services also supply you with other useful information, such as the sources of your traffic and the keywords used. You can then compare your marketing traffic to your site and sales.

We suggest you consider implementing some of the above simple, low-cost tracking ideas into your marketing efforts. Finding out how well your marketing is or is not working can be priceless. You do not want to waste precious marketing dollars on campaigns that are not working. You will likewise want to expand marketing campaigns that are working.

---

[3] Sometimes more than a single question is needed to obtain accurate tracking information. When I was the senior partner in a personal injury law firm, each Sunday we advertised in our local Cape Cod newspaper to generate additional business. The ad was headlined: "Hurt, Injured, or Disabled?" Each Monday the office was extremely busy with phone calls from new potential clients. Every new potential client was asked how they heard about us. Over 10 percent of the clients said they saw our ad on TV. One little problem: We never advertised on TV. The lesson here is that you may have to press the new clients to make sure they are giving you accurate tracking information.

4. It's the name, stupid.

EXECUTIVE SUMMARY: How you name yourself and your products matters greatly. Think things out carefully before deciding on a name. We suggest testing various names and getting feedback before the name is finalized.

* * *

One of the things we do in our business is train expert witnesses on how to testify more effectively, and one of the key techniques we teach these experts is that how you say something can often be more important than *what* you say. For example, anyone who has ever flown on a commercial flight that will travel over water has heard the following safety instructions: "In the unlikely event of a water landing, a personal floatation device is located … ." This message is purposefully presented in very low-key language that is intended to prevent passengers from freaking out. What the airlines could have said but didn't is: "in case we have to crash land in the ocean, we have equipment on-board that will help prevent you from drowning, an inflatable life jacket… ." Again, the point is that *how* you say something matters and can have a great effect on how others react to what you are saying.

We have learned the hard way over the years that the preciseness with which you name your products, company/organization, and/or services will affect how well you can market and sell them. Many years ago, we wrote a comprehensive text for expert witnesses on how to be an expert witness. This book covered all relevant areas, including law, procedure, how to testify, marketing, risk management, and so forth. The book received rave reviews and was very well received. Very few people who bought it, returned it. The one problem we had, however, was that the sales of the book were disappointing. The issue, we later discovered was that the name of the book, *The Comprehensive Forensic Services Manual: The Essential Resources for All Experts*[4] was ill-chosen. It was too long, and nobody could readily understand what it meant. Many experts thought that because the book included the word "forensic" in the title, the product was only applicable to physicians who perform autopsies.

A few years later, we decided to update the book and republish it under a new name. The new book was essentially the same as the old one, and the only major change was the title, which was *The A-Z Guide to Expert Witnessing*. Sales of the *A-Z Guide*, however, have been many times stronger than they were for its predecessor. In fact, the book is a perennial bestseller for us. All the difference in the world was made by simply improving the title.

---

[4] We won't bore you with the details of why we chose this name.

Ever since this valuable and costly learning experience, we take the naming of our products and services very seriously. What we do now is run various potential names by our customers, keep track of what they like and don't like, and set up informal focus groups to discuss potential titles. We never publish a product or develop a service unless we are confident that its name accurately and powerfully conveys what we are selling.

Here's another classic example of what can go wrong when naming a product. Jim's roommate in college was an international student from Mexico named Alberto. Alberto was a business major. His family was involved in many businesses in Mexico, one of which was an automotive dealership. One day Alberto had a good laugh telling Jim the story of how the Chevy Nova was an utter flop when GM tried to sell it in Mexico. What was the problem? Well, in Spanish *"no va"* means (roughly) "does not go." Not the best name for a car! GM had to change the name. Consider as well Ayds Diet Candy, which sold well in the 1970s and early 1980s. Unfortunately, when the disease AIDS became prevalent later in the '80s, sales of Ayds Diet Candy fell off sharply. This was bad luck for the manufacturer, as its product predated the AIDS crisis, but it is a clear lesson on the importance of a product's name.

It's not just the names of your products that matter. It's also the name of your organization. We (both of us lawyers) had a good laugh recently when the Association of Trial Lawyers of America (ATLA) changed its name to the American Association for Justice. This was a shrewd move with an obvious motive: many people distrust or even despise trial lawyers. The reputation of a trial lawyer is usually somewhere below that of a used car salesperson or a politician. If ATLA wanted to be more effective as lobbyists, they needed to change their name. That way, when people hear of their positions, research, or lobbying, they might trust it more.

5. Image is everything.

EXECUTIVE SUMMARY: Take stock of your image. It may well be worth the additional time and money to produce high-quality and polished websites, brochures, and business cards.

* * *

We pride ourselves on the fact that we run a low-cost operation and firmly believe that a penny saved is a penny earned.[5] That said, one of the lessons we have learned the hard way over the years is that it doesn't pay to skimp on

---

[5] For more on cost containment, please see Chapter 5.

your image. Image matters greatly and will directly affect your bottom line. Here are some examples of what we mean.

For many, many years, our business philosophy was to find the cheapest possible printer to print our conference brochures. There was a lot of money at stake because we mail out over 1,000,000 conference brochures each year, and we were quite successful at finding a cheap printer who specialized in printing newsprint-quality junk circulars. They gave us a very good price on our printing, and we were able to reach our niche market as cheaply as possible. Another way that we kept our costs low was by refraining to use any color in our pieces. Our logic here was simple as well: black and white is much cheaper than color. The more we save on printing, the more brochures we can mail out, and the higher our profit margin will be. Then, to round out our triumvirate of shoddiness, we used a low-cost graphic artist to design our brochures. He was a very nice man, and he was cheap as can be. The problem, however, was that he didn't design anything. He would do exactly what we asked (and we're clueless on design issues), and he didn't come up with any original ideas on his own. There was one little problem in all this: our designer couldn't design, our printer was low-quality, and our brochures looked like dog poop. We had a very small printing and design bill, but we weren't getting nearly as many people as we wanted to our conferences. So we decided to bite the bullet and try something a little different.

We hired a talented graphic artist named Jon. Jon cost four times as much as what we had been paying, but he turned out to be well worth it. He was smart, he listened to us, and he actually came up with high-quality, original designs for our brochures. Then we found a new printer that printed on high-quality glossy paper in full color. This was much more expensive than what we had been doing before, but again, we figured that we would give it a try and see what happened. We started to send out mailings that were professionally designed and printed in full color on a substantial paper stock. Then a funny thing happened. Our response rate and attendance skyrocketed. The increases in attendance for our programs were between 40 and 100 percent. The only thing that had changed was the brochures. The products we sold had remained exactly the same, but our image was now professional and polished. Sure, we had spent additional money on marketing, but our return far surpassed this cost. In fact, this one switch, which was completely superficial, was one of the breakout moments of our business and serves as a classic example of how your image, as reflected by marketing materials, can dramatically affect your bottom line. In addition, our image was now consistent with our brand.

Here's another powerful example of how a poorly thought-out image can stifle a business. A few years ago, we had a certain expert witness call and complain that he was not getting any new business, despite all the hard work he was doing to market himself. We looked into the situation and immediately surmised what the problem was. So we called up the expert. Here's about how the conversation went:

AUTHORS: Well, we think we know what the problem is.

EXPERT: OK, shoot.

AUTHORS: It's your website.

EXPERT: My website is my strongest asset. It defines me. You can't imagine how much time I have invested in it.

AUTHORS: You know we are straight shooters, so here it is. Your website reflects very poorly on you. It projects the image of your being rude and callous, and it insults almost everyone.

EXPERT: It's funny. It's brilliant.

AUTHORS: You have a photo of a man with a big flame coming out of his ass with a caption that reads, "I just ate Mexican food." Then you have a picture of a guy throwing up in a toilet with the caption, "I had a bad night last night." You also have a picture with a caption that reads, "Retards, we all know one." I could go on and on. This stuff is Kryptonite and it needs to come down immediately.

EXPERT: Gee, I thought you might have some good advice for me. You guys just don't get it.

This expert had made the very serious mistake, as we had, of being unaware of the image that he was projecting. We are quite confident that he would have done much better with a website that was low-key, respectful, and professional, despite the fact that such a site would be more conventional.

You can see examples of image projection in the marketplace, too. Go to an open house in a nice neighborhood and you will almost always see the real estate agent driving an upscale car, such as a BMW. Visit the office of a high-priced lawyer and you will often find fancy paneling, a prestigious address, high-end artwork, expensive furniture, and a beautiful view. In each case the image that is being propagated is one of success, that is, look at the money these guys have, they must be good. The retailer Target is also instructive. Target was stuck for years with a low-cost, low-style, discount store reputation and brand. It reinvigorated its brand and differentiated itself from WalMart and K-Mart by adding products by celebrity designers, wide aisles, a food court with Starbucks, and a celebrity make-up artist. Its image and brand are now more consistent with those of a modestly priced department store, as opposed to a strictly discount, big box store.

6. Understand how much a new client is worth.

EXECUTIVE SUMMARY: It is only when you understand the true value of a new customer that you can accurately evaluate when your sales and marketing efforts are cost effective. To calculate the true value of a customer, you need to always keep in mind the potential for repeat business from this customer. You should also consider the potential and likelihood of the customer generating positive word of mouth for you and thus greatly increase the possibility that your new customer will lead to additional new customers.

* * *

One of the most common and serious mistakes businesspeople make is failing to understand the true value of a new client. Let's say that you run a restaurant. A couple comes in to eat for the first time and they end up spending $100 on dinner. How much are they worth?

The answer is probably not just $100—and potentially a boatload of money. Let's say these people loved your restaurant, so they end up coming back four times a year for the next ten years. In addition, they leave your restaurant favorable comments on Yelp! and recommend your restaurant to their friends. Then their friends recommend your restaurant to other friends. Over a ten-year period, this one couple could be easily be worth many thousands of dollars to your business.

We see our expert witness clients make the mistake of undervaluing their new clients all the time. One of the services we provide, for a small fee, we list and publicize to lawyers all over the country the availability of expert witnesses to do expert witness work. But in providing this service, we often receive complaints from experts, who say something like, "This really hasn't worked well for me. I only get about one new case a year." When we receive these types of complaints, however, we have to remind the client of the *value* of a new customer. So we'll explain to our expert customer, "Look, your average case generates $5,000 in fees, and your listing only costs $495. That's a slam dunk right there. If you do a good job, this lawyer will hire you again in the future. He'll also recommend that his colleagues hire you. Finally, other lawyers will see you working on that case and may want to hire you as a result. The one new client a year you are getting is worth far more than $5,000—probably closer to $15,000 to $20,000." The argument is quite persuasive.

Those companies and businesspeople that do understand the true value of new customers will often go to great lengths to court them—and with good reason. New customers, as the previous examples have made clear, can generate substantial profits for your company. When I recently signed up for a certain Internet, phone, and TV package from a national telecom provider, for example, the provider was *very* aggressive in getting me to sign up and switch from its rival. How aggressive were they? I received on average one piece of mail from them a month for a period of many years. I also received numerous and frequent phone calls and multiple door-to-door, in-person visits from their representatives. All this marketing activity must have cost them a small fortune. Why could they afford to do this? Because the telecom company clearly realized the substantial value to them of a client that they can bill $100 to $200 each month, month after month, year after year. Every new client is a cash cow that is worth a fortune to them.

We recognize the value of new customers and make decisions accordingly. For example, the expert witness marketing service that we offer costs our clients $495 for one year. We are more than happy to spend $600 in marketing to get a new client to sign up for one year for $495. The reason for this is simple: the client is very likely to renew and to buy other products and services from us. As such, we've seen that each new client to us is really worth around $1,500, not $495. So, if we spend $600 to acquire a new customer who in reality is worth $1,500, we're doing well.

7. Find yourself a niche.

EXECUTIVE SUMMARY: There are tremendous advantages to operating in a narrow niche. When you do so, you will be able to define yourself as an expert in your field of choice and deliver superior products. Operating in a niche also may allow you to price your products and services at a premium rate. Finally, when you operate in a well-thought-out niche, you will be able to market your products and services in a more cost-effective manner.

* * *

One of the most effective marketing techniques we have utilized in our business has been finding the right niche in which to operate. By niche, we are talking about a distinct and relatively narrow segment of the market that has a unique appeal and fills an unmet need. The advantages of operating in a good niche are obvious. When you are a niche business, you are a big fish in a small pond. Because you have chosen a narrow niche, you are positioned to serve this smaller area better than your competitors. You also *appear* to have more expertise to potential customers because you hold yourself out as a specialist in the niche area.

By far, the most common and costly niche mistake that we and others make is defining our niche too broadly. The logical, but flawed, reasoning says: why limit our new product or service to a narrow segment of the market? Let's market and produce whatever we can for whomever we can. The flaw in the reasoning, however, is that broadening the appeal of your products and services dilutes their apparent value, thus making your offerings less desirable to your likely purchasers. Why should your customers trust you if you are a jack of all trades and do not specialize in an area? You will also find it challenging to produce a superior product in an area in which you do not specialize. Finally, defining your niche too broadly often makes targeted cost-effective marketing difficult or impossible.

Let me give you some examples from our own experiences: one of the niches in which we operate is the business of supporting expert witnesses through education, practice tools, marketing assistance, publications, and training. This is a very narrow niche, and we are clear leaders in this field in the United States. Because we focus on this relatively narrow area, we are able to spend the necessary resources to develop superb expertise in this field. As a result, our products and services are of the highest quality, which thereby supports our word-of-mouth brand marketing.[6] In addition, because we clearly specialize in the area of supporting expert witnesses, it is much, much easier for us to sell them our products and services. The reason for this is simple: our potential customers believe that our products and services are worthwhile investments simply because we specialize in a field that caters to them.

We quite frequently are asked by corporations, associations, and government agencies if we will train their members or employees in expert witnessing skills. The callers almost always say the same thing to us; namely, "I've been to your website. It was very impressive. We're clearly talking to the right people if we would like our experts trained." The fact that we specialize in a narrow niche is clearly making a positive impression on our leads, as specialization equates with expertise and quality in their minds.

Think for a moment how you would go about selecting someone to perform a service for you, where quality was a concern. For example, let's say you needed some estate planning done. You'd probably prefer a lawyer who specializes in this area as opposed to a general practitioner. The reason is simple: you want the job done right, and you are logically assuming that a specialist will do the job better.

Another huge advantage of operating in a narrow niche is that it greatly simplifies your marketing efforts, because your audience is smaller and more readily identifiable. For example, in our expert witness niche, there are a

---

[6] Please see Chapter 1.

limited number of people who are engaged in this type of work. As a result, we are able to precisely target this narrow market and thus save on our marketing dollars.

Here's another example: part of our business of supporting expert witnesses involves consulting with them on how to better market themselves and help expand their practices. A few years ago, a psychiatrist who specializes in treating the elderly—we'll call him Sol—hired us to help him expand his practice. We gave Sol some advice that he considered, at the time, to be counterintuitive: "Don't cast a wide net. Find yourself a niche." Sol at first resisted, but eventually he followed our advice. The niche we helped Sol identify and develop was serving as an expert witness in will contest cases.

Identifying his niche gave Sol a huge advantage over his competitors. First, he became a real go-to expert in will contest cases, thanks to the experience he had gained and the research he had conducted in his field. In addition, the niche he had selected involved big cases, which proved quite financially lucrative for him. Furthermore, because he was concentrating on a narrow area, he truly became an expert in his field and generated substantial word-of-mouth referrals as a result. Finally, he was able to target his marketing to the relatively few ($\approx$3,000) lawyers who specialize in will contests. This was a huge advantage for Sol, especially when you consider that there are around 1,000,000 lawyers in the United States.

In five years, Sol was able to build his part-time expert witness practice from nothing to a $500,000 business per year. It's gotten so busy, in fact, that he recently approached us for advice on another problem: he now has more expert witness work than he wants, so how does he get balance back in his life? Such is the power of positioning yourself in a niche.

Here's one final example that shows what happened to us when we made the mistake of straying outside of our niche. As discussed previously, many years ago we lost a small fortune when we developed a product, titled *Help Your Child Achieve*, for the parents of underachieving kids. We made many mistakes with this product, but some of the most important—and most costly—ones involved the niche audience we were reaching out to: parents of underachieving kids.

One problem with this niche was that there was no way to market to it in a cost-effective manner. We couldn't find a list of parents of underachieving kids we could send mailings to—or any other cost-effective way to reach them, for that matter. As a result, we resorted to shotgun advertising and threw ads on TV. These were, to say the least, not cost-effective. Another clear problem was that we had no brand or reputation in this niche, and we were involved in all kinds of other business activities at the time. As such, it was difficult for us to establish trust and credibility with our market. Had we been an organization with a recognized brand and a great reputation in kids' education beforehand, our results might have been much different.

How could we have done things differently? Maybe we should have defined the niche more narrowly. For example, let's say there was a way to identify and reach out to parents of children with attention deficit hyperactivity disorder (ADHD). If this were the case, our marketing costs could have been focused and greatly reduced. In addition, our product would have had much greater perceived value to this narrower market if it appeared to specialize in ADHD and was titled, *Help Your Child With ADHD Achieve.*

Finding lucrative niches need not involve sitting around, waiting for divine inspiration. In fact, the process of niche discovery can be planned—if you follow a protocol. We ask ourselves a series of questions when we are looking for niches to exploit, and we've adapted those questions for your use.

1. What are you really good at? A good niche will likely be something that you or your company is already really good at—and preferably something you know more about than almost anyone else.

2. Will the niche result in a lucrative product/service/customer base? A good niche will lead you to the right type of customers— those with the resources to pay a premium price for your product/service.

3. Can you do it "better" than the competition? What do we mean by better? Can you:

    •   Make it easier to use/more convenient?

    •   Customize it?

    •   Eliminate problems others have?

    •   Make the product last longer?

    •   Make it more valuable?

    •   Make it faster to use?

    •   Create something no one else has?

4. Is there a potential for repeat or allied business or product extensions? Here, the Holy Grail is to sell blades, not razors.

One successful niche product is good, but a product/service with potential logical extensions is great. For example, our expert witness niche, discussed earlier, has been developed by our company over the past 20-plus years. Our line of products for these experts includes:

- National conferences/preconferences

- Books

- Videos/audio programs

- White papers

- Directories

- Customized training

- One-on-one training

- Witness preparation

When we analyze a potential niche business opportunity in accordance with the above criteria, it reaffirms our commitment to looking deep and not just wide. What answers do we come up with when we work our way through the preceding exercise? Read on to find out.

1. What are we really good at? We have years of experience dealing with expert witnesses and excel at conference development, training, writing, producing, consulting, enduring material, and so forth.

2. Will our niche result in a lucrative product/service/customer base? Our customer base includes 50,000 plus experts who have the resources to attend conferences and purchase premium-based products and services. Many of those experts earn $300 to $500 an hour or more.

3. Can we do it better than the competition? We knew there was little competition for what we were planning, and we set out to deliver only high-quality materials and training. As a result, we have developed a blue chip reputation. We are not the cheapest (we don't want to be), but we are the best at what we do.

4. Is there potential for repeat or allied business or product extensions? The experts we service need to be at the top of

their game at all times. Experts can make six-figure incomes working one or two days a week, but one mistake can ruin a career, so the stakes for them are very high. These experts must stay current and ahead of their competition, which is why we continue to drill down and provide more and more narrow niche products for these experts.

You may wonder if it is possible to define your niche too narrowly—and the answer is yes. In most cases, however, we have found that the mistake most businesses make is in defining their niche too broadly, not too narrowly. Businesses in very narrow niches can thrive, as the following examples demonstrate.

Consider Chartwell Booksellers, a London-based bookstore that specializes solely in Winston Churchill materials, including books, photographs, signed documents, and so forth. The owner knew he was onto something when corporate raider, Saul Steinberg, called one day and ordered all the books in the bookstore's newsletter; first editions, bound in leather, and shipped as soon as possible. Price was no object or concern. Or think about the American Association for Justice, a plaintiff attorney organization. The AAJ has litigation groups/niches for personal injury cases related to climber tree stands, tap water burns, and welding rods. Although there may only be a few dozen or hundred plaintiff attorneys interested in these esoteric topics, the ones that are interested are very interested and will pay whatever it takes to gain an advantage in this field.

Baptist publisher Judson Press is another company that specializes in niche products, including practical church resources, books geared toward African Americans, and Hispanic/Spanish language books. Judson Press is in its 186th year of existence. Finally, the phenomenally successful website, FMyLife, receives almost two million readers a day, many of whom submit stories about their own misfortunes to help reassure (and sometimes amuse) others. FMyLife is the English language version of a similar French site, "Vie de Merde," which is one of the top ten websites in France. A sample entry: "I ate alone today in the college cafeteria. It was my birthday." Why would thousands of people send in these stories and visit these websites? You got me, but they do.

8. Consider premium pricing.

EXECUTIVE SUMMARY: In certain market niches, people will pay more for perceived quality. One way to increase the perceived quality of your product or service is to raise its price. The reason premium pricing works is that people will figure that they are getting a higher-quality product if they pay more. Consider finding a niche where you can use this technique.

* * *

There are certain products or services for which people will pay a premium for quality. Let's say you have a sick child who needs surgery. You find out that the surgeon you have selected charges the lowest prices around. How would that make you feel? It would probably scare you to death. If he's that cheap, there's probably something wrong with him, right? You want the most expensive heart surgeon because you presume that his rates are a reflection of the quality of his work. Or look at higher education today. Fancy private schools charge nearly ten times as much as comparably competitive state institutions do for an undergraduate education. How can they get away with that? Why don't people just flock to the cheaper state schools? Well, we'd argue that many people assume that private schools are simply better than their state school counterparts. A large part of that assumption is due to the logical but, of course, false thinking that if you pay more for something, it has to be better. Here's one final way to look at it: let's say that your child gets accused of a crime. If he is convicted of this crime, it will ruin his life. You are prepared to do whatever it takes to get your child the best legal representation possible. You interview three criminal defense lawyers, and one charges $20,000, one charges $30,000, and the final one charges $40,000. Who would most people hire? The answer, of course, is the $40,000 lawyer. Because that lawyer is the most expensive, they think, he *must* be the best.

It seems crazy, but we have found that a very counterintuitive way to increase our sales is to simply raise our prices. The key here is to find a market niche where people will pay for quality, which is basically what Apple has done to ensure its success. Apple focuses on the 20 percent of the marketplace that is willing to pay a premium for quality, and we suggest that you take a similar approach when pricing your products.

Let me give you some background. Lawyers hire expert witnesses to help them win their cases, and winning is extremely important to the lawyers. To paraphrase Vince Lombardi, it's the only thing that matters. We have found that lawyers who are involved in important cases don't overly care how much they pay their experts. We have also found that experts who raise their rates see increases in the *volume* of work they receive. The reason for this is clear: lawyers want to win. They therefore need the best-qualified expert witnesses, and they assume that the expert witnesses who charge the highest hourly rates are the best. We have surveyed a large number of expert witnesses and lawyers and have the empirical evidence to prove this.

The information age and the advent of the Internet have made it possible for businesses to greatly reduce their costs and greatly increase their productivity. The flip side of this revolution, however, is that pricing in many areas has become increasingly competitive. If your product or service is viewed as a replaceable commodity, it is very easy for a consumer to simply browse the Internet in search of the lowest cost provider. The perfect example of this price death spiral occurred when WalMart starting selling books at below their own cost (i.e., at a loss) in an effort to compete with Amazon.com. Amazon now uses this very same technique to sell some e-books.

Price war is a game that we have made a conscious decision to avoid. Let other people race to the bottom. We have found niches such as training, education, and consulting/professional services where people are willing to pay for quality. For example, the least expensive book we publish ourselves costs $100. Our writing conferences cost exponentially more than some of the conferences held by competitors. We are even able to charge $1,000 per day for one of our conferences. The point is that these premium prices can help sell your products because many people will logically assume that if you pay a premium for something, *it must be really good.*

Here's one final example: a few years ago we wrote and published a book on negotiating that was designed especially for physicians. We tried marketing and selling the book at a price of $100 per copy, which equals that of our other lowest priced specialty books but is obviously much higher than the cost of a nonspecialized negotiating book. Nothing worked. Jim and I had numerous discussions as to what to do. Here's about how they went:

JIM: Steve, we need to do something about the book. I think pricing is a big issue here.

STEVE: You know me, I'm an open-minded guy. I will keep my usual open mind, but I will not, under any circumstances, consider lowering the price. I would rather throw all the books in the garbage. This book is far too valuable to lower the price; its helps physicians save hundreds of thousands of dollars. Lowering our price will also hurt our premium brand and sets a bad precedent.

JIM: I figured you'd have that attitude, so I'm ready for you. Why don't we try *raising* the price?

STEVE: That I can agree to. Try it out and let's see what happens.

We raised the price of the book to $135, and a funny thing happened: it worked better than before. We sent out the same brochure to the same demographic. The only difference was the increased price. We sold more books and were paid 35% more for each book that we sold. We made a healthy profit. Raising the price and the perceived value of the book was our breakthrough marketing technique.

9. Deadlines make things happen.

EXECUTIVE SUMMARY: Deadlines are easy to implement and often boost sales. Customers tend to wait to make purchasing decisions until an offer deadline is near its expiration date, so you can expect a large spike in sales around that time.

* * *

One of our colleagues that we teach with serves as a federal trial judge. One day he was explaining the rules that lawyers must follow during litigation. He stated that there was a deadline for everything. The reason the court and the rules impose deadlines, he explained, is that without deadlines, nothing would ever get done. He was right: deadlines get things done, which is why we recommend putting deadlines on your sales offer. If you do so, you may find that your sales will increase. You may also find that the vast majority of your sales will come at or near the expiration of the deadline. Like many of the other lessons in this book, we have learned the importance of deadlines the hard way, through trial and lots of error.

For many years we have published various directories for the benefit of our clients. As previously mentioned, our directories follow the basic business model of the yellow pages. We would publish each of our directories once a year, and our customers paid us for the privilege of being listed in the directories. Once a year we print the directory and mail thousands of them to key persons across the country so that they can hire the clients that are featured in the directory. Because we were physically printing the directory once a year, there was always a deadline as to when clients needed to respond to make it into the directory. Each year we would market the directory near the deadline, and each year we would get a good response. In particular, we found that the majority of our listing sales occurred during the last few days before (and immediately after) the deadline.

We wanted to expand this product and increase its sales, so we decided that we should market and promote listings in the directory all year long. We sent out a number of costly mailings doing just that. Unfortunately, however, the response rate we received was atrocious. It was far worse than when we mailed at the closing deadline and not enough to generate a profit.

As discussed previously, one of the keys to marketing is experimentation. What if the deadline we have at print closing time is a key factor in getting people to actually pull the trigger and buy? Let's try sending out "off season" marketing that also has a deadline. So we decided to send out a direct mail offer with a deadline on it. The idea was that the customer would receive a valuable extra free service if he or she responded to our offer by a certain date. We sent out this test and an amazing thing happened: it worked. Our mailing performed many times better than it had before. We made money, and the valuable lesson we learned with regards to deadlines has allowed us to profitably market our directories throughout the year. This was an amazing breakthrough for us: our directories have grown in both revenue and profit since we made this switch to year-round, "deadline" marketing.

We have seen this deadline technique confirmed by one of the organizations with which we put on a small, targeted conference. About five weeks before the conference, we called to see how attendance was doing. Our contact at the organization said that only had eight people had signed up—which was less than one-fifth of anticipated attendance. But don't worry, she told us. Everything happens at the deadline. What the organization had done was give a small discount to everyone who signed up at least 30 days prior to the start of the conference. We called right after the deadline and were given an eye-popping update: 42 people had registered for the course! In two months, only eight people had signed up, but in the last week before the deadline, 34 people had signed up.

Using a deadline is by no means a novel idea. It is used over and over again by people who are trying to sell you something and encourage you to make a purchasing decision. It was purely a result of our own ignorance that we did not start using this tried-and-true technique to maximum benefit sooner. These days, a whole new series of companies are built on deadlines. The company Groupon sells a deal of the day, which offers discounts of 50 percent on goods and services targeted to direct locations near the customer, and the offers are sometimes good for only a 24-hour time period. Google Offers has followed suit with its own 50 percent offers, which are good for a very limited time—usually a week or less.

10. Offer a money back guarantee—and honor it.

EXECUTIVE SUMMARY: To boost sales, consider backing up your product or service with a money-back guarantee. Such a guarantee will help motivate you to produce the highest quality products and services. If you produce high-quality products and services, you will probably get very few returns. When you do receive a request for a refund, however, view the situation as an opportunity to build your brand as a stand-up organization by promptly issuing the refund without any hassles.

* * *

A bedrock business technique that we utilize is to stand by our products and services with a no-hassle, money-back guarantee. We have come to four conclusions regarding money-back guarantees. First, the promise of a money-back guarantee greatly enhances sales. Second, if you produce a high-quality product, you will get very few returns. Third, providing a money-back guarantee gives you even more incentive to develop and deliver products and services that are of superior quality and value. Fourth, honoring your money-back guarantee without hassles or hoops is an excellent way to further enhance your brand.

Let's talk about each of these elements in turn. First of all is how a money-back guarantee increases sales. We talk to and survey many customers, and one of the bits of feedback we often receive is that our willingness to offer of a money-back guarantee helps close sales. For example, it is very common to have a conversation like this with someone who is on the fence about signing up for one of our courses:

CLIENT: I want to sign up, but don't know if I'll be free on those dates.

AUTHORS: Well, if you sign up and need to cancel, we will give you a 100 percent refund up to two weeks prior to the start of the course.

CLIENT: That's fantastic, I have nothing to lose and will sign up.

We have conducted many focus groups and surveys with our clients, and in these forums, we ask for feedback on money-back guarantees. The availability of a money-back guarantee always comes back as a critical factor in customers' buying decisions.

Now let's talk about the second benefit: if you produce a high-quality product or service that delivers clear value to your customers, you will receive very few returns. It's that simple. Let me give you a good example. We sell a six-page contract that our expert witness clients can use when lawyers want to hire them. It costs $150, and we sell it on CD-ROM or via digital download so that it can be modified on a computer. The product is superb. We've sold over 1,500 contracts and have had only about four or five returns. Think about that for a second: this is a product that someone could buy, copy to their computer, return for a full refund, and then continue to use. It costs $25 per page, but almost nobody returns it because they feel good about their purchase. So, when you produce a high-quality product, you have a lot less to lose by offering your customers a money-back guarantee.

Offering a money-back guarantee can also help keep you honest. If dissatisfied customers can get all the money they spent on your product back, you will be highly motivated to make sure that your customers receive superior value for their money. Let me give you an example. We sell listings in our directories and offer a money-back guarantee if, eight months or so after the publication of the directory, the customer is not satisfied. In short, we stand by our product. We have the following conversation with someone who is considering listing themselves in one of our directories quite often:

POTENTIAL CLIENT: I am considering listing, but I want to know how much business I will get.

AUTHORS: Well, that no one can predict. What I can tell you is two things. One, since we offer a money-back guarantee, we are extremely motivated to make this work for you. We don't want you to request a refund. Second, for most people our directory works extremely well. We have over 1,300 of your colleagues in the directory, and only a handful of them request a refund each year.

POTENTIAL CLIENT: Can I sign up over the phone right now?

The last point I'd like to go over is how honoring your money-back guarantee without hassles is a great opportunity to help you build your brand.[7] To show you what I mean, let me relate a phone call I received recently:

CLIENT: I had some questions about which of your expert witness courses would be right for me.

AUTHORS: Tell me a little bit about yourself.

CLIENT: Well, I am a law enforcement expert witness. I do blood spatter, that type of thing.

AUTHORS: How did you hear about us?

CLIENT: I was actually in your directory last year. It didn't work out for me, and I received a refund promptly and without hassles the day I requested it.

---

[7] See Chapter 1 on building your brand by not jerking people around.

That greatly impressed me about your organization, and I made a note that day to attend one of your courses when they are being held nearby, like they will be this year.

After a brief, further discussion, the client signed up for $2,000 worth of training. Our history of standing by our guarantees without hassle had had a critical and positive influence on his buying decision.

The highly respected and successful company L.L.Bean has a unique and memorable money-back guarantee policy, called "Guaranteed to Last."

"Guaranteed to Last: Our products are guaranteed to give 100% satisfaction in every way. Return anything purchased from us at any time if it proves otherwise. We do not want you to have anything from L.L.Bean that is not completely satisfactory."

Not only does L.L.Bean stand behind its products for life, but the company goes above and beyond this policy to provide service to its customers. A few months ago I received an unsolicited email from L.L.Bean in which the company told me that they were not satisfied with the quality of the Egyptian cotton sheets I had purchased from them and offered to send me a replacement set at no charge. I had not even asked for a refund or replacement! Now *that* is standing by your products and treating your customer right. I'll be buying from them again, and again, and again.

11. When someone tries to sell you something, sell them something.

EXECUTIVE SUMMARY: Grabbing potential customers' attention is one of the biggest problems businesspeople face when they try to sell their products or services. Whenever someone from an allied field is trying to sell you something, look at the possible things you might be able to sell *them* or their company before you blow them off. Turn the potential problem or hassle of being sold something into a sales opportunity for your business. The person who contacted you will listen to you, because they initiated the original contact and need to be nice to you.

* * *

Perhaps the ultimate coup in the sales process is when you are able to take someone who is trying to sell you something, turn it around, and get that person to buy something from you instead. This is a technique that we pride ourselves in. It's a simple and practical business strategy.

Here's a typical example of what we mean. I recently received a voicemail message from an accountant, and in the message, the accountant told us that he was an experienced expert witness and thought he would be a good teacher for us. He was suggesting that we hire him as a teacher on a volunteer basis. We get many requests from people who want to teach for us, and their requests are usually motivated by the fact that teaching for us can give someone tremendous exposure and credibility. The problem, however, is that many of these "volunteers" are either looking for an honorarium that is greater than what we pay or are looking to use our courses as an opportunity to sell something to our attendees. We take great lengths to avoid speakers who want to turn one of our conferences into a commercial for his goods or services.

The sum of all of this is that we are quite suspicious of volunteers and only rarely use them. In light of this, an easy way to handle the accountant's message would have been to ask my assistant to request his resume and tell him we would keep it on file and consider him for future work. Basically, this is a polite way of saying no without *actually* saying no. Of course, we didn't become successful doing things the easy way. What I did instead was research this man and his firm, and when I found out that he worked for a large forensic accounting firm, I called him back. During our conversation, I suggested to him that his firm might be interested in the training services we offer, which started a discussion that went on for a few weeks. In the end, the accountant's application to work for us turned into a lucrative training assignment for us. He tried to sell us something, but we ended up selling him something instead.

Here is another example of this technique in action: We recently had a physician inquire as to whether our company would publish one of his monographs. We returned the call and patiently and politely explained to him that we do not publish monographs. By actively listening to him, we were quickly able to figure out that he was passionate about writing. We suggested to him in a low-key way that as a writer, he might want to look into our Fiction Writing for Physicians conference. He was excited to learn of the conference and later registered to attend. We were able to turn what many would consider a nuisance call into a $1,700 sale. Now, we are not suggesting that you talk to every salesperson who cold calls you, trying to sell you copy paper or a timeshare in the Dominican Republic. The key to not wasting your time is to get a sense of who you are dealing with. If we are approached by an allied business that might realistically buy something from us, we'll talk to them. If they are selling chopomatics, we won't.

Here's another typical example: because I am an attorney, I have received solicitations, direct mail, and advertising for many years from a company that supplies expert witnesses to attorneys. This company makes its money as a middleman/broker between the experts and the attorneys. One day a representative from the company called me up to try to sell me their services. I figured I'd see if I could turn them into a customer. I asked some questions, and the salesperson (who was trying to suck up to me and get me to use their service) was very cooperative. I discovered that this company had 5,000 expert witnesses on its mailing list. This was obviously important and valuable information because my company sells product and services to expert witnesses. I then asked for the contact information of the person who was in charge of their marketing. Again, because the salesperson thought I might buy something from him, he was very cooperative. I received a good deal of information about the company.

After the call, I followed up with the owners of the company, and we set up a meeting. Eventually, this company became one of our distributors, and they have bought and resold a large number of our products. All this was made possible because I pounced on the opportunity to sell something to someone who thought he could sell me something.

12. Pitch to your customers when their wallets are already open.

EXECUTIVE SUMMARY: Make it easy for your customers to buy additional products and services from you when you are closing the sale. We have found that once your client has his or her wallet open for a sale, it is much easier to get that person to buy additional products and services from you. Design a protocol or a system for asking your customer if he or she would like to add additional products or services to their order. This is a very cost-effective way of increasing sales.

* * *

One of the most valuable lessons we have learned in business is that one of the best times to sell a product or service to your customer is when they are already buying something else. What makes this technique particularly valuable is that it is easy to implement, inexpensive, and can often be wildly profitable. Of course, we had been in business for more than 15 years before we figured this out.

After Jim had been working with me for a couple of years, he came to me with an idea. Here's approximately how the conversation went:

JIM: Steve, I have something I'd like to try out with our big annual two-day National Expert Witness Conference, an idea to make more money.

STEVE: OK, I'm listening.

JIM: Well, every year we send out 100,000 or so brochures at a cost of $50,000 to promote the conference.

STEVE: Yes, go on.

JIM: Well, we get 150 people to sign up, they pay $500 each, and after we pay for the hotel and speakers, there's very little—if anything—left over in profit.

STEVE: Exactly. That's why I'm strongly considering no longer running the conference. Too much work, too little profit.

JIM: We don't want to raise the price and drive attendance down, but what if we offered, in the same brochure, a one-day "preconference," which will take place the day before the main conference. We charge $250 for it. The marketing costs are zero—we'll sell it in the same brochure we already send out.

STEVE: I don't know if people will want to sit here for three days. That's a long time.

JIM: Can we try it out? We have little to lose by seeing what happens, right? The upside is huge, though. If this works, we could also use this technique on our other conferences as well.

STEVE: OK, the potential rewards far outweigh the risks,[8] so let's give it a try.

We tried out a single preconference and an amazing thing happened: That year over 50 percent of the people who came to the conference signed up for the extra day. This increased our revenues by 25 percent *but resulted in our profits going up several hundred percent.* A program that was about to be cancelled became instantly profitable because we were able to sell our customers more—that is, an additional course.

As Jim had suggested, the results of this test were widespread and dramatic. We next tried adding preconferences to our other annual conferences. This worked well, too. Next, we started adding more than one preconference on the day before the main conference. Finally, we started adding more than one day of preconferences, with multiple preconferences occurring each day. In the end, we had found a way to dramatically increase the profitability of our

---

[8] See Chapter 6.

conferences by simply selling extra courses at the same time that we sold the main product. This one simple sales technique has literally made us additional millions of dollars in profits over the last 15 years.

Here's another dramatically effective example from our experiences: As part of our business, we sell high-priced ($100+) professional books to doctors, lawyers, and expert witnesses. Since 2005 or so, the majority of our book sales have come through our web store. We would mail out a flyer promoting Book X, and then we'd get a bunch of sales of Book X through our website. The problem, however, was that customers were only buying Book X and nothing else. One day our young partner Alex came to Jim and me with an idea. What if we programmed our web store to suggest other products that the customer might be interested in? For example, if a customer was viewing a particular book for expert witnesses, the web store would suggest to the customer that he or she might also be interested in the other products we have for expert witnesses. The web store would also make it easy for customers to add these suggested products to their order. Alex said he could get our programmer to set the web store up in this way for $3,000. We analyzed the situation and saw that if this worked, it would be well worth the $3,000 investment. There was little risk and a large and ongoing potential upside, so we quickly decided to proceed.

We invested the money and built the system, and the results were dramatic. Instantaneously, over 10 percent of the orders we received through our web store were for multiple products. Many customers were now buying three, four, and five or more products. We earned back our $3,000 investment in the first month, and we have made hundreds of thousands of dollars in additional profit from this simple, low-maintenance, nonongoing-cost technique.

We are not the only business that has a fondness for selling to the customer while his or her wallet is open. I was in the post office the other day, and the poor clerk was forced to ask every customer that went through the line if he or she wanted a post office box, mailing supplies, stamps, and so forth. Go to buy a piece of office equipment and you'll be asked if you want a service plan. Try buying a car and see all the add-ons the dealer will try to sell you (floor mats, extended warranties, etc.). Many businesses understand that to increase profits, it is helpful to try to sell your customers additional products and services at the same time that they are buying something else. The technique is doubly effective because it's very low cost to try to sell something to your customer once he or she is already buying something. They are already right in front of you—all you need to do is ask.

13. Capture and add to your database the names of potential customers.

EXECUTIVE SUMMARY: Find ways to capture the contact information of leads who have expressed an interest in your products or services. Then add to your database this information and use it to solicit their business. Your payoff in additional sales can be quite dramatic.

* * *

It's a heck of a lot easier selling products or services to potential customers that actually have an interest in your products and services than to those who don't. This is not a startling statement, but it is an extremely important one. The mistake that we often see—and the mistake that we have made ourselves—occurs when companies fail to employ effective systems for capturing the contact information of those who have expressed (or implied) interest in their products or services. The related mistake is not following up with these individuals after their contact information has been captured.

The value of maintaining a database of potential customers can be quite large. We often measure a response rate of 10 to 20 times *or more* greater from qualified persons who have expressed an interest in our products over those who have not. As such, the contact information of people who are interested in your products is worth its weight in gold. Gather this information in any way that you can, and make sure to solicit your potential customers regularly.

Unfortunately, it took us many years to get serious about collecting contact information from our potential customers. When Jim first joined SEAK, he started asking some questions of the staff. One day, early on, he asked, "When someone calls up for information about one of our seminars, what do you do?" The answer came back: "Well, we mail that person a brochure." That sounded good, but Jim's a good lawyer, so he asked a few follow-up questions: "OK, and what do you do with their contact information? Where is it stored, and how do you follow up?" "It isn't. If they want to come, they will. They know where to find us." Needless to say, it took me about an hour to calm Jim down after he heard this answer. He let me know, in no uncertain terms, that we were throwing money away by not capturing these names and following up. I pled guilty and agreed to change our ways. As a result, we started a system whereby, if anyone inquires about a particular product, we ask if they would like to be placed on our mailing list (the vast majority do), and then we enter them into a database, tagging them as a lead for the product line they asked about. Then we aggressively and regularly follow up with these leads through direct e-mail and snail mail solicitations. We track the sales from these "requests" lists, as we call them, and they perform extremely well.

The procedure of capturing names may need to be drilled into your staff repeatedly. You may need to stress the importance of doing so. If need be, you can have a test person call up and pretend to be interested in your products to see if your staff follows protocol. One thing we have trained our staff to do is to always offer to send a brochure or free giveaway to a lead on the phone that has not specifically requested to be put on our mailing list and isn't ordering something. The idea, of course, is simple: get the lead to provide you with his or her contact information. Another simple thing we did a few years ago was to add a form for "Join Mailing List" to our various websites. Interested people click on the link, type in their contact information, and submit it to us. Our little company receives around five of these requests on average per day, and the leads are incredibly valuable. Even better, the cost of capturing these names are virtually nonexistent—just a small, one-time cost of a few hundred dollars to program the website. I am amazed at the number of business websites I visit that don't explicitly feature this option.

Recently, we've tried another technique to gather the contact information of those who are interested in our products and services: we give away a short article on a topic of interest if people will write in for it via e-mail. For example, we run a course for physicians on how to leave the field of medicine and transition to an alternative career, so we placed on our website a notice for a free, short, 1,000-word article that we wrote: "The Biggest Mistakes Physicians Make When Transitioning to a Non-Clinical Career." Each day, one or two doctors request this article and provide us with their contact information. We then add their contact information to our database and follow up with every lead we get; as a result of our efforts, we have tracked a high conversion rate (up to 5% and more) of clients that eventually attend our Conference on Non-Clinical Careers (which costs between $1,300 and $2,300). The bottom line is that giving away a free teaser product can be a good way to capture the contact information of an even greater number of people who are interested in your products or services. If the teaser is high quality, it can also help build your brand and close the sale.

Looking around the marketplace, you can see many examples of companies that successfully capture the contact information of leads or customers. For example, a few days ago, I called to cancel my cable service. The rep asked me to provide an e-mail address so that she could send out a confirmation of the cancellation, and when I told her that I was not interested in receiving spam, she informed me that they don't rent their names to other companies. What was unsaid, of course, was that they had every intention of bombarding me with spam of their own.

Go to a chain restaurant, and you will often be asked your e-mail address when you pay the bill—sometimes to join a rewards program. Visit an exhibit booth at a conference, and you will often see raffles of valuable and attractive prizes. All you need to do to be eligible to win, of course, is provide a business card with your contact information.

14. Follow-up.

EXECUTIVE SUMMARY: One of the most common sales mistakes that companies make is failing to follow up with their leads. Never quote a job and then fail to follow up with either an e-mail or a phone call. Following-up is a simple and effective technique to increase your sales. Develop a protocol and calendar system to follow-up with your leads so that nothing falls through the cracks.

* * *

Often times someone will express an interest in your products or services but then refrain from buying on the spot. Maybe they have to think about the purchase. Maybe they are waiting on other quotes to filter in. Maybe they have to talk things over with their family members or colleagues. Whatever the cause of their hesitation may be, it is critical that you maintain a system for following up with potential customers. I can't tell you the number of businesspeople who have quoted a job for me and then never bothered to follow up.

Recently, Jim decided to put a significant addition onto his house. He received bids from four contractors, and of those four, only two of them ever followed up to see if he would like to proceed or ask additional questions. This was mind boggling to Jim. How could these people not follow up on a six-figure proposal? A similar thing happened recently when Jim investigated the possibility of installing a security system in his house. He received a quote from a very nice man with whom he hit it off. The security vendor e-mailed the quote over, but then Jim never heard from him again. It is shocking, but this sort of situation happens all the time.

Consulting constitutes a large part of our business, and when someone expresses interest in our consulting services, we typically sit down and have a conversation with that person. After that conversation, we e-mail out a written proposal, and sometimes the client will immediately accept the proposal. More often, however, the client will write back to let us know that he or she will consider our proposal, and most often, we receive no response at all. Our protocol then is to follow up with these leads until we get an answer, yes or no. Following-up can be as simple as shooting over an e-mail to the client and asking if he or she would like to proceed with the proposal we sent over. We also sometimes ask when the client would like to proceed.

After persistent nonresponsiveness, we will often send over a note asking if we should close our file.

We have found that the simple follow-up techniques described above can be very effective in getting your leads to make the decision to buy. We don't know exactly why this occurs, but we have seen it time and time again. The bottom line is that following up with potential clients is a simple and easy technique that will help you increase your sales. Use an effective calendar system, and make sure to follow up.

15. Make it simple and easy for your customer to buy from you.

EXECUTIVE SUMMARY: Make it as easy as possible for your customers to buy your products and services. Don't make them fill out complicated forms. Keep it simple. If you need to get further detailed information from your customer, do it after the sale. Simplifying an order form or ordering process can greatly enhance your sales.

* * *

One of the lessons that we have learned the hard way is that the easier you make it for your customers to make a purchase from you, the more likely it is that you will be able to close the sale. Let me give you an example. Recently we developed an enhanced way for our clients to list and promote themselves in our online directory. We called the new product a "Featured Listing," which in some ways is similar to Google's familiar AdWords, which appear on the side and top of a Google search. How the product worked was somewhat complicated, and it required us to gather a good deal of information from anyone wishing to place a Featured Listing.

We started off by selling the new Featured Listings through a very complicated form, which included detailed instructions (about as clear as a tax form) and gathered all of the information we would need to pull together the listing. Once the customer filled out all the information on this form, we would be able to get them up and running without having to contact them for further information. Basically, getting the customer to give us this detailed information made our job of delivering the service much easier. We then began marketing our new Featured Listing service, but the response we got back was very weak. Just a few people had signed up using the complicated form. A pointed internal discussion ensued, and we decided to try a different, much simpler order form.

The new order form was greatly simplified. Basically, it said that all the customer needed to do was provide their payment information, and then we would get them additional online exposure they wanted. There were no complicated forms to fill out and no confusing directions. We made it as easy as possible for the customer to say yes; just say that you want this, we told them, and we'll take the lead from there.

The downside of this new approach, of course, was that it required us to contact each new customer after the sale to obtain the additional information we needed to enhance their web presence (e.g., how many and what search terms they wanted to be associated with). This was extremely time consuming, but it ended up being well worth it. With our new simple order form, which made buying our service monumentally easier, we were able to increase sales of our Featured Listings by a factor of more than ten. This one simple change instantly transformed a marginal product into an extremely profitable one.

In the time since we learned this lesson, we have simplified many of our ordering processes and have seen corresponding increases in sales. We don't worry if we have to commit additional time and resources to make it easy for our clients to finalize a sale. We have learned the hard way that the easier we make the purchasing process for our customers, the more likely we are to close a sale.

You can see many examples in the marketplace of companies successfully using this "simplify the sale" technique. States offer transponders so that tolls can be charged automatically to their credit cards and people don't have to reach into their pockets and open up their wallets. Amazon, Apple, and other online sellers offer purchases with just one or two entries on a phone or computer. Business-to-business sales are often offered on credit: tell the supplier what you want and he'll send you a bill. Car dealers offer sign-and-drive, no-money-down deals. As you can see, making it easier for your customers to buy your products and services is a proven and effective marketing technique.

* * *

To be successful, you're going to need to excel at marketing and selling the products and services you produce. The more you will be able to sell, the more you will be able to make. An additional way to increase profits is to improve your productivity and decrease your costs. And that is the subject of our next chapter.

Step 5: Control Your Costs and Increase Your Productivity

Most businesses ultimately do not have any absolute control over how many of their products or services will be bought. The truth of the matter is that you just can't make somebody buy your stuff. Where you do have some control, however, is on the cost side of the equation.

Cutting costs is a surefire way to make more money because the money saved translates directly into an equal amount of increased profits and directly benefits your bottom line. How compelling is the power of cutting costs? After the financial meltdown of 2008, the world entered the worst recession it had seen since the Great Depression. Meanwhile, the stock market rallied in 2009 based on increased earnings from companies. These earnings were, in part, due to companies' decision to aggressively cut their costs.

1. Do not fear technology; embrace it.

EXECUTIVE SUMMARY: Using technology is a proven way to increase your company's efficiency and reduce its costs. If you are a technophobe, add a technophile to your team. There are simply too many ways to reduce your costs and improve your efficiency through technology to forgo this technique for making more money.

* * *

One of the most important ways a business can dramatically increase its efficiency and significantly reduce its costs is by embracing technology. And don't forget: lower costs means higher profits. Now, I'm not one who is comfortable interacting with technology. Give me a computer, and I'll crash it. I have no patience for reading directions. I've been very skeptical of technology my whole life and derisive of those who fall in love with technology without concentrating on what can make them money. These very same attitudes that I've held onto for so long, however, have been a mistake. As a result of inviting younger partners to join my business, my eyes have been opened wide in terms of the advantages that can be gained from technology. Let me give you some examples of what I mean.

Our company's core marketing media is distributed through direct mail. In fact, we mail out over a 1,000,000 pieces of direct mail *each year*. As mentioned in Chapter 4, one of the first projects that I put Jim in charge of when he joined me full-time was marketing. At the time that Jim began working with me, all of our mailings were done by hand by a soccer mom who lived down the street from me. Jim complained to me that we should be using a mail house that was capable of sending the mail out in an automated fashion. I curtly explained to Jim the concept of, "If it ain't broke, don't fix it." We've been doing it this way for 13 years, I told him. Let's not mess with success. This went on for a couple of years, but Jim kept asking for my permission to switch to a mail house so that we could send out our mailings with automation. I kept telling him no.

In December of one year, we were getting ready to send out a big mailing of 200,000 pieces. I was recovering from oral surgery and needed some help, so I asked Jim to drive down from Boston. We rented a big truck and proceeded to our office, where there were hundreds of bags of mail that had to be lugged up from our basement and loaded onto the truck. It was four degrees above zero. The walkway was a sheet of ice. Eventually, after much slipping, work, and cursing, we loaded up the truck and drove it to the post office. We then spent another two hours at the post office unloading the truck, after which we were physically and mentally exhausted. Finally, we handed the paperwork to the foreman at the post office, who then looked us straight in the eye and said, "We can't take this. It's all wrong. It will have to go back." I thought Jim would kill me on the spot.

After exhausting all of my powers of persuasion, I was able to convince the foreman to accept our mailing. As for Jim, after this episode I had to give in.

He selected a local mail house, and we started sending out our mailings using their automated equipment. The differences were astounding. Because this mail house used automated equipment, working with them was actually cheaper than hiring the soccer mom. They also could get out the mailing about four times as fast. Finally, there were no more truck rentals, and there was no need for Jim and me to schlep around mail bags. We could concentrate on making money.

This pattern has been repeated over and over again in our business. Jim and the other younger partners push for a switch to technology, and I push back. It's not that I don't have good reasons to be resistant. First, if you rely on technology, it has to work. I remember as it was yesterday the doctor who gave a talk for us at one of our conferences about using technology to increase productivity. The doctor, in front of hundreds of people, couldn't get his computer to work. I have also seen countless hours wasted on technology that wouldn't work. Then there was the time our server went down for a week right before our largest conference of the year. Very recently, following knee surgery, I had to languish in a hospital bed many hours past when I should have been discharged because the hospital's computer system had crashed. When you can get the technology to work, however, the results can be dramatic. Here are a few more examples.

Jim and I travel a good deal for business, and we are often on the road, consulting and teaching. One day we took a business trip, and I saw Jim using his iPhone. On seeing this, I asked, in my typical techno-cynical fashion, "Having fun playing with yourself?" Jim glared at me and retorted, "I am getting you one of these, and then you can play with yourself, too." A few weeks later, Jim dragged me to get my iPhone and showed me how to use it. And I have to admit: My efficiency has increased significantly since I started using it. I get my e-mails on the road and can respond promptly. I was even able to continue working while I was recovering from knee replacement surgery.

Seeing me accept the iPhone, Jim figured he'd push a little more and see how far he could get with me. Jim knew that I get a lot of phone calls—probably 20 to 30 per day—and he was constantly observing me calling into my voicemail and scribbling down phone numbers and messages. I spent a good part of my day doing this. So, one day, Jim showed up and declared, "I'm getting you something to help you with your messages. You WILL try it, and you will love it. It will save you a load of time. If you don't love it after one week, I promise to remove it." Jim then proceeded to set up a service whereby my voicemails are automatically transcribed and then e-mailed to me. Again, he was right: I loved it, and it saved me a load of time. My messages are pushed right to my iPhone, and I never have to scribble them down or worry about reading my own handwriting. This one little bit of technology probably saves me at least one hour a week, which is the equivalent of having an extra week's productivity each year.

The list of technological improvements we have successfully implemented to increase our productivity and decrease our costs goes on and on. We developed a web store with e-commerce, and now orders are processed automatically and can be taken 24 hours a day, 7 days a week. We replaced written confirmations through the mail for our conference attendees with ones sent via e-mail. We replaced paper certificate of completions with e-mailed ones. In fact, we don't use paper anymore, don't pay for postage, and as a result, clients receive their information much faster. We scan and e-mail instead of faxing, which saves us costs related to paper, toner, and fax charges. We save storage costs by digitizing our records. Our bookkeeper saves time, postage, and supplies by paying our bills online. We have even begun to offer web-based videoconferencing for some of our consulting assignments to save travel time and expense.

The marketplace is replete with examples of technology being used to improve businesses' productivity and reduce their costs. As US President Barack Obama famously pointed out, ATMs have, to a large extent, replaced bank tellers. Robots have replaced many assembly line workers and will soon replace many warehouse workers. Many credit card sales can now be completed without the need for a signed paper receipt. It is good business practice to vigilantly look out for opportunities to increase your productivity and decrease your costs through the use of technology.

2. Shop around for the best deal and use vendors based in low-cost areas.

EXECUTIVE SUMMARY: The more you shop around, the more you'll find how simple and effective shopping around can be. Put the time in and shop around, especially if you are dealing with a significant or ongoing expense. For the best chance of getting a great deal, concentrate on vendors who are based in low-cost, rural areas. You'll save tons of money by not helping to pay for your vendor's inflated overhead and labor costs.

* * *

If you want to save money, shop around. Shopping around is a simple process; all it requires is a little bit of time, and the amount of money you can save by doing so can be eye popping. If you want the best deal, don't pay extra for your vendor's inflated overhead, taxes, or labor costs. Be geographically flexible and concentrate on low-cost venues. Be wary of vendors based in high-cost areas. You would be shocked at how much prices vary from place to place and how much money can be saved if you just shop around. If you yourself do not like to shop around, find someone in your company who enjoys it and is good at it, and assign the project to them. Let me give you some examples of the power of shopping around.

Many, many years ago, I hired Jim to help me produce a series of educational videotapes, and when all the videos were shot and edited, it was time to duplicate the tapes and ship them to our distributer. We were selling the videos for $100 each, and our fancy, downtown Boston production company offered to duplicate the tapes for us for $10 each, leaving us with a good margin. I wanted to get the tapes duplicated immediately and proceed, but Jim wasn't at all satisfied. He asked for 48 hours to see what he could come up with, and though I really wasn't interested in wasting time to save a few pennies per unit, I indulged Jim. "Forty-eight hours, no more," I told him.

I got a call from Jim two days later. He had put in a good amount of time, calling potential vendors (this was before the Internet) and asking for recommendations, and he told me that he had found a vendor in rural Maine that would duplicate the tapes for 80 percent less, or around $2 a tape. I was very skeptical and suspected he was foolishly allowing himself to be taken by either a fraudulent company or one that produced a shoddy product. At the same time, however, I felt a little nervous at the thought that I might have been very close to grossly overpaying for something. After some heated back-and-forth discussions between Jim and me, I agreed to ride up to Maine with Jim and kick the tires of the vendor he had found.

We met with the owner, Matt, who was a stand-up guy, and he showed us his immaculate and well-organized production facility, which was essentially running 24 hours a day, 7 days a week. We met his professional staff, too, and we saw his low-overhead building in the middle of nowhere in Maine. We were impressed; Matt got the contract; and we saved 80 percent in costs by shopping around. Needless to say, we were very pleased with ourselves. We have been using Matt's company ever since, and the money we have saved over the years from duplication alone has been over $100,000.

Shopping around is a simple and easy way to save (i.e., make) money. All it requires is a little bit of time and, ideally, an employee that is obsessive–compulsive about finding the best deal. As can be seen in the above example, we have also found that the best-priced vendors are usually those that are based in rural areas of low-cost, low-tax states, so if you want to get a good deal, concentrate your search in these locations. For example, a very low-priced printer we regularly use is based in the boonies of Wisconsin. We love it. Why would we want to pay extra to help our vendors cover their rent or the labor costs associated with operating in a big city? Using the Wisconsin printer has saved our company $200,000 over ten years. That's money that goes directly to our bottom line.

Here's one final example from our business that really shows the startling amount of money you can save just by shopping around. Recently we were looking for a new web developer to develop a simple website for us, so we called around to get prices. It was really all quite predictable. The prices we were quoted were wildly different, and the closer the developer lived to a big city, the more expensive he or she was. We got several quotes in the $20,000 to $30,000 range from Boston developers, but we ended up paying $2,000 to a vendor from Utah *for the exact same service.* That's a savings of up to 93 percent, and we were only able to realize these savings because we took the time to shop around.

Looking around the marketplace, you can easily see countless examples of businesses that operate in low-cost environments to boost their bottom line. For example, while GM and Chrysler were having major problems, closing union plants, and taking billions in taxpayer bailouts, foreign automakers were opening more and more assembly plants in the United States in rural, right-to-work states with lower taxes and lower labor costs. Businesses are leaving high-cost states, such as California, and relocating to low-cost states, like Texas. Boeing recently and famously tried to expand into South Carolina—another nonunion, low-labor-cost, right-to-work state. And finally, it goes without saying that Apple's wildly successful products are assembled in lower-cost countries overseas.

3. Develop long-term relationships with vendors.

EXECUTIVE SUMMARY: There are tremendous advantages to be gained from establishing long-term relationships with your vendors. Long-term vendors will know your business, your needs, and your quirks, and as a result, you can spend less time telling them what you need and more time running your business and making money. You also have tremendous leverage over long-term vendors and should be able to obtain and receive superior service, pricing, and concessions from them.

* * *

We have found it very advantageous to develop long-term relationships with our vendors. The advantages to this approach are numerous:

- Long-term clients are valuable to vendors, and as a result, we are able to obtain superior pricing and terms.

- We reduce the time spent shopping around.

- We don't need to constantly renegotiate.

- The vendor knows our needs and is able to provide us with superior service without our needing to nag or hold the vendor's hand.

- Because we are a very important client, the vendor is there for us in a pinch.

- We are able to develop relationships with the key decision makers at the vendors so we are able to get what we want, when we need it.

All our leverage over our long-term vendors comes from the same inescapable fact: as a long-time good client, *we are extremely valuable to our vendor*. The last thing the vendor would want to do is lose our account. Our explicit or implicit threat to do so is usually enough to get pretty much anything that we want, within reason.

Let's talk about terms and pricing. As a long-time client, we expect and command superior pricing, and to keep our vendors honest, we regularly obtain competing bids from their competitors. For example, we've been using the same mail house to process our marketing brochures for many years. Recently we received a bid from one of the mail house's competitors for a lower price. We shot the owner of our mail house a note with the pricing we received from his competitor, and his response back to us was typical, considering how valuable a client we have been to him over the years: "I will do whatever it takes to keep your business." He then proceeded to beat the competitor's bid. The whole "negotiation" took about one minute.

Sticking with the same mail house is the ideal solution for us. Our long-term vendor knows exactly how we want things done, so we save a tremendous amount of time by not having to explain to them our job specifications over and over again. We also save time by not having to monitor them as closely. It's very similar to having an experienced employee versus a new hire. With a new hire (or vendor), you need to spend extra time getting them up to speed and monitoring their progress. But when we stick with long-time vendors, we spend less time supervising them and can in turn spend more time creating products, selling products, and serving our clients. In other words, we can spend more time making money.

Here's a good example of what we mean when we say that we can save a significant amount of time when we work with a long-term vendor. We've been doing business with one particular hotel for years, so when we put on one of our conferences at this venue, we save huge amounts of time. Instead of having to painstakingly explain the exact details of everything we want in terms of how to set up the room, what food to serve, how to serve the food, and so forth, we simply instruct them to run things "the same as we always have." That frees up a tremendous amount of our time, which in turn saves us money.

Here's another short story that reveals the tremendous advantages of dealing with long-term vendors. Many years ago we established a long-term relationship with a certain hotel. We had put on many successful conferences at this hotel over the years, and both the hotel and our company were making money. It was a mutually beneficial arrangement. In this instance, however, we ran into a problem. Because we had fallen in love with our own idea and failed to follow a proper product development protocol[1], we created a seminar called *Testifying Skills for Chiropractors* that nobody wanted. Even though we spent $50,000 promoting this seminar, only two chiropractors signed up for it. What we needed to do was cancel the course, cut our losses, and move onto something new. Unfortunately, however, the contract we had signed with the hotel in question called for heavy penalties if we were to cancel.

We were an exceptionally important client for this particular hotel, so we decided to see what could be done. We called up the general manager of the hotel, and although he wasn't available at first, he returned our call promptly.[2] We explained the situation very stoically and then paused, without asking for anything. The general manager immediately said to us, "How I can help?" We then asked if it would be possible to let us out of our contract. The general manager's response was both immediate and gracious: "No problem, consider it done. Is there anything else I can help you with?" We were let out of the contract because we were a valuable, long-term client, but if we had not contracted with a long-term vendor, it is very, very unlikely that we would have been able to get out of the contract. The more likely scenario is that we would have faced tens of thousands of dollars in penalties. The reason for this is simple: what incentive would a hotel we had never done business with in the past have to waive the penalties that were due?

The advantages of working with long-time vendors cannot be overstated. If necessary, they will bend over backward for you. Recently, we needed some brochures printed for us on an emergency basis so that we could distribute some time-sensitive materials. We sent the brochure over to our contact at our long-time printer, but her response was that they were too busy to help us. So we called up the owner, who took our call. After a brief, 30-second conversation, he agreed to bump other customers and take care of us. The

---

[1] See also Chapter 3.

[2] Another advantage of being an important client.

reason for this was clear: we were an extremely valuable, long-term customer, and he didn't want to do anything to risk killing his golden goose. As a long-term customer, you are in a strong position to receive special treatment when emergencies arise and you need help.

4. Keep a low overhead and avoid large, fixed expenses or commitments.

EXECUTIVE SUMMARY: Try where possible to avoid long-term commitments/contracts and large, fixed expenses, such as mortgages, debt, and salaries. Such a policy can give you much-needed flexibility when faced with a crisis or changing business conditions. It will also give you greater leverage over your vendors and save you money.

* * *

Many years ago we hired a computer specialist, Harvey, to develop our first server-based customer and lead database. He was based out of state, and all of our communication was on the phone or through e-mails. Through the course of the project we became friendly with Harvey, and Harvey in turn gained a keen understanding of our business and came to admire it. As part of the deal, Harvey was required to come to our home office, install the database, and train our staff—and the day Harvey arrived was one to remember. Let me give you some background. We rent an office on top of a sushi restaurant. There is no elevator, and the entrance is hidden around the side of the building. Our rent is only around $1,500 per month, because this is obviously not the most desirable office space in the world.

Starting around eleven, you can smell the food cooking in the sushi restaurant below. In the past, we have had occasional problems with rat infestation and have needed to call an exterminator. The office itself consists basically of one big room with four work stations, a tiny office with a door, a tiny room for storage, and a bathroom. Our rug is worn. There is no conference room. The paint on the walls is in need of touching up. There's no mahogany paneling or fancy artwork on the walls. So when Harvey got to the top of the steps and looked around, there fell a look on his face that was some strange combination of disbelief and admiration. I still remember the exact question he asked me, before he even said hello: "You guys generate millions of dollars a year in sales *out of this?*" I quite proudly answered in the affirmative.

One of our mantras is to keep as low an overhead as possible. We believe in overpaying our staff[3]—but not in an inflated overhead. Our office is a good example of this philosophy. Our business is conducted over the phone, through the mail, and over the Internet. As such, there is no reason to spend money on a fancy office to impress our clients, because our clients *never* see our office and have no interest in helping us pay for a fancy office. What we need is an office that gets the job done. Money spent beyond this is taken directly out of our profits. We don't need to impress anyone.[4]

Another business philosophy that we strictly follow is the avoidance of long-term commitments. We *never* sign multiyear contracts with hotels or other vendors. There are two main reasons for this. First, once you are locked in, you lose your leverage with the vendor, because you can't threaten to walk. Second, you lose your flexibility. Circumstances can change—and they can change quickly—and you can become tremendously disadvantaged by committing yourself for the long term and eliminating your flexibility.

Here's a quick example of how you can get in trouble with long-term contracts. We do business with an allied organization that puts on conferences similar to ours. In early to mid-2008, this organization signed a two-year contract to hold its annual meeting at a fancy hotel, and one of the stipulations of the contract required the organization to guarantee the hotel a certain amount in sales. Then the financial crises hit in the fall of 2008, and the bottom fell out of the conference industry, as companies cut back on training and travel. Not only did the organization face a tough situation and lose money with its 2009 meeting, but it was contractually locked into the 2010 meeting as well. This was problematic given the changed circumstances, and this is the exact situation we try to avoid.

Fixed expenses can be business killers because you either pay them or you are insolvent. In fact, fixed expenses are just that: hard or impossible to reduce. In tough times, they can sink you, so we try to avoid as many fixed expenses as we can. The reason is clear and simple: when times are tough, you may need to reduce your expenses, but fixed expenses can't be reduced. As a result, we have no mortgage. We have no debt. Sure, our avoidance of fixed expenses may have resulted in slower growth at times, but it has also given us the ability to weather economic storms and our own dumb mistakes. Consciously deciding not to borrow money to grow our business is very 1930s and contrary to much of the current thought, but it has worked well

---

[3] If need be, staff can be reduced, but overhead is much more challenging to reduce when needed.

[4] Do you think Warren Buffett worries about who he fails to impress by being based in Omaha, Nebraska?

for us. We sleep easy at night and have the flexibility to reduce costs when we need to. We also feel that the consequences of the debt-fired Great Recession have vindicated our approach.

The final thing I should mention is compensation. It is our philosophy to overpay our employees, and this is discussed in detail in Chapter 7. *How* we overpay them is another matter, however. Wherever possible, our philosophy is to provide a modest base salary combined with incentive compensation, bonuses, profit participation, and the like that can be reduced or will automatically be reduced if the business suffers. Maintaining this flexibility gives us both much more flexibility to weather storms and helps us motivate and retain our staff.

Many companies now substantially hold down their fixed expenses by requiring that all employees work out of their homes. The *Wall Street Journal* reported on September 9, 2012, that companies such as Automatic, Inc., with 123 employees, and Kalypso LP, with 150 employees, have no corporate offices and require all employees to work out of their homes. No rent, no commuting, and less downtime. This is a win–win for both employers and their employees. In risky economic times, it can pay to think creatively about reducing costs.

5. Watch your vendors like a hawk.

EXECUTIVE SUMMARY: Watch your vendors like a hawk. A responsible and compulsive person should be in charge of regularly reviewing the deal you are getting through research and competitive bidding. You will unfortunately find that these audits will often reveal that you are no longer getting the superior terms and pricing that you once enjoyed. If you have a competing bid in hand, you most likely will be able to get your vendor to quickly beat that bid. As a result, you will have instantly saved (i.e., made) money.

* * *

When you are involved in a business, you will tend to use the same vendors over and over again. As discussed above, developing long-term relationships with vendors is a technique that we believe strongly in. However, these vendors need to be monitored closely to ensure that you are still receiving the highest level of service for the lowest cost. This is especially true of vendors affiliated with big, nameless, faceless corporations. One of the big corporation's classic techniques is to sneak through new disadvantage price terms and hope the customer doesn't notice.[5] Let me give you some examples.

---

[5] Think credit card companies, banks, and telecoms.

We accept credit cards, and the processing company charges us a percentage of the sales as a fee. A few years ago, however, we decided to renegotiate our credit card processing rates, and Jim, after much shopping around, was able to obtain what looked at the time to be a good rate in the mid twos. We were quite pleased with the results of our due diligence. Then, when the financial crisis of 2008 hit, we immediately focused on reducing our costs. Vendor pricing was an obvious area of concern, so we took a look at all of our relationships.

At this time, Jim once again looked into our credit card fees. He got the latest statements from our bookkeeper and discovered that our rates were now in the 3.25% to 3.5% range! This was costing us an extra $20,000 to $30,000 per year directly out of our profits and was totally wasted money. What had happened? The credit card processing company had slowly kept raising our rates over the years. We didn't notice or complain, so they kept doing it. We were paying a ridiculously high rate, and it was our fault because we had not kept an eye on them. How bad were we being gouged? Jim called around and got competing quotes in the 2.45% range. When we called our vendor, they immediately agreed to beat this price. Now, let me be clear: Jim and I would *never* sneakily raise the costs of one of our clients and gouge them. Unfortunately, however, the credit card processing company doesn't share our values in this regard. Our laziness and false trust cost us dearly. As such, ever since this debacle we have implemented a procedure where we audit our credit card statements every month to make sure we are not taken advantage of again.

We also implemented annual audits with competitive price checking of all our vendors' pricing. These audits continue to turn up shocking examples of bait and switch. Here's another typical story. One of the ways to make money out of nothing is to try to earn as much safe interest as you can from any working capital you have on hand with which to run your business. With this in mind, we negotiated a favorable interest rate with our long-time bank, where we keep significant sums of money. Unfortunately, our bank is another one of those nameless, faceless corporations that runs on a business model of changing the deal to your disadvantage and hoping you don't notice. On a recent audit we found that the bank had reduced our interest rate to far below market rates. We called to complain, and the bank immediately increased our interest rate *by a factor of ten*. Clearly they could have paid us this market rate before, but they were hoping our laziness and lack of attentiveness would result in a windfall. For a while it did, and it was our own fault.

Here's one more example. A few years back we made a point to negotiate favorable rates with our telephone company. We patted ourselves on the back and went back to concentrating on making money. Then we stopped paying attention to our phone bills because we had gotten such a good deal. The end of this story is very predictable. After a year or so, the phone company started slowly increasing our rates. They also came out with much cheaper plans that they did not switch us to because we never asked. When it came time to audit our phone bills a few years later, we found out that we were grossly overpaying for our phone service. We shopped around, threatened to bolt to a competitor, and as a result, the phone company reduced our rates. Our failure to diligently monitor our vendors had cost us dearly once again.

6. Consider buying over renting.

EXECUTIVE SUMMARY: Do your homework and make an informed decision as to whether you are truly better off renting or buying. In some cases you can save (and thus make) tremendous amounts of money by buying as opposed to renting.

* * *

One of the easiest ways that you can overpay for something over time is by renting instead of buying. Let me give you a typical example. Many years ago, we were putting on a conference at a fancy hotel in California. Two of our speakers, who were speaking during different time slots, wanted to use an LCD projector for their PowerPoint presentations. We didn't know anything about LCD projectors at the time (they were fairly new), so we rented one from the hotel. After the conference, we received the bill from the hotel, and as it turned out, renting an LCD projector cost $400 *per room per day*. They charged us double because this piece of equipment, which was about the size of a toaster, was moved 50 feet at lunchtime. In addition, the bill included a service charge and tax on top of this. The total rental charge was over $1,000. When we received the hotel bill, we nearly had a stroke, but we shouldn't have. It was our own fault for not doing our homework before we decided to rent.

We did some quick research after we received the bill, and we found that we could have *bought* a brand-new projector, better than the one we rented, for $1,500. Other rental equipment was even worse. For example, the hotel charged $50 per room per day for a laser pointer (plus service charge, plus tax). You could buy these at the time for around $10 or less! So we resolved that day to never again make the mistake of renting when it makes more sense to buy. Prior to making this decision, we had rented a cordless microphone 20 times over the course of a year. At $200 per day, the total cost of our rental amounted to $4,000. You can buy a superb cordless microphone for $500. The list goes on and on.

We have saved tens of thousands of dollars by buying and bringing our own AV equipment to our conferences, as opposed to renting such equipment from the meeting facilities that we use. There is a downside, of course. First, you need to get the equipment there and back. Second, you need to know how to use it. Third, if it breaks, it's your problem, not somebody else's.[6] Nonetheless, we deal with shipping the equipment, and we even hired a contractor AV tech to go with us to our major meetings. We also take on the risk of the equipment breaking because there's so much money to be saved.

Office equipment is another area in which we have found buying over leasing to be effective. Paying $3.00 per month for a phone doesn't seem bad. Consider, however, that if you keep the phone for ten years, you'll end paying $360 for a phone that could have been purchased for $150.

7. Read the fine print.

EXECUTIVE SUMMARY: Carefully review each and every word in contracts before you sign them. Don't just focus on the price. Never assume that the fine print is not important and does not matter. The fine print can and will cost you a lot of money.

* * *

Whenever you are presented with a contract for a business proposition, it is very important to read the fine print. The devil is often in the details, and those details can end up costing you a lot of money.

Many years ago, we put on a series of training conferences at a fancy hotel in Florida. The conference wasn't that highly attended—we had about 40 doctors participate—and a few days after the end of the conference, we received the bill from the hotel. When we saw the bill, we almost had a stroke: The hotel had charged us around $25,000 for continental breakfast and lunch for 40 doctors for four days! We investigated the bill, and it turned out that one of our former employees had signed a contract with the hotel that included a fine-print clause with a complicated formula that spelled out how much money we were required to spend on food and beverage. Because we didn't have a large number of attendees at our conference, this clause kicked in, and we were forced to live up to the agreement we had foolishly and blindly signed. This, of course, was a valuable learning experience for us. Ever since, Jim, a lawyer by training, signs off on all of our contracts, and he is especially careful

---

[6] Please see Chapter 6 on problems.

to read every word in every contract we sign. Where fine print exists that could come back and bite us in the backside, he gets that fine print removed or watered down.

Now, not everyone will be lucky enough to have a lawyer on staff to review all their contracts. You are fortunate if you do. If you do not, you must get yourself into the habit of reading every word of every contract. You must also understand every word of every contract that you sign. You don't need to be a lawyer to do this, but you do need to be a careful and active reader. The bottom line is: when reviewing contracts, don't just focus on the price. When you find a particular clause objectionable, try to get it taken out or weakened. You will find that you often can. As we have learned the hard way, the fine print in contracts can cost you a lot of money.

***

Every dollar that you save goes directly into your business's bottom line. When you increase productivity and reduce unneeded costs, you will make more money. Chapter 6 covers tips and techniques that can be applied to many functional areas within your business, including sales, operations, marketing, product development, and human resources.

Step 6: Take Charge

This chapter contains several general administrative and management techniques. We found that each technique discussed here is both easy to implement and capable of yielding powerful results. In sum, they are simple and easy to implement real-world ways to help your business succeed.

1. Watch the little details.

EXECUTIVE SUMMARY You need to watch the little details. Little mistakes can and will create huge problems that will cost you a lot of money. Everybody makes mistakes. To minimize mistakes we suggest that you create and follow a protocol of checks that helps avoid these costly and easily preventable mistakes.

History is replete with examples of little mistakes or errors that lead to horrific consequences. For example, in 1941, the United States broke diplomatic codes sent by Japan, and based on the intercepted diplomatic messages, which were decoded very early on December 7, 1941, the United States strongly suspected that the Japanese would attack that morning. So the US Army Chief of Staff, George Marshall, sent a warning message to Pearl Harbor. Because of an error or mistake, this warning message was not marked "urgent." As a result, it was not received until well into the attack, when it could not be of use.

Perhaps our favorite recent historical example that demonstrates how little mistakes can turn into big problems occurred back in 1999. The best and brightest rocket scientists of NASA designed and launched the unmanned

Mars Climate Orbiter to explore Mars at a mission cost of $125,000,000. Then, after it had completed its ten-month journey, the orbiter crashed into the planet on arrival and was lost. What was the problem? One set of NASA rocket scientists had used the metric system, and another used the imperial system. After the cause of the failure was determined, NASA released a statement that read, in part, "People sometimes make errors. The problem here was not the error, it was the failure of NASA's systems engineering and the checks and balances in our processes to detect the error. That's why we lost the spacecraft." We couldn't agree more.

Success or failure in business also depends greatly on getting the little things right. This is a lesson we have learned the hard way over the years. One little, simple mistake can cost you and your business greatly. In some cases, it can even damage your brand. For example, many years ago, I asked Jim to develop a direct mail brochure to help us sell a new continuing educational product. We had spent tens of thousands of dollars and many months developing this product, and Jim designed a nice-looking, glossy, four-color brochure to market it. We mailed it out to 50,000 people, but after two or three weeks, we had not received a single phone call expressing interest in our new product, so we started to ask ourselves what might be happening. Eventually, we discovered that we had inadvertently printed the brochures with a telephone number that ended in 7083. Unfortunately, our actual number ended in 7023.

Now what? Well, after giving Jim an earful, I asked him to look into whether we could add the telephone number that ended in 7083 as a new line. No dice; someone already owned 7083. It turns out that we had printed and mailed 50,000 brochures with an ordering telephone number that belonged to a little old lady that lived in our small Cape Cod town. I had Jim call her up. It was actually quite amusing, watching him pleading into the phone and trying to explain to this elderly woman who we were, what we did, and what had happened. He apologized profusely and asked her to refer any calls she might get to us. She actually agreed to do this. What a nice woman.

The important point from this debacle was that we learned our lesson. We immediately implemented a protocol in which at least four different people must sign off on the contact information on each brochure we send out. In the years since, we have sent out over 15 million pieces of direct mail, and we never again printed incorrect contact information on any of these mailings. We take this one step further as well; in every brochure that I proof, I actually call up all the numbers listed to see if we have the correct numbers for the hotel, reservations, and so forth. You would be surprised how many mistakes we have avoided by doing this.

Another time many years ago, we were closely monitoring registrations for our second biggest conference. In those days, the vast majority of our registrations were faxed into our office. Every day we would check with the office and ask how many registrations we had received and each day the report came back—none. We were greatly concerned that something had gone wrong with our mailing. Maybe the mail house messed up the lists we had sent them? So we began to execute an emergency plan to invest $50,000 and remarket the conference while there was still time. We were just about to financially commit to this marketing campaign when we received a somewhat sheepish call from one of our employees. Our fax machine had been out of paper. She just put in some new paper, and the fax machine immediately spit out dozens of fax orders from the last two weeks that had been saved in the machine. A simple, easily avoidable error of not filling up a fax machine with paper had almost cost us $50,000. Once again, we had learned our lesson. We immediately created and enforced a protocol whereby the fax machine's paper was filled up at the end of each day. This problem has never reoccurred.

Here's another example: many years ago we were involved in a very emotional and potentially costly dispute with someone with whom we had done business in the past. We'll call him Henry. Fortunately, we were able to resolve the dispute amicably, and so we asked our corporate counsel to take care of executing documents that would finalize the settlement. He did so and faxed the documents to Henry and us for execution. A couple of days later, however, we received an angry call from an agitated Henry. "Why in the settlement agreement do I indemnify you," Henry erupted, "but you don't indemnify me as well? What are you trying to pull? I thought you were operating in good faith?" We were puzzled, so we said we would call Henry back. As it turns out, the clerk at the law office had not been careful when faxing the documents. The fax machine had jammed, and the page where we had cross-indemnified Henry never went through. To make matters worse, the clerk was lazy and did not include a fax cover sheet specifying how many pages should have gone through.

We called Henry and explained what had happened. He took it well and actually laughed. The settlement was finalized, but once again, a failure to pay very close attention to the little details almost caused a disaster. These days, if we are faxing anything of importance, we do three things: first, we use a cover sheet that specifies the number of pages that are being sent. Second, we have the person sending the fax stand over the machine and look for paper jams. Finally, we ask the person sending the fax to call the recipient to make sure that the fax went through. Ever since we have instituted this protocol, we have not had any additional problems.

One of our lines of business is developing and teaching courses that train doctors, engineers, accountants, and others on how to be effective expert witnesses. We drill into these experts the importance of watching the little details, right on down to typographical errors. One day, when we were teaching a course for experts, we basically scorched one of our attendees for the presence of credibility-damaging typographical errors in the report he had written. At the end of our tirade, a student in the back row raised her hand. We called on her, and she calmly asked, with a smug grin, "Do you realize that you have a typo in the very first sentence of your chapter on the importance of avoiding typographical mistakes?" The whole class laughed. We were caught not practicing what we had preached. The fix to this problem was simple: from that point on, we hired a professional proofreader to proof all our training handbooks before publication. In the time since we implemented this procedure, no similar problems have reoccurred.

2. Answer your phone and return phone calls promptly.

EXECUTIVE SUMMARY: Answer your phone and return your phone calls promptly: doing so will prevent you from missing fruitful business opportunities and will help you build your brand.[1] Your customers will appreciate this rare courtesy. You should return calls promptly even when it looks as though the person you are responding to is not looking to buy something from you. This will help your reputation immensely and may give you an opportunity to turn the conversation into a closed sale.

* * *

We have two simple policies when it comes to our telephone. First, we actually answer it—ourselves—without gatekeepers. Second, we return phone calls. Based on our experiences over the last 20 years or so, our clients and contacts greatly appreciate that we conduct our business in this manner—and with good reason. I cannot even begin to estimate the number of people that we work with who do not answer their telephones or promptly return phone calls. It's downright scary. It's also often inexcusable. Here's a typical example.

A few months ago, we were looking to buy $100,000 worth of services in conjunction with one of the conferences we were putting on. We called *the sales department* of ten vendors, but we were only able to actually talk to two people. We left messages at the rest and mentioned that we were interested in buying their services. Of the remaining eight people, two called back within 24 hours, three more took more than 24 hours to call back, and the three

---

[1] For more on branding, please see Chapter 1.

remaining never called back. And these were salespeople, who were presumably working on commission!

Even professionals such as expert witnesses, who can and do make $300 to $500 or more an hour, often do not have a good method for handling their phones. Here is an example (exaggerated for emphasis) of what could and actually does happen:

ATTORNEY CALLING EXPERT WITNESS: Hello, may I speak to Dr. Westlaw please?

CHILD ANSWERING PHONE: Mommy, it is for you.

DR. WESTLAW (SCREAMING): I told you to never pick up that phone. It is for Mommy's business.

LAWYER: I want to talk to her about a class action lawsuit. Can she come to the phone?

CHILD: Mommy, it's a lawyer about an ass action. Isn't that a bad word? Mommy is in the bathroom. She went to a Mexican restaurant last night and said, "Never again." I think she is going to be in there a long time.

DR. WESTLAW (SCREAMING): No ... Stop talking ... Ask him if he can hold ...

CHILD: I have to fold now (hanging up).

We conducted independent research and determined that experts lose a substantial amount of business because they do not have a professional answering their phones. Despite the fact that the lack of professional phone conduct is economically foolish, can result in lost clients, and can ruin a company's brand, many businesses sadly do not prioritize their phone calls.

Here's another typical and sad example. Two years ago, Jim was looking to install an irrigation system in his house. It was approximately a $5,000 job. He called three vendors that were listed in the phone book, and only one called back. Jim hired him. Then, *two weeks later*, a second vendor called back. He apologized and said that he had been busy coaching little league at night. He was shocked and upset when Jim told him that he had hired someone else because he had never heard back from him. He asked Jim if he would reconsider, because he really needed the business. What planet does somebody like that come from?

Nonresponsiveness had become such an epidemic that we now do not use a vendor that does not pick up the phone when we call to inquire. The thinking is this: if they don't pick up the phone when you are looking to hire them, how much harder will it be to reach them when something goes wrong and you really need them?

Recently, we were looking to hire a developer to create a new customized website in support of one of our product lines. After unsuccessfully trying to get a referral for a trusted vendor, Jim resorted to the phone book. He called ten vendors again, and only three picked up the phone. Jim didn't even bother leaving messages for the other seven vendors. If they weren't smart enough to have an employee answering their phone, we didn't want to do business with them.

Recently my phone rang on a Friday at 5:30 p.m. I had already finished working for the day and was heading out of the office, so I easily could have let the call ring through to voicemail. Instead, I picked up the phone, and it turned out to be a potential client that was calling from the West Coast. He ended up hiring us for a lucrative consulting assignment. God only knows if we would have gotten the job had I not picked up the phone that Friday evening. Would he have called back? Would he have hired someone else? Who knows, but this much is clear: The simple act of answering our phone was integral in our gaining an important client. I also recently received a phone message at home at 6:30 at night. (Remember, I have my voicemails automatically transcribed and forwarded to my e-mail.) A client was looking to talk to me and left his cell phone number, and I called him back right away. The client was extremely appreciative and impressed at my responsiveness. I provided him with some free advice and let him know how we could help him if he wanted to hire us as consultants. He called back the next week and hired us for a lucrative consulting assignment. Again, the simple act of promptly returning a phone call proved very helpful to us.

Picking up your phone and returning phone calls has many advantages. First, as shown above, if someone is trying to hire you, you are well advised to pick up the phone when they call. If you don't, they might just forget about you and hire someone else. Second, picking up your phone builds your brand. Who hasn't been aggravated when their call to a company is picked up by a computer that offers the dreaded menu, "Press one for Spanish, press two if you are an existing customer ... I'm sorry, I didn't understand your response ... " People *despise* these menus. As such, we distinguish ourselves by having a live person who speaks understandable English promptly pick up the phone and ask how he or she can help. You can't imagine how many compliments we have gotten with respect to our phone conduct. Our customers appreciate that we don't waste their time and treat them with respect. Another simple way to build your brand is to return customer calls right away. This is especially important in situations where a customer is not placing an order but instead has a question or complaint or is looking for free advice. We return such phone calls immediately, and the reaction is almost always the same: the customer answers with a startled voice and thanks us profusely for returning his or her phone call so promptly. Essentially, the customer is impressed that we return their call promptly even when we aren't selling them anything. For this reason, returning phone calls promptly is a simple and remarkably effective way to build your brand. Finally, the third reason to pick up your phone and return phone calls promptly is that it can often be good for business. You really never know what a contact, especially one in an allied field, will turn into.

Here's a good example: a few years ago I received a hard-to-understand, heavily accented message from someone who said he was researching an area in which we had expertise and was wondering if I knew an obscure statistic that he could use in his research. I realized that he was from an aligned business, and I actually called him back. The researcher was very grateful, and it turns out that he had called because he was investigating whether his organization should get into our line of business. I suggested to him that instead of reinventing the wheel, his organization should hire us instead, because we knew how to do what they wanted. After a few weeks of negotiations, they agreed and hired us for a lucrative contract.

The above is the epitome of simple, usable advice that will help you succeed in business. Most busy professionals would have just deleted the voice message, as there was nothing apparent in it for them. Not us. We did the unthinkable and called back. It is often small gestures as returning a simple phone call that make all the difference between success and failure in business.

Here's another example that demonstrates how profitable it can be to simply return phone calls from people who are not looking to buy anything from you. Recently, I received a voicemail message from a professional who wanted to speak at one of our conferences. The conference was already full, so I couldn't use him, but I called him back promptly anyway. This was common courtesy, and I sensed we might have an opportunity to work together in other ways. While we were on the phone, I Googled his company to see what they did, got a sense of his situation, and suggested that he hire us as a consultant to help grow his business. We were eventually retained for a lucrative consulting contract, and this was only possible because I returned a phone call, even though doing so did not appear to yield me any benefits.

Somebody in a related field that actually wants to talk to you is a golden opportunity. Just because they originally wanted to talk to you about one thing does not mean that you can't turn the conversation into one that is focused on how you, your products, or your services can help them. This is a simple but effective strategy.

3. Keep your eye on the ball.

EXECUTIVE SUMMARY: Keep your eye on the ball. There's only so much time in a day, so spend it wisely on things that will make you money, not on what you like to do or what feels good. Don't have too many meetings; they can waste a tremendous amount of time. Also, resist the temptation to litigate or get in protracted disagreements with people. This is most often a losing proposition and will only cost you more time and money in the end.

* * *

If you want your business to be successful, you need to keep your eye on the ball. What do we mean by that? There are only so many hours in day and your funds are limited, so you absolutely must focus your time and money on things that are going to make or save you money. If you stray from this principle, you can run into many problems. Let me give you a couple of examples of what I mean.

A somewhat embarrassing but instructive example occurred during our largest conference of the year. Jim, our resident cost cutter and penny pincher, got involved in a heated discussion with the hotel manager about the hotel charging us $200 to rent some power strips. While this $200 dispute was being played out, he inadvertently authorized an unplanned lunch for all 500 of our attendees at $30 a head, which cost us $15,000. We saved $200 on the power strips but ran up $15,000 because we were distracted and took our eye off the ball.

Here's another good example. Many years ago, we had a partner we'll call Fred, who was a very bright, high-powered MBA. At one point early on in our partnership, we decided that it would be a good idea to hold a meeting without any distractions, because the company was going through a very serious cash flow crisis. We had important things to decide and tough decisions to make, so we set up an off-site meeting on Nantucket, which is a short ferry ride away for us. We were each tasked with producing a short agenda that detailed how the company should proceed in light of the acute situation we faced.

We made it out to Nantucket and started our meeting around 7:00 a.m. the next morning, and Fred presented his agenda first. He had prepared a beautiful spreadsheet with color charts that showed how we would be making tens of millions of dollars in profits if we sold 20,000 to 50,000 units each of some of the books and educational programs that we had developed. This would solve our cash flow problem. No mention was made of *how* we would sell 20,000 to 50,000 of each unit, however. Jim and I sat in stunned silence. Fred then proceeded to show us the new way he had trained himself to update our web page. Now, keep in mind that Fred was drawing a $200,000 yearly salary, but he thought a good use of his time would be to spend a week learning this web work because he loved technology and computers. It was something we could have hired a college kid to do for $20 an hour. Fred never explained how his web training would solve our cash flow crisis. After presenting these two top agenda items, Fred turned to us and asked us for our thoughts.

I responded as gently and diplomatically as I could, considering how disappointed I was in what Fred had spent his time on. "Our ship is sinking," I said. "We don't have time to rearrange its deck chairs. Here is a report from our bookkeeper. Each month we are taking in less money than we spend. We will be insolvent in three months unless radical cost cutting takes place. I propose," I continued, "that we immediately eliminate our salaries until the crisis abates. We also need to agree, here and now, to spend all our time on projects that can and will generate cash NOW or will save us money NOW. As to the financial projections, those are somewhat interesting, but in 15 years of business, we have never sold anywhere near those quantities, and you have not presented any suggestions as to how we could do so in a cost effective manner. We need to raise cash now and reduce expenses or," I concluded, "we'll be out of business in three months."

Fred had made the classic mistake of taking his eye off the ball. There is no question that he had worked very hard on the projections he had gathered and the web page training he had undergone. But he was putting in 12- to 14-hour days working on projects that, although he found them satisfying and interesting, ultimately were not helping our profitability. He took his eye off the ball. The meeting shocked him a bit, and he was able to refocus for a while. For our part, we took tough actions, and the company survived.

Here's one more Fred story. About a year after the Nantucket meeting, we decided that we needed to have a meeting so that we could once again focus all the partners on producing and selling profitable products and services. Fred stated that he needed two weeks to prepare for the meeting, but when we tried to call him during the two weeks prior to the meeting, all we got back were e-mails: "Too busy to talk ... You're gonna love it." Then the day of the meeting arrived; we all gathered in the little conference room we had booked at a hotel in Boston. Fred took charge of the meeting and revealed the fruits of his last two weeks: "Item #1," he proudly said, "Let's define who we are." "Well, I am Steve, he's Jim, and you are Fred," I responded.

Fred chuckled and went on to explain that this was a process he had learned in business school; all the top business minds now used this process, he explained, and so we should bear with him. For the next hour, Fred discussed who we were, and Jim and I grunted in assent, hoping he would move on to something relevant. Eventually, he did move on. "Item #2: What's our mission statement?" Jim, beginning to lose what little patience he had left, responded quickly: "To not go bankrupt and hopefully make some money."

Fred chuckled again and explained that we *still* didn't understand the high-level process he learned in business school that he was now guiding us through. So we indulged Fred and let him drone on and on about mission statements. The meeting had started at 8:00 a.m. Finally, at 11:30 a.m., Fred unveiled Item #3. "What's our vision statement?" he asked. I saw Jim take a deep breath and try to hold back what he wanted to say. Finally, not sure he could control himself any longer, Jim just walked out of the room.

I caught up with him in the bathroom a few minutes later. He explained to me that he couldn't take it anymore. "We're trying to make money," Jim exclaimed, "and all Fred is doing is droning on and on about mission statements and visions statements. We pay Fred to spend over one hundred hours working on this [expletive]? I cannot spend another minute wasting my time listening to this drivel," Jim concluded. "I'll have a stroke." We eventually made our way back to the meeting and explained that Jim wasn't feeling well. We suggested that we take a lunch break, and we did. After lunch, we asked that before we got back to Fred's agenda, maybe we could talk about some other things, because time was short. Fred was disappointed, but he agreed. His agenda, filled with vision statements and SWOT[2] analyses, was based on what he had learned in business school.

Then Jim and I took charge of the agenda, and the recommendations we made were based on what we learned in the school of hard knocks. We discussed the costs and benefits of new product ideas we were proposing. We discussed marketing ideas. We kicked around ideas for saving money. In short, we turned the focus of the meeting back on making money. The meeting, which turned out to be the last partners meeting we ever had with Fred, ended at four in the afternoon without any further talk of vision statements or synergy. We simply couldn't afford to waste our limited time like this again.

Allow me one little aside about meetings: they can be a huge waste of time if participants take their eye off the ball. For example, one time, during a 90-minute conference call in which I participated, 60 minutes were spent discussing when we would have our next meeting! I'm sure you can understand why I resigned from the organization that had initiated the call shortly after that infamous incident, which stands as the worst waste of time I have ever experienced.

---

[2] Strengths, Weaknesses/Limitations, Opportunities, and Threats.

Here is another example of what I mean when I say that meetings can often be colossal wastes of time. I was the only lawyer on the board of a new professional organization. A high-powered strategic planning meeting was set up in Aspen, Colorado, so the board and I flew in and met at a beautiful meeting facility bright and early the next morning. The room was ultramodern, the entire front of the room was covered with whiteboards, and the executive director had purchased large, poster-sized pads you can write on and then stick to the boards. For hours, the board members came up with idea after idea of what the organization could and should be doing. After four to five hours, the entire room was covered with dozens of ideas (few of which were practical or any good). It looked like a war room for an army primed for failure. Every board member felt compelled to contribute his or her ideas, regardless of whether they were any good.

When asked my take on the meeting proceedings, I stated: "It would take us 25 years to implement all of the ideas posted. Many of these ideas, to be charitable, are not viable. I suggest we come up with five realistic, practical, good ideas and concentrate on those." The board agreed, and we eventually got our eye back on the ball and actually made some progress. I now utilize a special technique whenever we have one of our rare meetings: I make everybody stand. Doing so encourages people to get to the point and not waste any time.

I want to mention another commonly tempting distraction in business: getting involved in protracted fights or litigation with people. Jim and I are both former litigators, so we understand that the only people who win in a litigation situation typically are the lawyers. Litigation and fighting with people take your eye off the ball and hurt your business. Here's a quick example.

Many years ago, we employed a single mother—we'll call her Sally—who struggled to get by, overwhelmed, and experienced declines in her performance. We had to let her go near the year's end. In January, we received a bill from an office store where we had an open account. Someone, without our authorization, had bought a laptop computer and some computer games. We strongly suspected that the source of the charge was Sally, who perhaps wanted to give her kid a merry Christmas. We contacted the store and told them the charge was fraudulent, and the store reversed our bill. That took about 30 minutes. What we didn't do, however, was march down to the police station and file a complaint. We kept our eye on the ball. We didn't want to spend countless hours battling in court and filling out affidavits. We also didn't want to antagonize someone who might be close to the edge and could come back and burn down our building—or worse. So we sucked it up and moved on because that was the shrewdest business decision to make.

Stories like Sally's happen all the time in business. A customer stiffs you. A contractor rips you off. Somebody acts like a jerk and makes you angry. Our advice is to refrain from fighting or filing litigation unless it's absolutely necessary. When you weigh the costs of fighting in terms of time and money against the probable benefits,[3] you will see that taking the high road is usually the best way to go.

4. Develop a protocol, along with a system of checklists to make sure you follow it.

EXECUTIVE SUMMARY: Checklists, protocols, and procedure are very helpful ways to prevent mistakes. Develop protocols and procedures, and make sure that they are followed. Checklists and sign-offs help you avoid the need to rely on the memory and/or attention of the person you have tasked with a specific project. Following these simple steps will prevent myriad of problems and save you a good deal of time, money, and aggravation.

* * *

If there's one lesson we've learned over the years, it's that, just like a pilot, you should always use checklists and follow protocols. There's really no cheaper or easier way to avoid costly mistakes than to create and follow tried-and-proven checklists and/or protocols. You would be amazed at how easily business problems and mistakes can be prevented and avoided if you simply follow a protocol. Here are just a few of the many examples of how well-thought-out protocols and checklists have assisted our business.

We market our professional directories to potential clients via direct mail and e-mail, and an embarrassing, yet preventable, problem used to occur occasionally when we marketed these directories. Namely, we would, from time to time, send out a solicitation to invite a potential client to buy a listing in the directory only to later realize that we had sent this invitation to someone who had already paid to be listed. This screw-up caused many problems. First, we looked like idiots to our customers, who were left to wonder why we weren't smart enough to know that they were already listed in the directory. Second, it forced our customers to contact us and confirm that they were already listed in the directory, which wasted both our time and our customers' time. Third, we were wasting good money by mailing a 50-cent brochure to someone who had already signed up. Clearly, sending out

---

[3] Please see later in this chapter on cost-benefit analyses.

brochures to clients who had already signed up for our directory was not the best way to build our brand or instill confidence in our customers.

The sad thing is how easily preventable this problem was. Because we had made this mistake in the past, we actually developed a protocol whereby we remove from solicitation mailing lists anybody who was already listed in the directory. It's a great system, but it only works if we actually use it. To make sure we don't repeat this mistake again, we developed a written checklist that we use when assembling directory mailing lists, and two people at our company must sign off on the checklist before any mailings are sent out. Since instituting this new policy, we have not had a reoccurrence of the problem.

Here's another quick example of how establishing and following a protocol can easily prevent potentially big problems. Many of our conferences take place all over the country. While we are at one of our conferences, we typically collect $10,000 or more in credit card charges for on-site registrations and book purchases. The way we handle these on-site sales is by writing down the credit card numbers and then running them in our system when we get back to the office. That means, of course, that if we lose the credit card numbers before they are run, we are out of luck.

A few years ago one of our (former) employees took in over $20,000 worth of credit card information and had the relatively simple responsibility of taking the card numbers back to the office for processing. The stack of paper involved was about half an inch thick and weighed well less than a pound. It was so simple a task, what could go wrong? Well, in a thoughtless moment, she went ahead and checked these receipts in her luggage and handed it over to the airline. You know what happened next. When our former employee got off the plane in Boston, she found that the airline had lost her luggage. We were out $20,000 and had potentially breached the credit card security of numerous customers. It wasn't a great day for my blood pressure.[4] However, we learned from our mistake. We now have instituted and follow a written protocol regarding how to send orders home from a conference. This protocol requires making backup copies and personally carrying the receipts in hand. To make this protocol even more effective and idiot-proof, we have developed and now utilize a written checklist that details how to ship materials back from our conferences.

Here's one final example. At the end of every conference we put on, we hand out evaluation forms so that our attendees can give us feedback. In many instances, we are required to provide these forms so that we can maintain our accreditations. They also contain valuable feedback. In sum, it's very important

---

[4] Luckily, she did eventually get her luggage back with the orders still inside and apparently undisturbed.

that we hand them out and get them back. Unfortunately, however, at one of our seminars a few years back, we forgot to hand the forms out. The reason for this failure was simple: we did not establish and follow a protocol. Nobody was in charge of handing out the forms, we had established no set way of doing so, and it fell between the cracks. In response, we once again developed a protocol to address the situation. Now, whoever is responsible for assembling the conference handbooks is also responsible for physically attaching the evaluation forms to the books with a clip or rubber band. This way the forms are automatically handed out when we hand the conference handbooks out and can't be forgotten. This procedure has also been included on our conference preparation checklists. Since establishing the protocol and including it on our checklist, we have not had any additional problems in this area.

The key when developing protocols and checklists is to review and incorporate the solutions to all past problems. Before finalizing the protocols and checklists, sit down and anticipate all of the things that could go wrong, be overlooked, and result in disaster. A well-thought-out protocol/checklist should cover almost all contingencies.

5. Weigh likely benefits against potential risks, and don't bet the farm.

EXECUTIVE SUMMARY: It is absolutely critical to carefully weigh the likely possible upsides of a business decision against the potential risks. Unfortunately, predicting the future is more art than science, so you will always be making your decisions on imperfect and less-than-complete information. Regardless, remember to periodically review your protocols to see if they can be improved on. If you want to be in business on a long-term basis, always avoid making decisions that open your firm to the risk of serious failure. Don't ever bet the farm.

* * *

Unfortunately, because you can never predict the future with 100 percent accuracy, almost every business decision you make will involve its fair share of risks. Predicting what will happen regarding critical questions—how many people will buy this product? What will the economy be like when this product is launched? Could the response tarnish our brand? Will we get sued for this?—is a fine art. There are no precise formulas for predicting the future, nor can you look up what the future will bring on the Internet. Many businesspeople must confront the harsh reality of constantly making decisions without having all the information and answers they need or would like to have.

The key to making good business decisions involves a balancing act in which you must weigh the likely benefits of a course of action against the potential risks. To reduce mistakes and potential disasters, this analysis should be made in every important business decision you face. The process itself appears to be simple but has many nuances and variables. Ask yourself:

- **What is the potential upside if things go well?** When analyzing this factor, also consider the potential secondary gain from new customers, opening new markets and lines of business, extension products, and so forth.

- **What would be the likely and potential time and cost involved?** Consider as well how much work and distraction are involved. Could your time and effort be more profitably spent elsewhere?

- **What are the risks of proceeding?** Keep in mind the risks of affecting a current product line or customer base.

- **What are the risks of not proceeding?** Maybe someone will beat you to it, or a golden opportunity could slip by.

- **What is a worst-case scenario?**

- **Could this course of action potentially put you out of business if things don't work out the way that you had planned?**

Perhaps the most important of these questions is the last one: If things don't work out, could you go out of business? If the answer to that question is "yes," we do not and will not proceed. We've been in business for over 30 years, and we are planning on staying in business another 30 plus years. The reason we've been able to stay in business that long is that we haven't bet the farm on any one project and have been very careful in our risk analyses.

We use the above series of questions to vet every important business decision that we make. For example, we recently were deciding whether to develop and launch an additional directory product, which would promote physicians who are interested in publicizing their ability to review medical charts for insurance companies and others. Here's how our internal discussions went amongst the three decision makers.

JIM: I have completed my analysis of the needs assessment data we sent out, and there appears to be strong interest from our physician customers in a directory to promote their availability to do file review work. I think we should proceed.

STEVE: What happens if we launch another *Titanic* with this one? Could it put us out of business?

JIM: I have considered that, and the answer is a clear "no." I have structured the initial marketing push so that it only costs us $20,000. That and $10,000 in web development costs will be our major expenses. If not enough doctors actually respond, we will simply refund their money, fold shop, and cut our losses. A $30,000 hit won't come close to putting us out of business.

ALEX: There's a ton of work involved in setting up the website and designing the marketing pieces. That's a big cost, so we'd lose a lot time, too.

JIM: Agreed, but the risk is manageable and within our control. More important, we need to consider the potential upside. A directory is a subscription product. Once someone signs up, we usually get most people to renew for years. Because of this, directories can be extremely profitable. There is also potential for advertising and extension products. Finally, if this works, we might be able to create other products for consultants that we can later sell. There is a large but capped and manageable cost involved, but the potential upside is enormous. That potential upside justifies the time, cost, and risk. Plus, the data we have gathered shows a solid likelihood of success.

STEVE: What if the listed physicians don't get assignments from their listing? Won't this poor result tarnish our brand?

JIM: We will promptly refund the money of unhappy clients. As has been proven before, standing by our product in this way will build our brand, not tarnish it.

ALEX: Some of our customers might get upset if we try to sell them another directory listing.

JIM: I agree, that is a possibility, but the potential reward justifies this risk. We are in the middle of a Great Recession here. The seminar and conference business has been severely affected. We also need to consider the risks of *not* proceeding. This is the only viable idea we have for this year to make a big score. The upside, in my opinion, justifies the manageable risks involved.

STEVE AND ALEX: Agreed. OK, let's try it.

Any time you are facing an important business decision, you should conduct an analysis that is similar to the one detailed above. Look hard at both the risks and potential upside, and then make your best decision. Keep in mind, of course, that sometimes the risks are not a simple and direct function of the money you might lose on a project. For example, as mentioned in Chapter 1, trial experts often ask us to teach them how to research, cross-examine, and destroy opposing expert witnesses. This service is in demand. Lawyers would pay for it, and we'd make money selling the service. The reason we haven't jumped into this line of work, however, has to do with the risks it would entail. Our bread-and-butter business is serving the needs of expert witnesses. If we tried to play both sides and taught lawyers how to go after experts, we would rightly face a huge backlash from our expert clients. It could destroy our reputation and cost us a fortune. Because this is a huge risk, we have never seriously considered working with attorneys to help them attack experts.

In situations where both the risks and costs are low, our general attitude is, "Sure, let's try it out and see what happens. What do we have to lose?" In situations where the risks are greater, however, we need a much larger potential pot of gold before we proceed. Finally, in situations where the risks are so great that they could reasonably put us out of business if things went south, we pass, regardless of the potential upside. Our philosophy is old fashioned, but it has served us well. Our goal is to run a profitable business year in and year out that will last indefinitely. One of the ways we accomplish this goal is by never betting the farm.

6. Keep in contact with the competition, and cooperate where you can.

EXECUTIVE SUMMARY: Keep your competitors close. Build mutually beneficial relationships with them. There are many benefits to keeping the lines of communication open with your competition and staying on friendly terms.

* * *

In *The Godfather*, Don Corleone followed the maxim, "Keep your friends close, *but keep your enemies closer.*" Businesspeople do not have enemies, but they do have competitors and potential competitors. Keeping in contact and cooperating where you can with the competition may seem counterintuitive, but it can be a very effective strategy for improving your bottom line. There are numerous advantages to this approach.

- By keeping in contact with the competition, you have a direct way of finding out what they are up to, and you can share with and obtain from them useful information.

- A competitor you keep in touch with may refer you business.

- In turn, saying nice things about the competition will reflect well on you and build your credibility with your customers.

- You may be able to join together with your competitors to face a common threat, such as governmental action, or meet a common goal, such as expanding the size of a market or building awareness of your products or services.

- If you ever want to sell your business, your competitor is a natural potential buyer.

- If you ever want to switch jobs, a competitor is a natural fit, and building a relationship in advance is how most jobs are filled.

- There are, in fact, many win–win propositions that can come from working collaboratively with a competitor. Not everything in business is a zero-sum game.

We'd like to add three additional quick points about competition:

1. If you believe in the free market, you should not be upset by having competition. This, after all, is how the system works.

2. Competition can be a blessing in that it brings out the best in you. That is, the way you should respond to competition is by doing things *better* than the competition.

3. Sometimes having competition will raise the marketplace's awareness of a given product or service and result in more potential business for everyone in that space. As the saying goes, "A rising tide lifts all boats."

Here are some examples of how keeping in contact with the competition has proven advantageous for us. We are based on the East Coast, and there is an organization based on the West Coast that also provides some expert witness training and has its own smaller expert witness directory. As such, this organization—we'll call it Acme—can be considered a competitor of ours. Instead of fighting with Acme, getting into price wars with them, and cannibalizing a market that is already quite small, we have decided to take a different approach. Namely, we stay in touch with Acme. To avoid directly antagonizing them, we have not held any of our conferences on the West

Coast. In turn, they have reciprocated this gesture and have refrained from putting on any conferences outside of the West Coast. Direct competition between Acme and our company would not be in either organization's interest, as demand for such training can simply not support a large number of courses. We also have found that working collaboratively with Acme has been financially rewarding for both organizations. Instead of competing with Acme on the West Coast, we have worked together to put on a series of joint courses, and as a result, both organizations have profited. Acme also resells a significant number of our books.

Think about all the innumerable trade associations that exist in this country. Many of the people or companies that are members of the same trade association are actually direct competitors with one another. Despite the competitive nature of their relationship, however, they still join together in an association because it is much easier to expand and defend an industry if its constituents are united, rather than divided. In addition, information and research shared can be extremely valuable to all concerned. As such, what we are suggesting when we advise you to keep in touch with the competition is that you should, in effect, form collegial and informal trade associations with your so-called competitors. Try to work together where you can. Share information that helps build the market. You'll obviously want to protect your own interests, but there are clear advantages to staying on good terms with the competition and keeping the lines of communication open.

Here's another example of how we work with our competitors. Perhaps our biggest competitor in the expert directory field is a small company—we'll call them Beta—that publishes an online expert directory. Beta has a good product. It is reasonably priced, and it works. We're not afraid to tell people that, either. We are also on very good terms with Beta's owner. We refer him business, and when somebody asks where, besides our directory, they should be listed, we refer them to Beta. In turn, Beta's owner has shared useful information with us. We have worked together to sell our books (Beta doesn't publish books of its own), and Beta's owner has both promoted and presented for us at our conference (Beta doesn't run a conference). He has also referred us business. We speak regularly and brainstorm about industry trends, problems, and solutions, and we know that if we ever wanted to sell, Beta would be a natural firm to approach. By working together with Beta where we can and keeping the lines of communication open, we have raised our own bottom line.

Here's one final example. One of our lines of business is working one-on-one with other consultants to teach them how they can expand and develop their consulting practices. There is a woman—we'll call her Lisa—who does the exact same thing as us. We keep in very close contact with Lisa and work collaboratively with her wherever we can, which has been a win–win situation for both of us. We refer Lisa clients who balk at our fees (Lisa charges less and does things a little differently than we do). In return, Lisa refers to us a large number of clients that she is unable to work with. She calls us for help, and we call her to pick her brain. Lisa is also one of our biggest distributors. She sells our books and other products through her e-zines, blog, and web store. She has spoken at our conference. In short, she's a great person and a good friend, and the fact that she is a competitor has not blinded us to the wisdom and advantages of keeping in touch with her and working with her when we can.

7. Win the war, not the battle.

EXECUTIVE SUMMARY: There's often very few profits to be made in proving you were right. Always keep your eye on your ultimate goal, which is the success of your business. Be very careful to only fight battles that move you closer to your goal. Concentrate on winning the war, not an individual battle.

* * *

It's been a pleasure to mentor Jim over the years. I am 20 years Jim's senior, and we have a very close relationship, so the advice I give him is not restricted to business matters. For example, on the eve of Jim's wedding, I sat him down and told him the most important thing I had learned in almost 30 years of marriage: "Whatever you do, don't ever win an argument with your wife." Jim looked at me like I had three heads. I had told him some strange things in the past, but this one took the prize, he later told me. I reassured him, "Listen, I know you are a lawyer and like to argue and have been trained and paid to win arguments. Forget about all that. What you need to think about is not whether you are right or whether you can win the argument. Instead," I continued, "you need to think about the consequences of winning an argument with your spouse where you prove her wrong. Trust me," I concluded, "it's not worth it."

The point of this story is as follows: in the business world, you will often be faced with situations where you disagree with a customer, client, vendor, or partner. You may very well be 100 percent right, and the other party may very well be 100 percent wrong. That does *not*, however, in any way mean that you should go to the mat to prove that you're right. What I'm getting at is this: in the business world, it is extremely important to pick your battles. The goal of fighting a battle is to win the war. Pyrrhic victories are not helpful. As such, before you start a battle with someone, you should very carefully consider whether winning that particular battle is in your business's best long-term interest.

Let's go over a couple of examples from our own experience in which refusing to win the battle was the wisest long-term decision we could have made. Many years ago, we were producing hour-long educational videotapes on VHS that retailed for $100 apiece. We sold the tapes through an exclusive distributor—we'll call them Exclusive—and in the first couple of years of our relationship with Exclusive, we sold them a boatload of videotapes, which they later resold at a profit. We each were making hundreds of thousands of dollars from the relationship.

Eventually, the sales of the tapes we had produced started to slow. We were interested in producing a new tape, so we set up a meeting with the powers that be at Exclusive. We diligently prepared for the meeting, sent Exclusive a detailed agenda on the purpose of our visit, and flew half-way across the country to meet at their headquarters. When we got into the meeting, however, it was clear that nobody had even read our proposal. We were actually asked if there was an agenda for the meeting, despite the fact that we had sent Exclusive a well-thought-out and carefully prepared agenda. Nobody had even bothered to look at it! In fact, the person in charge of our account—we'll call him Tony—was reading the sports pages and eating a donut during our meeting. He wasn't even listening to us. The meeting went nowhere, and Jim and I were quite perturbed at the lack of common courtesy we had been shown. We had spent thousands of dollars and many hours preparing and traveling, but for what? We felt insulted and disrespected.

Exclusive obviously had a lot to lose by not listening to us. We had supplied them with hot-selling products, which in turn had made them a lot of money. We were so mad that we wanted to send a letter to Tony's boss, telling him that Tony was lazy, rude, and foolish. In this regard, we would have been correct. Tony might have been reprimanded as a result—or maybe even fired. To be sure, it would have felt good at that moment to stick it to Tony. The problem, of course, was that doing so would not have been in our best interest. Let's say we got him fired: how cooperative with us do you think his replacement would have been? The bottom line was that we were wronged, despite the fact that we were in the right. The key, however, was figuring out that this battle was just not worth fighting. Ultimately, we wanted Exclusive to buy our next product more than we wanted to get Tony in trouble, so we swallowed our pride and continued to make nice with Tony. Eventually, after many months of prodding, he did in fact focus on our proposal. Exclusive bought our next videotape, and we've been doing business with them ever since. Sure, we had passed on the battle, but the end result was positive for us.

Here's a final example. I was the rainmaker and managing partner at my old law firm. When I retired from practicing law, I came to a financial agreement with my old partners: In return for my leaving my clients to them, they would pay me $1,000,000 at the rate of $50,000 a year for 20 years. All went well for the first couple of years after I left, and I received my payout on schedule. When year three came along, however, I did not receive my money. Because of numerous managerial decisions and events, the firm was no longer successful. In fact, it was disintegrating. In a short period of time, head count went from eight lawyers down to two and then eventually only one.

I was faced with a decision. My old firm clearly owed me the money. I was right. I also was of counsel to the firm, and that's how I continued to receive my health benefits. I could have hired a lawyer and sued them, placed a lien on their cases, and foreclosed on their building. But I didn't do any of these things. It was more important to me that I maintain my health insurance through them. While I had every right to sue them and put them out of business, doing so would have caused me to lose my health insurance, and it was unclear how much of my payout, if any, I could have recovered from a now marginally profitable firm. The best decision was to refrain from fighting the issue. Sure, it would have given me some initial satisfaction, but it would have left me worse off in the end. As it turned out, the firm ended up staying in business, I continued to receive my health insurance, and I didn't waste time and money on litigation that only would have created bad feelings.

8. Attack little problems aggressively and don't let them turn into BIG problems.

EXECUTIVE SUMMARY: You are always going to be faced with problems in your business. Your goal should be to prevent little problems from turning into big problems. Doing so often requires active listening, awareness, and aggressive and immediate action once you have identified a little problem. It also requires carefully thinking through potential solutions to make sure that you won't just make the problem worse.

* * *

Let's say you have high blood pressure. This can be a relatively minor health issue, or it can kill you. The differing results are largely caused by how you deal with the problem. By immediately taking the proper steps to deal with this little problem (such as exercise, cutting down on sodium, taking your medication, etc.), you can prevent it from turning into a big problem, such as a heart attack or stroke. The same principle is very true in business. Business people are confronted with numerous problems all the time. The key to dealing with these problems effectively is to aggressively attack little problems before they metastasize and get out of your control. The idea is to do whatever it takes to contain the situation and prevent a manageable, little problem from morphing into an unmanageable, big problem.

Two classic examples of how to deal and not deal with problems are provided to us by Tylenol and Toyota. In 1982, Johnson & Johnson was faced with a severe crisis. Seven people in Chicago had taken extra-strength Tylenol and died within minutes. It was later discovered that the Tylenol these individuals had taken was laced with cyanide. Johnson & Johnson dealt with this problem head-on and effectively and immediately recalled 31 million bottles of Tylenol at a cost of over 100 million dollars. They put customer safety first, worked with the FBI to discover who had tainted their product, offered a $100,000 reward for information leading to the perpetrator's arrest, and exchanged recalled Tylenol for safe products. Johnson & Johnson, after assuring customer safety, then launched a national marketing campaign featuring a new tamper-proof triple seal. The company also arranged for over 2,000 of its salespeople to make safety presentations across the United States. Within six months, customers regained confidence, and sales of Tylenol rebounded dramatically. The lesson here is that by dealing with the problem head-on and with honesty and transparency, Johnson & Johnson was quickly able to overcome a problem that, if left to fester too long, could have destroyed Tylenol forever.

Toyota, on the other hand, did not appear to put safety before profits when acceleration problems cropped up in its fleet of automobiles. From 2003 to 2009, the company denied, delayed, and disregarded numerous accidents and deaths that were allegedly due to sticky gas pedals, problem floor mats, accelerators, and possible electrical computer problems. As the deaths increased and the pressure for action spun out of control, Toyota, six years later, finally recalled over eight million vehicles. The damage to its brand from the publicity of the delayed recalls is incalculable. Whether or not Toyota had actually done anything wrong in design or manufacture was neither important nor remembered. What lingered was the company's apparent stonewalling.

Here are a couple of examples drawn from our own business experiences that further make our point. Back when I was running a busy law office, I found out that someone (we couldn't prove who) was opening up and looking into their colleagues' pay stubs to see how much money they were making. This was obviously a problem that needed to be addressed. An obvious reaction to the problem could have certainly been to conduct an investigation to find out what had happened. The problem with this approach, however, were numerous and serious. By publicly revealing what happened, there would be tremendous distrust in the office. We would never really know who did this unless they confessed. What if we fired the wrong person? Did we really want to begin a process that could potentially make employees feel as though they were not being paid enough? What if we found out the person responsible was otherwise a model employee? How much time would be wasted on the investigation? How distracting would this all be? How low would morale sink?

It quickly occurred to me that I had a little problem that could very well turn into a bigger problem if we handled it in the wrong way. What I decided to do was instruct our bookkeeper to no longer leave pay stubs anywhere in the office. The stubs were to be mailed directly to each employee at his or her home. In implementing this solution, our hope was threefold. First, the new procedure would prevent a reoccurrence of this problem in the future. Second, it would send a powerful yet veiled message to the perpetrator that we knew what had happened and were not pleased. Third, it would prevent the situation from potentially getting larger and much worse. In the end, our plan worked. We had no further incidents. The problem did not spin out of control, and we were all able to get back to the business at hand—making money.

One of the ways to ensure that little problems are dealt with before they spiral out of control is to foster a culture at work where people are not afraid to bring problems to your attention. Employees may try to cover up problems that they are afraid to mention, but these hidden, little problems are potentially very dangerous because you often cannot deal with them until it is too late. For example, in my law office I noticed that one lawyer's desk was almost completely paper-free, giving the impression that he was caught up and on top of things. Further investigation, however, revealed that he placed notices of key court dates and other crucial, time-sensitive documents under his desk blotter so no one would know he was behind. This potential big problem waiting to happen was headed off with a stern talking to and the removal of his desk blotter.

Here's a final example. We had an elderly and crusty lawyer speak at one of our conferences many years back. Around 500 people attended this conference, and the vast majority of them were female nurses. The lawyer got up and, to my horror, told a sexist joke that disparaged of women. When he made the remark, you could hear hisses coming from the audience. Four to five attendees turned to me in the back of the room with an angry look that said to me, "Do you approve of this??" It became pretty clear to me that if this relatively little problem was not addressed immediately, it could develop into quite a big problem. There would be many complaints. We might appear complicit. Our brand would be tarnished. People would be angry. It would be a major distraction. We'd spend the next three days fielding complaints. So I did something that I had never done before at a conference. I went onto the stage, while the speaker was still speaking, and asked if I could have a word with him. The speaker excused himself, and I explained to him in no uncertain terms what had happened and what needed to be done. In about 60 seconds, the speaker was up on stage again and gave a sincere apology.

By attacking this relatively little problem aggressively and early on, we were able to ensure that it remained a little problem—not a big one. There was no insurrection. There were no complaints on the postconference evaluation forms that we received back from our attendees. Our brand was preserved, and we had successfully intervened to stop a little problem from turning into a big problem.

9. Recognize what is and what is not your problem.

EXECUTIVE SUMMARY: The first question to ask yourself when confronted with a business problem should be, "Is this my problem or somebody else's problem?" You should *not* automatically ask yourself, "How do I solve this problem?" Just because you can solve a problem does not mean it is in your interest to do so. This ability to diagnose what is and what is not your problem will save you time and money. It may seem harsh, but you have enough problems of your own to deal with. You are not helping yourself by taking on additional problems.

* * *

By now you know that part of what we do is train expert witnesses on how to run their expert witness practices. At almost every course we have put on for experts, we get a question along the lines of, "Jim, I know you said we should get our money up front, but what if the lawyer is a solo practitioner and says that he won't have the funds to pay us until the case settles?" Whenever we receive a question like this, we always do the same thing. We don't say a word. Instead, we go over to the flip chart in the room. We then proceed to draw a line vertically down the length of the paper. To the left of the line, we write: "My Problem." To the right of the line, we write: "Somebody Else's Problem," and under the latter heading, we make an "X." When we are done writing on the flip chart, we explain to the class that there are only two types of problems in the world. The first type is your problem. The second is every other problem. Our technique is a bit harsh, but it's extremely effective and memorable. It also teaches our experts a critical lesson.

A crucial component of problem solving in business is determining what is and what is not your problem. A lawyer crying poor is not an expert witness's problem. It's the lawyer's problem. It only becomes the expert's problem when the expert lets himself or herself get into a situation in which he is owed money by the lawyer and has trouble collecting. At the conclusion of every class we teach, we hand out evaluation forms for the attendees to fill out. On these forms, we always ask our attendees to tell us the most important thing they learned at the course. Invariably, many people respond, "My Problem/Somebody Else's Problem."

Businesspeople also should figure out which problems are rightly theirs and which are somebody else's. As a businessperson, you will often be faced with problems that you can solve. The mistake many people make is trying to solve a problem before first asking themselves the most important question: namely, is it in their best interest to solve this problem, or is this really somebody else's problem? For example, we often get calls from potential customers, telling us that they can't afford our products or services and would like to get them at a discount or for free. Some of these people are just trying to get something for nothing. Others have legitimate problems, such as unemployment, divorce, health issues, and so forth. It is certainly within our power to solve their problem of not wanting to pay full price for our products or services. It's not, however, in our interest to do so. We recognize that these are not our problems. They are somebody else's problem, and as such, we do not hesitate to just say no (politely, of course).

In a similar vein, we used to deal with a distributor who was chronically late or deficient in paying us what we were owed. Sometimes she had some pretty creative and believable excuses. Often she did not. We recognized, however, that the fact that she had difficulty paying us was really her problem, not ours. We could have solved her problem by sending her more products that she might never pay for. But we recognized, of course, that her problem would only become our problem if we kept extending her credit. We cut off her credit and stopped doing business with her, which was a harsh but necessary step. We didn't want her problem to become our problem.

Another common occurrence is when somebody asks us to do a favor for them.[5] We are all in favor of helping out when we can do so. Many times, however, we get requests that could only be met at high cost. For example, our contacts often ask us to blast out information about their services to our large e-mail list of customers. Could we do this and solve their publicity problem? Sure. But it's not our problem. If we agreed to send out these types of e-mails for our contacts, someone else's problem would *become* our problem, because doing so would violate our privacy policies, clutter up our customers' inboxes, and make them mad. We politely respond to these requests with a no and offer to help out in other ways if we are able to.

---

[5] Please see Chapter 2 on networking.

10. Do not rely exclusively on e-mail; pick up the phone.

EXECUTIVE SUMMARY: Don't be afraid to pick up the telephone. In many instances, using the phone is a better way to communicate than using e-mail. There are many advantages to phone communications. They help you and your business stand out, they are generally more efficient (depending on subject matter), they give you a chance to shine and bond with the person with whom you are communicating, they give you a read on the person you are talking to, and they ensure that your message isn't misunderstood or lost in a spam filter or overstuffed e-mail inbox. To make certain that people can easily call you, you include your telephone number in your e-mail signature.

* * *

In today's age of e-mails, texts, and tweets, your ready willingness to use the telephone can give you a significant advantage over your competition. We have come to the conclusion that far too many people these days rely almost exclusively on e-mail for their business communications. In my opinion, this is a mistake. Reliance on electronic communication has gotten completely out of control in some cases. The perfect example of this is the number of e-mails we receive with questions from clients. We find it far more efficient and accurate to respond to many types of questions by calling the client up to talk. There's one little problem with this approach, however. In many instances, the person who has sent us an e-mail has failed to include his telephone number in the message. For this reason, we suggest that you include your telephone number in your signature line of your e-mails so as to make it easier to start a phone conversation with someone you are doing business with.

The epitome of this phenomenon occurred a while back, when we received an e-mail from a computer expert regarding some potential business. Of course, this computer genius did not include his telephone number in his e-mail. We hunted down his number and gave him a call. The computer expert was taken aback. His first words were, "How did you get my number?" You could readily sense how discombobulated he was when talking to someone in person. This fear and loathing of using the telephone was obviously not helpful to this person.

In most cases, however, picking up the phone to call someone has a number of advantages. First of all, you stand out. Phone calls that have not been previously scheduled are such a rarity these days that you will often set yourself apart from the competition by making them. Showing that you care to take the time to call can leave a positive impression on current and potential clients. Second, phone calls can be the most efficient use of your time. There are some communications that are straightforward and can be easily and appropriately handled by e-mail. However, many communications require more of a back-and-forth conversation. Such communications can be inefficient, awkward, or even dangerous when they are conducted through e-mail. Third, speaking on the phone allows you to make a good impression on the person with whom you are dealing. You can demonstrate how easy you are to work with, and you can show off your personality and knowledge. You can also start to form a bond with the person to whom you are talking. Fourth, e-mails are notoriously unreliable. Whenever you send an e-mail to somebody, there is always the risk that a technical glitch or human error might prevent the message from getting through. You also run the risk that of a spam filter wrongly capturing your e-mail. As a matter of fact, just today I learned from our graphic artist (by talking on the phone) that an important e-mail he sent to us yesterday did not go through because the file was too large. Fifth, you are likely able to get a better sense of the person you are dealing with when you speak to them on the phone, as opposed to exchanging e-mails with them. For example, does this person have any annoying manners? Do they sound enthusiastic? Are they well-spoken? Do they sound knowledgeable? Do they have a speech impediment or indecipherable accent? Finally, everybody today is overwhelmed with e-mail. People answer e-mail from smartphones while walking, exercising, waiting in line, and so forth. This means that first, they may well be distracted when responding to your e-mail. Second, they may be too busy to carefully consider your e-mail. In either event, they are not paying close attention to your message.

Picking up the phone and calling your contacts can also quickly and simply resolve communication ambiguities. Here is an example of what I mean. Recently, we were planning on conducting a two-day training session with a client, and the price for this session was set at $20,000. Just prior to the session, however, we received an e-mail from the client, telling us that he was bringing a check for $10,000 to pay for the session. We looked back and actually could not locate the e-mail in which he had agreed to our $20,000 fee. We wondered if the client was simply trying to cut our fee, and we were on the brink of sending out an e-mail that expressed our feelings. Instead, we picked up the phone and discovered that the client had already sent us a check for $10,000, and our bookkeeper had not informed us of his payment. A quick phone call cleared the matter up quickly—without any embarrassment or hard feelings.

We are not shy about using the telephone, and we feel that this simple practice has monumentally helped our business. We almost always try to call anyone with whom we want to do business. Using the telephone allows us to show our stuff, get a read on the person with whom we are communicating, get our message through, and, in many cases, communicate more efficiently and effectively.

* * *

Take charge by using the techniques in this chapter, which can help you in many aspects of managing a business. Of course, to paraphrase someone famous, nobody ever built a business alone. Most businesses have employees. The next chapter contains the lessons we have learned regarding recruiting, motivating, and retaining a superior workforce.

Recruit, Motivate, and Retain a Superior Workforce

The success of any business with more than one employee depends on recruiting, motivating, and retaining a superior workforce. This chapter provides the techniques for doing so that we have learned the hard way.

1. Give interviewees a test assignment.

EXECUTIVE SUMMARY: Testing can be a very effective technique when making hiring decisions. Requiring the completion of a pre-interview assignment can and will separate out those candidates who are hungry, resourceful, and motivated from those who are not. The testing process can also yield priceless evidence as to what the candidate is actually capable of doing—which is better than trusting the unsubstantiated claims they make on their resume. Another effective way to test a prospective employee is to try them out on a contract basis before you hire them as a full-time employee.

* * *

I was listening to sports radio the other day after my team, the New England Patriots, lost their second regular season game in a row. The Patriots fans were ranting and raving about these losses. How could this happen? Well, the consensus (which I agreed with) was quite simple: the team simply did not have the talent to win the Super Bowl. They just weren't good enough. In the same vein, when you are running a business, your team is made up of your employees. When you have a talented, dedicated staff that gets along well and is highly motivated, your business will be far more likely to succeed. If, on the other hand, you don't find a way to field a team of talented employees, you will find it exceedingly difficult to succeed in business.

Let's focus on finding the employees with the talent and motivation to help your business win in the long term. Now, we've all read countless resumes. The good ones usually claim that the candidate can walk on water. This, combined with the fact that many businesspeople make the false assumption that they can conduct a traditional interview and intuitively select the best applicants for a position, can be costly to your business. For this reason, a simple technique that we live by is to put the candidate on the spot by giving them an exam or test so that they can show exactly what they can and cannot do. As with many of the techniques discussed in this book, however, this one was learned the hard way. Many years ago, we were in need of an extra admin. We believed (and still do) that everybody should have a say in the hiring of a new admin, so we asked the three admins on staff to select the individual we should hire. They picked a lovely person from the local community, but there was only one tiny little problem: she couldn't use a computer. We had to fire her after two days and start from scratch, which wasted a huge amount of time and was an unpleasant experience for all involved. From that day forward, every admin interviewee is first given a computer test to screen out unqualified applicants.

Recently we decided to hire a law clerk to help us write and proofread one of our books. We followed our standard technique and sent the candidates a short assignment. Two candidates, each boasting blue-chip resumes and great grades from top law schools completed the assignment. One was riddled with typos, the other was perfect. It was easy to decide whom to hire. After all, we write for a living. It is hard to imagine how damaging it would have been to our brand, our reputation, and our book if we had hired a sloppy clerk. Fortunately, the test we gave helped us screen out incompetency.

Giving interviewees a pretest can also help to quickly and easily differentiate hard-working, motivated people who really want the job from people who are less motivated or less interested in the position. A billionaire money manager was once asked what type of candidates he preferred to hire. His response was simple, direct and immediate: "PHDs, and by that I mean POOR, HUNGRY, and DETERMINED. The more PHDs you have on your staff, the more you will succeed." We have taken this money manager's advice to heart, which is why we use an unusual technique to find out if someone is a PHD: we send them out a written assignment to be completed as a condition of being interviewed. If you do this, you will immediately be able to identify the candidates who aren't highly motivated, because they will refuse to complete the assignment. Of the people that do complete the assignment, you will also get a good sense of how much each candidate actually knows, as opposed to what they claim to know.

Many years ago we were hiring a seminar coordinator to help us plan and manage the logistics of the continuing education seminars and conferences that we sponsor. This is an important job that needs to be done correctly. We placed a few ads, received dozens of resumes, and then sent the top ten candidates a one-page written test on seminar coordinating. Only three of the candidates bothered to complete it and send it back to us. Those were the three we interviewed. Of the three candidates we interviewed, one had taken the time and effort to research and provide extremely good answers to most of the questions. This showed us that she was very well motivated, and that's who we ended up hiring.

Another variation of this technique is to use the interview process to give somebody an oral exam. The obvious advantage to this technique is that the interviewee cannot cheat by asking someone else to help them. The other advantage is that you can get a great sense as to how the interviewee reacts to stress and whether he or she is able to think on his or her feet. For example, many years ago we were looking to hire a sales and marketing executive. As part of the interview for this position, we asked a test question: "We are thinking about creating such and such a product. How would you sell that for us?" Again, the answers we received were highly relevant in separating the candidates who merely *claimed* they could help us from the candidates that *actually showed us* that they understood sales and marketing.

This oral test technique has been used against me to great effect. When I was first getting out of law school, I interviewed at one of the top personal injury firms in Boston. The main part of the interview was an unannounced test, where I was to take a mock deposition, and I didn't do well. The firm ended up hiring a friend of mine who was very, very good at mock trials—so good that she had won our school's mock trial competition. The firm had successfully used the testing technique, made the right decision, and hired the best trial lawyer. My friend, for her part, rapidly rose to partner and is now one of the top personal injury lawyers in Boston. As for me, even though I didn't get the job, I learned a priceless lesson: if you want to see what people can and can't do, give them a surprise test during their interview.

One final variation of this technique is to try a prospective employee out on a contract basis and see how they perform. This extended test can be conducted on a short-term basis—perhaps a week or two—and for a small, fixed fee. Seeing the prospective employee's work style and ability to produce can be very revealing and helpful. Here's a quick example of "try before you buy." I was writing a technical book for lawyers and needed a good deal of research help. I also had to write a short article, which did not require as much help. What I decided to do was hire a clerk to first help me write the article as a test.[1] I did so, and the test went well. After the article was completed, I was able, with a good bit of confidence, to offer the clerk a full-time job working on the large technical book.

More and more companies (up to two-thirds) are using online and in-person tests as part of their interviewing and hiring processes. Timken Co., an Ohio company that manufactures bearings and lubrication products, uses online testing to assess its applicants' math skills and attention to detail. Google is famous for the online problems it poses to applicants and its off-the-wall tests, the latter of which are administered at its in-person interviews. Large consulting companies base the majority of their hiring decisions on how well applicants perform when tested. Consider testing job applicants. It just might help you pick a winning team.

2. No employee is ever too old—or too young.

EXECUTIVE SUMMARY: Be open-minded about hiring students, recent graduates, and retirees. The very young and retirees can provide your organization with tremendous value.

---

[1] The phone interview with my law clerk was a good test, too. It's what I call a stress interview, and it's designed to see how tough someone is and how they deal with stress. The interview was very short. Here's how it went:

STEVE: I am writing an article on the following statutes. I need you to summarize each of them for me, footnoting everything. Nothing is to be missed. I need this in two weeks without fail. It must be perfect. I am a busy man, and I don't want you calling me up, asking me any questions. Keep track of your hours and expenses and send me your bill with research. Any questions?

CLERK: None. You will have it on time and as requested.

* * *

One of the biggest mistakes you can make in leveraging human capital is to maintain preconceived notions or biases about prospective employees based on their age. We have found over the years that you often get incredible bang for your buck when hiring students, recent graduates, and retired persons. Let's discuss each of these in turn.

We are in the business of selling information. The more information we can gather and package, the more products we can sell. The problem, of course, is the cost of gathering that information. One technique that we have utilized over and over again is to hire law students to assist us in gathering legal and other research. We simply post an online ad at the local law schools and are flooded with resumes. The law students are almost all smart, hungry, college graduates from top schools, and eager to make some money and build up their resumes. Best of all, we pay them less than we pay the administrative assistants in our office. The result: incredible bang for the buck. Many businesses even hire students or recent graduates as interns, and many of these internships are unpaid. Smart young people will give their time to gain experience, and it can be a win—win arrangement for both parties.

In terms of paid employees, we have found that graduate students from top schools can be real gold for our business. These people are usually very sharp, and they are often very hungry as well, because they are heavily indebted from all their educational expenses. For example, a few years ago we were looking to hire someone to help us write a complicated textbook on a topic that combined both law and medicine. By posting an ad at the local law schools, we were able to find a student who had earned a PhD in microbiology from Stanford and was studying to become a life sciences patent attorney. She was much smarter than both Jim and I, and she worked for $15 an hour. Her work over the summer helped us finish a very profitable book. As you can see, grad students can provide tremendous value to your business.

Never be afraid to hire someone right out of school, either. Sure, they don't have any real-world business experience, but they are usually hungry and malleable, which means that you can train them to do things the way you want them done without struggling to undo bad habits and ingrained ways of operating. Also, because they don't have any experience, you can get people fresh out of school relatively inexpensively.

We have had good luck when we hire recent graduates. The key, as we see it, is to refrain from limiting your expectations of an applicant or employee on account of his or her age. For example, many years ago we launched a new and promising line of business in which professionals such as engineers, accountants, and physicians would pay us to promote their availability to serve as expert witnesses for lawyers. We originally put someone with 20 years of professional experience in charge of this new line of business, but despite the large amount of money we paid this person, which was commensurate with his experience, the service struggled. We fired that person and hired a different professional, who also had 20 plus years of experience and whom we also handsomely paid, but she needed intense handholding and couldn't make the service fly. After two years, we decided to fire her as well and hire a young and hungry 25-year-old recent graduate, who had only one year of previous work experience as a call center customer service rep under his belt. Because this person was a recent graduate, we were able to hire him for much less than what we were paying his two predecessors. Sure, he had zero experience in our field, but he was eager and learned quickly. Within three years, he helped build this line of business into one of our most profitable products. We paid less and got more, which is a pretty good business model. The key to our success in this case was not letting youth and lack of experience blind us in our hiring decision.

Here's yet another example of how tremendously valuable recent graduates can be to your business. Many years ago we signed a contract with a national nonprofit organization to produce a series of educational videos for their members. When the videos were delivered, the organization would compensate us with a minimum payment of $150,000, and then we would receive 50 percent of the revenues the videotapes brought in if sales reached a certain level. As always in business, however, there was one catch: we didn't know how to make videos, and our existing staff was tied up with other work. As such, we decided to find a young and hungry recent law school grad to take over the project. Because the individual we eventually selected for this project couldn't find another job, we were able to contract his services for the ridiculous price of $7,000. Combined with the great deal we had negotiated with the production company we had hired, we were able to produce the videos in short order for $45,000 total. We were so happy that we sent the recent grad a $5,000 bonus—which, to him, was like hitting the lottery. We made a $100,000 profit, and the law student eventually agreed to stay on with the company and completed many additional projects as well. The lesson is clear: your best value is often a recent graduate.

When we say potential employees are never too young, we mean it. When I was a busy personal injury lawyer, I was neighbors and friends with a prominent scientist. His exceptionally bright 14-year-old son—we'll call him John—was too young for a summer job and was driving his parents crazy, so I "hired" him to help me at my law office three to four days a week. I would pick John up on my way to court, and during the three to four hours a day that I spent driving, John would read me the typed summaries from my files for minimum wage. In this way, he helped me prepare for my cases, and he also helped me carry my briefcase. His parents were ecstatic. John put his stint as my "legal assistant" on his resume, and I put my hours of driving to good use.

Our experience has shown that retirees can also prove to be valuable hires and present many advantages to your business. First, because they are likely to be on Medicare, they probably don't want or need health benefits, which simplify matters and greatly reduce your costs. They are also usually very talented and accomplished. Next, their schedules are quite flexible, so you can generally call them in as needed, and they will be available. Finally, you can hire them for less than you might otherwise have to pay a younger employee. Many retirees have pensions and other sources of income, so they don't need a huge pay check. Their motivation is not money but rather getting out of the house, breaking up the day, feeling useful, and doing something a little bit different with their time.

Here's a quick example. Many years ago, we needed to enter a large amount of information into one of our databases in a short amount of time. In the past, we had hired freelancers, usually work-at-home parents, to do this type work. We came to the conclusion, however, that these freelancers often delivered a poor-quality product, could not produce a large volume of work when needed (they had other time commitments), and demanded a relatively high rate of pay (they had a family to support and needed money). After many years of utilizing this more conventional approach, we decided to do something a little different and tried out some retirees. The results were phenomenal. We paid the retirees 50 percent less than we had been paying our freelancers and received far better work in exchange. The retirees were also able to push harder when we needed output, because they generally had fewer side commitments.

Here's one final example. Our company does a lot of marketing via direct mail, so we often send out high-end, personalized pieces to our thousands of clients. The work comes in bunches, and often our full-time staff can't get the mailings out in a timely manner. We could hire temps through a staffing agency to tackle our direct mailings, but we found that for about half the cost, we can bring in some retirees, who are more than happy to stuff envelopes for us. Because the retirees are contractors, we don't have to pay them benefits, nor do we have to dole out payroll taxes. This is just another example of how being open minded about a worker's age and experience can help save (i.e., make) you a lot of money.

We aren't the only organization that is using retirees to fill positions successfully; government and private industry are doing so as well. In New York State, retirees are hired liberally for many positions and for many different reasons. They fill seasonal jobs, serve as emergency fill-ins, and work as subject experts. In Massachusetts, judges can be recalled after they have retired to serve on a provisional basis at 80 percent reduced pay and with no benefits. Retail stores such as Target, Kohl's, Nordstrom, Macy's, JCPenney, and Sears all make liberal use of retirees during the holiday season. These retirees are dependable, seasoned, and have a good work ethic.

3. Mercilessly get rid of the bad apples on your staff.

EXECUTIVE SUMMARY: One of the most unpleasant tasks that any manager must undertake is letting go of one of his or her employees. It's just not a fun thing to do. As such, some managers delay what needs to be done far too long. The problem with this approach is that one disruptive or unproductive employee can create jealousies within your organization. Other problems will inevitably cascade down from this individual and can poison the morale of your entire staff. Bad apples need to be terminated as soon as they are identified. Unpleasant as it may be, you must protect the business. You are responsible for feeding too many people to shirk this important responsibility.

* * *

A few years ago, I was on vacation in the Caribbean. As I was sitting on the beach, I met a nice gentleman and his wife, and it turned out that this gentleman owned a successful small business as well. We chatted very pleasantly about business philosophy and exchanged ideas. At one point in the conversation, he said to me, "I'm responsible for feeding over 40 people. Every day that I go to work, I think of that responsibility." I couldn't agree more with his statement or his philosophy. He had about 12 employees at the time, which is about as many people as our firm employs. But many of his employees were the household heads. As such, they were responsible for feeding their children, spouses, and other dependents, so, actually he most likely underestimated the immense responsibility he has.

The economic ripples of owning a successful business are far greater than just your gross revenues. If you own a successful business, you can feed your employees and their families. You can also feed the families of your vendors, help your customers succeed, and generate tax revenues that are used to feed and assist the elderly and needy as well. As a business owner, however, how successful you are at feeding those who depend on you relies, to a large extent, on how talented your team is. If your team is able, motivated, and enthusiastic, you will be positioned to succeed.

One of the hard lessons we have learned over the years is that one bad apple on staff can quickly and insidiously destroy the morale of an entire department or firm. Bad apples must be dealt with firmly and should be immediately terminated. Nobody likes firing people, but in the case of bad apples, it has to be done. Because you want your firm to be successful and you want to continue feeding everyone who depends on your firm's success, you must respond with firm action where there is a morale buster on your staff. Here are a couple of examples from our own experience.

Many years ago, we hired an employee who showed tremendous potential. This person—we'll call her Sandy—was very bright and very nice, and she had a blue-chip education. The problem with Sandy, however, was that she had a corrosive effect on our other employees. She was habitually late, which made the other employees feel like suckers for getting in on time. She didn't pitch in and help out outside of her job description, which caused further resentment. She brought her dog to work, which wasn't a problem (we're laid back and love dogs), but the dog had fleas that infested the office and other employees. When this happened, she didn't even apologize, nor did she lift a finger to mitigate the flea infestation. It got to the point where our staff's productivity was nose-diving. We were spending time every week trying to placate the staff and alleviate friction, but what we were really doing was avoiding the unpleasant job that had to be done—terminating Sandy.

The economy took a turn for the worse shortly after the flea incident. Not only that, but Sandy's absenteeism was really getting to be a problem and was eviscerating staff morale, so we made the decision to terminate her. We went into the office around ten in the morning to perform this unpleasant task, only we couldn't fire her because she hadn't shown up for work yet! Talk about confirming any doubts we had about what needed to be done.[2] We terminated Sandy, and morale in the office quickly returned, but there was an added benefit as well. On the managerial side of the business, we were no longer spending valuable time figuring out how to manage the Sandy problem. We were concentrating on making money.

We had another person—we'll call him Fred—who worked with us as a partner for a period of time. Fred was very smart and very talented, but the problem with Fred was that his personal situation required a high guaranteed salary. Our position was that, in a small business, salaries should be much more conservative. One should first draw a modest salary and *then* share in whatever profits the business brings in for a larger payout. Fred was (and is) also a very dear friend, which further complicated things.

---

[2] There's one further confirmatory epilogue to this story. Sales constituted a large part of Sandy's responsibilities in the office. Her production is this area left much to be desired. To give you an idea of how little she was accomplishing, after she was terminated, we had her calls forwarded to us. In all the time since she was terminated, we never received one call from someone looking for her.

When Fred was working with us, he demanded a salary that was commensurate with those that big corporations pay, which turned our company into a cash-draining, losing proposition. The staff couldn't get a decent bonus because we were bleeding money, and no one could get a raise. Fred, who actually wanted more than he was making, also wasn't happy. He took a job moonlighting on the side, which negatively affected his work performance. The other partners had to loan the company cash to keep it in business, and morale was near zero. Every day the partners had a discussion about how to placate and manage Fred, and every day they fought about dividing up the pie instead of trying to make a bigger pie. People were very resentful, productivity plummeted further, and key staff was getting ready to bolt.

We were avoiding what should have been done sooner. We had a meeting with Fred and told him that things weren't working out. It was tough. After all, Fred was a friend. We eventually offered to buy him out, however, and he accepted. In the end, we were all far better off. Fred started a highly successful business, where he wasn't constrained by more cautious partners, and we were able to focus on our business, customers, and making money—not on managing Fred. Morale returned very rapidly, and so did our profitability. The unpleasant task of separating ourselves from Fred should have been done much sooner.

Here are two more quick stories. Many years ago, we had a person—we'll call him Kevin—who was working in our office and becoming increasingly disruptive. Kevin had been working for us for a number of years and had always been a very good employee. Then something happened, maybe a personal crisis, and things started to change. Almost daily, Kevin would call up complaining about one of his coworkers, and while everybody wanted to cut Kevin slack, his complaining was really getting disruptive. The next odd thing that happened is that Kevin started taking time off around once a week to go to funerals of nonrelatives that he "had to attend." His absenteeism engendered resentment in the office and became a running joke. At one point, one of our employees called up to tell us that her printer died. We asked if Kevin was going to the funeral. The final straw came when Kevin got into a serious fight with his long-term office friend. Productivity in the office came to a halt, and it became clear that we had to act, so Kevin was fired. The strange thing was that his desk had already been completely cleared of personal effects. We think he wanted to get fired and was expecting it. After Kevin was terminated, morale quickly returned to the office.

How seriously do we believe in getting employees that hurt morale out of the office? Here's the final vignette: for almost 20 years, a very bright woman ran our office and was instrumental in growing our business. She was tough as nails and sharp as a tack. When she started out and for many years after, she was very easy to get along with. Toward the end of her tenure with us, however, she became very disruptive in the office. When we would hold meetings, she would make faces when we said something she didn't like. She was constantly complaining. She cursed. She talked back when we asked her to do something. She clearly was not happy at work anymore but did not want to quit and leave us in the lurch.

As it turned out, her husband had become very successful, she didn't need the money anymore, and she really just wanted to stay home with her kids and beloved dog. I discussed the situation with my partners, and the decision was made to let her go. I came into the office to talk to her and give her the news, and as soon as I had finished firing her, an immense smile opened up on her face. She was thrilled not to have to work anymore. She gave me a big hug and kiss, walked out, and asked if I wanted anything special for dinner that night. I was in the somewhat unusual position of firing my own wife.

4. Overpay your staff.

EXECUTIVE SUMMARY: It may seem counterintuitive, but you may be able to improve your efficiency and increase your profitability by overpaying your staff, as doing so may allow you to decrease the total size of your staff, thus reducing your labor costs. You also will not suffer from turnover problems and are likely to have a well-motivated staff that you can count on when you need them. Overpaying your staff can also make you feel good about your business and the work that you are doing.

* * *

Staff turnover is a continuous problem in many businesses. The problems with turnover are clear. First, time and money are wasted when you are forced to find a replacement employee to fill your open position. Second, the enormous time that must be spent training a replacement employee can drain your business's bottom line, and for a long time (and maybe forever) they will be less capable than the person they are replacing. Third, the replacement is unknown, may not fit in well with your staff, and could cause friction or worse. Fourth, much institutional knowledge can be lost due to turnover.

How valuable can a long-time, knowledgeable employee be to you and your business? Here's an example. We took a staff member to a three-day conference that we were running, and the staff member helped coordinate the conference and made special accommodations for attendees with visual impairments, hearing loss, bad backs, and so forth. The staff member also chatted with the attendees at breaks and assisted them. At the conclusion of the conference, a box arrived for the staff member at the office with a gift of smoked salmon from one of our attendees who was from Alaska. As you can see, a happy, long-term employee can be invaluable to your company. These types of employees get to know your customers and their likes and dislikes, and many customers will come to bond with them. As such, we suggest that you overpay the longstanding members of your staff that have proven to be vital assets to your business.

Now, let's be clear: our attitude on compensation used to be rather stingy. We took the view that we should just find the best person for the job and then hire him or her at the lowest possible price. We figured that doing so would obviously generate the biggest bottom line for us. The result of our stingy hiring practices, however, was that we were constantly losing good employees, who left to find better paying jobs. Our employees also weren't very motivated to put in a hard day's work. Why should they bust their hump for a crappy job that they could easily replace? To make up for our employees' lack of productivity, we ended up hiring additional staffers, which, of course, *cost us a fortune*. We finally realized that being stingy on compensation was a losing proposition for us, and we decided to take a different approach that was much more satisfying: we began overpaying our employees. In other words, we pay each of them more than they could command in another job for which they would be qualified.

Now, we know this sounds foolish, but we have found that there are many advantages to overpaying our employees. First, turnover has been completely eliminated. We haven't had one staffer leave for another job in the over eight years since we adopted this approach. The elimination of turnover has saved us a tremendous amount of time because we no longer have to dedicate days on weeks to locating, hiring, and training replacements. The staff that we have is experienced and motivated, and they perform superbly. The second advantage is that by overpaying our employees, we have been able to *decrease* our compensation costs. This sounds crazy, but it's true. By only hiring competent, motivated people and overpaying them, we were able to reduce our support staff from five people to three. That's a 40 percent reduction, and the result is reduced overall labor costs. The third advantage is that when you are paying someone well, they will be more likely to cooperate with you when you really need their help on a project. Let's say you need something done at night or on a weekend. An employee who wants to keep his or her well-paying job will be much more likely to agree to pitch in. The final advantage of overpaying your staff is that doing so is fun. One of the biggest satisfactions we derive from running our business is that we are able to help out our employees. Treating them well financially *just feels good*.

Nobel Prize-winning economist George Akerlof and his wife (and future Federal Reserve Board Member), Janet Yellen, have found evidence supporting our compensation approach. In a study conducted in the 1980s, Akerlof and Yellen found that employees who worked at companies that paid them above-market wages had higher morale, lower turnover, and higher productivity. Try overpaying your staff a little. It may turn out to be a very shrewd investment.

5. Treat people you terminate with compassion and respect.

EXECUTIVE SUMMARY: Treat your employees with compassion and respect when you terminate them. Do not criticize them. Do not fight their unemployment benefits. Do not humiliate them. Provide a generous severance package, and don't screw them out of their bonuses. Treating people you have to fire with compassion and respect is the right thing to do. You will feel better about yourself, and you will also reduce the significant risks that former disgruntled employees can pose to you and your company. Your current employees will be watching you, and they will appreciate the compassionate way you dealt with a difficult situation.

* * *

Jim and I are both lawyers, and though we are not employment lawyers, we do have a good friend is who is a superb employment lawyer. She once told us, in one sentence, everything we needed to know about employment law. Namely, although there is no such thing as a "gruntled" former employee, *dis*gruntled former employees can cause a lot of problems.

Both Jim and I have worked for managers who have treated us poorly. I was fired one day after my boss—a lawyer, no less—found out that I was Jewish. Jim once worked for a man—we'll call him Tony—who was not at all likeable. Tony was greedy and cared nothing for his employees. One day, Tony showed up for work in sweat pants, a tee shirt, and slippers, despite the fact that he usually wore thousand-dollar suits. It turned out that his house had burned down the night before. Tony was so challenging a boss that Jim immediately assumed that the fire was set by disgruntled former employee.[3] To Jim's knowledge, not one employee visited Tony's office that day to ask how he was doing and express their regret. Needless to say, to this day we both have very strong feelings about people who we worked for that did not treat us right, which is part of the reason why we believe in treating our employees with compassion and respect, from the day that they are hired to the last day they work for us.

---

[3] It turned out that the fire was not set by a former employee, but rather by someone with a mental illness who was not purposefully targeting Tony.

Speaking of the last day an employee works for you, sometimes, as mentioned previously in this chapter, you have no other choice but to terminate an employee. Even if you did everything within your power to ensure that you hired the right candidate, whether by interviewing them, testing them, or even trying them out on a contractual basis, sometimes people change. They may experience a personal crisis that causes their performance to permanently deteriorate. Maybe your business may need to cut costs, or perhaps there is bad blood between you and the employee because of mistakes they have made or problems they have caused. The employee may even be angry at you. Whatever the case may be, it is our policy to treat the people that we are forced to terminate with compassion and respect.

Treating those we terminate with compassion and respect has turned out to be a prudent business policy for us. We have minimized disgruntlement to a large extent, and no former employees have ever filed any type of complaint against us. They've also never taken retaliatory action against us, such as badmouthing us or trying to harm our business. In fact, they've always cooperated in transition. So, the bottom line here is simple: although it may feel good to try to get even with an employee who has cost you time, money, and aggravation, just don't do it. If they come back and burn down your office building, sue you, delete your computer data, or worse, you will have paid a steep price for indulging in revenge.

Let me give you an example of what I mean. We have a good friend and client—we'll call him Bill—who runs a highly successful small business. We were doing some consulting work for Bill on how he could grow his business and sell it so that he could a break from working so hard. We were getting ready to do some more work for Bill when we called him up to get things going and found out that he couldn't proceed. As it turned out, all his money and time were being eaten because he had to defend himself from a wrongful termination and discrimination lawsuit from a deranged and disgruntled former employee. His liability insurance didn't cover lawsuits of this nature, and things were so stressful that Bill ended up having a heart attack. This is exactly the type of situation that our policy of compassion and respect is meant to avoid.

Here's another quick example. For many years, Jim's wife worked at a large, publicly traded corporation, and she would regularly read a blog maintained by a disgruntled former employee of this corporation. This blog contained information about management that was, to say the least, not complimentary. The blogger was a thorn in the side of management, and the blog certainly wasn't helping the corporation's share price. Would this blogger have been angry enough to spend all this time trashing his old employer if he had been treated better? There's no way to know for sure, but that's certainly a good question to ask.

What exactly do we mean when we say our policy is to treat people we are forced to terminate with compassion and respect? Here are the specific policies that we follow. First, we never, ever, ever talk about the past when we fire people. We don't blame people, talk about their poor performance, or tell them how much their performance lapsed and how much money they cost us. Conversations of this nature are losing propositions that are only going to throw fuel on the fire. We simply tell the employee that we need to let them go, and no reason is given that reflects on their performance. Instead, we stress nonantagonizing reasons, such as cost control and reorganization. Second, we don't fight the employee's unemployment insurance. There is nothing more likely to anger a former employee than trying to revoke their unemployment benefits. Third, we provide generous severance benefits. Many people live paycheck to paycheck. Our solution is to recognize this fact and give people far-above-average, generous severance benefits. Going one step further, if the employee would have been due a bonus had they remained with the company, we pay their bonus on a prorated basis. Our employees recognize this gesture and appreciate the fair way we treat people, even when we have to let them go. Fourth, we handle the actual termination as compassionately as possible. We come in and talk with the person when nobody else is around so they are not embarrassed. We neither escort them out of the building nor watch them as they pack up. We treat them with respect. Finally, we do not provide poor references. We didn't go into business to end careers. If someone calls us up to ask us for a reference, we tell them that our lawyer told us that we can only provide dates of service. Doing so allows us to avoid providing a potentially poor reference.

Not only has nothing bad happened to us as a result of our former employees, but a number of good things have happened as well. We directly attribute these good things to the way we treated the person when we terminated him or her. A former employee of ours—we'll call her Barbara—serves as a good example. When Barbara was with our company, she was working two jobs to support her two teenage sons. She was also going through a divorce and dealing with an elderly father who was having many health issues. Needless to say, Barbara was under a lot of stress. She was also just an exceptionally nice person.

Barbara was put in charge of one of our most important lines of business, and though she tried her best, the product line did not thrive under her charge. We decided that we needed to make a change. The job just wasn't a good fit for her skill set. We were very concerned, however, about what would happen when we terminated her. Would she freak out? How upset would she be?

Would she still talk to us? We all live in a small community. Would she be cooperative with her replacement during the transition period?

I came in to fire her one evening after everyone else had left. I didn't want her to be embarrassed. I praised her efforts, and I told her how hard it was for me to fire her, because she was so well-regarded within the company. I reinforced that she did nothing wrong, told her we would help her with the transition, and offered her six months of severance salary. Keep in mind, now, that this is a woman who had only worked for us for around two years. Most big companies give terminated employees one week of severance for every year of service they have given to the organization. After a difficult discussion and some tears, I left her.

During the next few months, Barbara and I kept in touch. I helped her find other work and mentored her. Eventually, another job opened up at our company that Barbara was uniquely qualified for, and we offered her this position. She accepted and continued to work for us for over ten years. She has even helped us network and make some very profitable deals. As you can see, treating Barbara right when we terminated her paid us huge dividends, both personally and professionally. Who knows what would have happened with her and with the transition had we treated her poorly? Two things are for sure. First, we wouldn't have been able to hire her back, and second, we would have had trouble sleeping at night.

What about when an employee decides to quit working for your company? What do you do then? Jim and I follow the same rules we adhere to when we are terminating an employee. We treat them with respect, talk about the future, give them more than they are entitled to, and then go the extra step and throw them a party and wish them well. Let me give you an example. Many years ago, we employed a young lawyer—we'll call him Gary. One day Gary came into the office and told me that he was leaving to pursue his dream of becoming a trial lawyer. Because I had served as a trial lawyer for 20 years, I patiently explained to Gary the numerous problems that can arise when you work as a trial lawyer. He quit anyway, and we threw him a going away party and wished him well. He kept in touch, so when his boss threw a telephone at him, he called me for advice. I asked him if the phone had hit him, and he said no, so I advised him to go to Sears, purchase a toy rubber phone, put it on his boss's desk, and go back to work. After several more months, he had had enough. He asked for his old job back, which I happily gave him. The bottom line: treat employees right, even when they quit or you have to terminate them.

6. Be flexible with your staff.

EXECUTIVE SUMMARY: One of the absolute keys to profitability in business is being able to minimize staff turnover. One way to do this is to be flexible with your staff regarding their hours and their desire to work from home. Many employers are not flexible and cannot be so, but if you can be flexible with your staff, you can gain a competitive edge in the labor market. If you can find win—win flexible working solutions for you and your employees, they will be very unlikely to leave you. The reason for this is simple: your employees will be hard-pressed to find similarly flexible situations in any new job they might find.

* * *

Our focus as small business owners is on our customers. As such, our goal is to spend as much time as possible developing and selling products and services that help our customers. We also want our customers to have a superb, helpful, and efficient experience when they interact with one of our employees. A cornerstone of our ability to focus on our customers stems from the measures we take to prevent staff turnover. The less time we spend hiring and training new staff members, the more time we can spend focusing on our customers. The less turnover we have, the better the customer service our clients will receive from our staff.

One way to prevent turnover is to be flexible with your staff and give them benefits and perks that money can't buy and/or they can't get elsewhere. Namely, because many employers will not be flexible with their staff regarding working hours and work-from-home arrangements, if you can be flexible about these matters, you will gain a huge competitive edge when it comes to retaining valued employees. Let me give you some examples. One of our employees—we'll call him Darrell—serves as our bookkeeper. Darrell has been working for us for over 30 years. He sets his own hours and usually works from 5:00 a.m. to around 8:00 a.m. each day, which allows him to have the rest of the day free. Darrell gets his work done. He never complains. He's smart. He's precise. He doesn't constantly agitate for more money. We trust him with the checkbook. And best of all, he's been working for us for 30 years and does not need any training or supervision.

It is certainly not ideal for our bookkeeper to work such odd hours. For example, if a question arises on an accounts payable or receivable during the day, Darrell is not at his desk to answer it. However, this isn't the end of the world. We have made the decision to be flexible about Darrell's hours, and it is a win—win situation for both him and us. The job gets done, Darrell is happy, and most important, we don't worry about bookkeeping. The job is taken care of, and we are free to focus on our customers and making money.

When we say we believe in flexibility, we mean it. Consider this. Many years ago, I hired a bright new lawyer—we'll call him Jerry—to work for me. Jerry graduated from a Boston law school and was happy to stay in the Boston area after graduation. He was smart, hardworking, and industrious. After several years of working for me, Jerry came into my office with a sad face and said he was going to have to quit because he was relocating to California to be with his fiancé. We talked about the problem, and I finally authorized him to rent space and open up a California branch of our company in Oakland, California. The calculus of this decision was simple: we decided that Jerry would still get the job done for us in California, so we agreed.

Jerry continued to work for me. He expanded our presence and reach to the West Coast, so it was a win–win situation. He also created a very profitable conference for us that is still running to this day. How loyal is Jerry? Let me give you an idea. Recently, I suffered a serious injury that rendered me unable to travel. I had to teach a course on the West Coast in a week, so my inability to travel was presenting a big problem for us. We called Jerry, who now runs his own super busy law firm in the Midwest, and Jerry, without hesitation, agreed to cover for me on the West Coast. The primary reason Jerry was so extremely helpful to me in this situation was that he felt that I had been very good to him.

Here's another example. One of the admins on our staff—we'll call her Rachel—is a young and extremely bright recent college graduate. Rachel is a go-getter who earned her degree in night school while working full time—which is an impressive accomplishment. As a well-qualified college graduate, she could certainly earn more money if she were to do a different job for someone else. Yet, she's been working for us for over four years since she graduated from college. We think that part of the reason Rachel has been so faithful to our company is because of the flexibility that we give her.

Here's what we mean. Rachel's husband owns a restaurant, and his only day off during the week is Tuesday. Rachel obviously would like to spend Tuesdays with him, so she proposed the following to us: Would it be OK for her to work whenever she is needed on weekends and holidays so that she could take Tuesdays off as comp days? Our answer was yes, as long as there is enough coverage in the office on any given Tuesday. This has worked out well for all concerned. Rachel has taken many, many Tuesdays off, we've received extra coverage on holidays and weekends, and we haven't had to hire and train a replacement. In this case, I guess you could say that it's been a real win–win–win situation!

Here's a final example. I once hired a law student—we'll call him Joe—to work on a new product for me. Joe did a very good job, so I contracted him on a part-time basis for several additional projects, all of which went very well. Joe graduated from law school and went to work for a law firm in Boston. I wanted him to come work for me, but I knew he didn't want to live out on Cape Cod, where we are located, and I also knew that he wanted to practice law. So I decided to see what some flexibility could buy me. I offered Joe a full-time job, a salary that was competitive with that which he was receiving at his law firm, and the opportunity to work out of his home in Boston. Joe accepted. After all, there probably weren't too many other places where you could make a lawyer's salary and work out of your home. It was one heck of a perk. Joe started for me 17 years ago, and he's still working for us out of his home. Instead of spending our days hiring and training a constantly revolving staff, Joe and our team can spend our time focusing on our customers.

One more note about working from home: if one of your employees is a self-starter and the work involved is amenable, we have found that working from home can be a great arrangement for all involved. The employee gets convenience and doesn't have to commute. We get low overhead and a happy employee who is unlikely to jeopardize losing this perk. In fact, here's something that might interest you: no home-based employee has ever left our company. That's right: allowing our employees to work from home has been a 100 percent effective strategy for preventing turnover. That's a pretty tough statistic to argue with, isn't it? Work-from-home arrangements have worked so well for us that half our staff is currently based out of home offices. Moreover, the technology that facilitates working from home is getting better all the time.

We're not alone in our decision to extend flexible working arrangements to our employees. Many companies have successfully leveraged flexibility to build a great team and grow their businesses. The law firm Axiom rapidly grew to over 900 lawyers in part by allowing many of their lawyers to work from home some of the time. Many former call center jobs are now staffed with home-based representatives. Executive Health Resources has grown rapidly since its founding in 1997 in part by attracting a talented and satisfied team of often home-based physician advisors. And as early as 2008, almost 27 percent of insurance giant Aetna's employees worked from home. Clearly, giving your employees the option to work from home is something you may want to consider if you are not already doing it.

7. Pay for performance.

EXECUTIVE SUMMARY: There are many advantages to basing your employees' pay on their performance results. Each employee under the eat-what-you-kill model is paid exactly what they are worth to the company. As a result, they will be well-motivated to generate profits. In addition, you won't need to renegotiate their compensation every year. Finally, if you have multiple employees under your employ, they can each get the exact same deal, which will minimize jealousies and prevent the need for secrecy. To make pay-for-performance work, the formula it is based on must be fair and not subject to unfair manipulation by the employer.

* * *

Before I discuss pay-for-performance, I want to provide you with a little helpful background information about my prior career, when I served as the senior partner in a medium-sized personal injury plaintiff's law firm. In this capacity, I had to deal with a lot of egos—which was unpleasant in and of itself—but no responsibility of mine was more unpleasant than negotiating the compensation of our lawyers. When I first started managing the firm, I made many mistakes regarding compensation. First, I would negotiate a salary with each lawyer separately. This was problematic in that neither one of us was usually ever happy with the result; I thought I was paying too much, they thought they were getting too little. Second, every year I had to have a contentious and distracting compensation renegotiation with each lawyer, and again, neither party generally left that conversation feeling very satisfied. Third, the lawyers didn't have a financial incentive to bring in fees. They'd make just as much money if they just pushed papers around their desk all day long. Finally, there was a lot of jealousy among the lawyers. One attorney thought he should make more than the others, because he had attended an Ivy League school. Another thought he should make more, because he put in long hours. You get the idea.

The bottom line was that I spent far too much time fighting with my lawyers about money—and there is nothing more unpleasant than fighting about money. Furthermore, my staff wasn't as well-motivated as I knew they could be, and our contentious compensation conversations were distracting. Nobody was happy with this arrangement, which is why I eventually decided to switch to a pay-for-performance model. Here's how it worked: every lawyer was paid exactly the same rate. They each got one-third of the gross income that they generated. The more money the lawyer made for the firm, the more money the lawyer made for himself or herself. In this way, our interests were aligned, and the lawyer was well-motivated to generate fees. Even better, I never had to negotiate compensation with a lawyer again, because their compensation was always the same. If they wanted to make more money, they just needed to generate more in fees. There was no further jealousy, because everyone had the same transparent and fair deal.

The results of instituting an "eat-what-you-kill," pay-for-performance model at my firm were dramatic. Our profits soared as the firm collected much more in fees, and my aggravation level nose-dived. The lawyers focused on bringing in money, and I never had to spend another minute negotiating compensation with a lawyer. It was a real win–win situation for us, which is why I have applied the concept of pay-for-performance in my business wherever possible. Here are a couple of examples.

Many years ago, during the dot-com boom, we decided that we needed to start selling our products online, as we thought by doing so would make the company much more valuable. In those crazy days, it seemed like anybody with a website was going public and cashing out big time. We only had one problem, though: we didn't know anything about e-commerce, and we were busy running our business. So we approached one of the young lawyers on our staff—we'll call him Caleb—and asked him if he would be interested in building and maintaining an e-commerce-enabled website for us. Caleb responded that he was a lawyer, not a programmer. We shot back that we would pay him 10 percent of every sale that was generated from the website, above and beyond his salary. Caleb was now a very happy web developer.

Because Caleb was very motivated to start receiving his 10 percent cut, the website was developed in a rapid fashion. We didn't even have to prod or chase him. Over the next two years, we grew our e-commerce sales from zero to over $200,000 per year. Caleb was happy, and we were happy—not only because we had made substantial profits from our web store, but also because we didn't have to renegotiate compensation with Caleb for the remainder of his tenure with us.

Here's one final example. Many years ago, before Jim and I began working together, I hired a very accomplished young lawyer—we'll call him Joe—to work for me at my business. Joe was qualified to command a high salary working elsewhere, especially as he gained more and more experience. When I hired him, however, I did not want to have to renegotiate Joe's salary every year. I remembered that compensation renegotiations had been losing propositions at my law firm, so I made Joe an offer. "Here are our books," I said. "Last year, without you, we made $300,000 in profits. With your help, however, I think we could make a lot more." So I offered Joe a small base salary, plus 10 percent of our company's profits. Joe was smart enough to realize that my offer effactually made him a partner in my business and gave him unlimited earning potential, so he accepted. I was happy, because I figured that I would never have to renegotiate Joe's compensation again. I was also very pleased that he would be motivated and happy to be working for me. Unfortunately, however, I was wrong on both counts.

At the same time that Joe joined our team, Fred, who I have mentioned previously, was hired as a partner. Fred was a very talented, experienced, and accomplished professional, but he was also saddled with a good deal of fixed expenses. As such, he did not agree with my eat-what-you-kill salary philosophy, whereby Fred and I would split 45 percent of the company's profits and Joe would receive the remaining 10 percent. Fred insisted on a guaranteed salary of $200,000 per year, which is what he could command if he were to work for a different company. To keep things fair, I had to increase my salary to $200,000 per year as well, but Fred and my humungous salaries absorbed all of the firm's profits (and more). As a result, Joe's 10 percent of the profits turned out to be worthless.

After the first year, Joe was expecting a nice $30,000 to $40,000 bonus, so when I told him he was getting nothing, he was understandably pretty upset. He basically felt that he had been cheated and that his compensation formula had been manipulated to screw him over. I sensed that Joe was ready to walk, and I also felt badly about what had happened, so, to see how sharp he was, I jokingly proposed that we renegotiate his 10 percent bonus. I asked him if a bonus that amounted to 20 percent of the firm's profits would be satisfactory. Joe, of course, was not amused. I apologized and proposed that we use a new formula going forward—one that could not be easily manipulated. Instead of offering him 10 percent of our profits, I suggested that we pay Joe 2 percent of our *gross income*. The year before, we had generated $1,500,000 in gross income, which meant that, if the new formula had been in place at that time, Joe's bonus would have worked out to $30,000. Fortunately, Joe accepted my offer. That was 17 years ago, and he's been working with us ever since. I should mention here that in the time that has passed since I revised Joe's bonus formula, I have never once had to renegotiate compensation with him. When the company grows, he shares in it, so he is motivated to work hard. Best of all, his formula is transparent and objective. It is not easily manipulated, as "profits" can be, and as such, Joe knows that he is being treated fairly.

Even though pay-for-performance is perhaps most widely and obviously used to motivate employees who work in sales positions, many other professions and companies employ this payment model as well. Servers at restaurants, for example, are paid based on their performance. In addition, many professional sports contracts include performance incentives, as do the contracts that bankers who work on Wall Street. Pay-for-performance is also being tested in education, with the idea being that a teacher's compensation and job security should be linked to how well his or her students perform on standardized tests. Indeed, merit pay is the basis for much of the billions of dollars provided by the federal government in its "race to the top" initiative. So, think about it. You may just want to consider implementing a form of merit pay in your own organization as well.

* * *

You're going to need productive and motivated employees to succeed in business, but if you follow the suggestions in the chapter, you should be able to put together and retain a successful team of employees. Of course, a successful business requires customers as well as employees, which is why improving your interactions with customers is the focus of our next chapter.

Deal with Customer Complaints Head-On

Interacting with your customers in an optimal manner is a critical component of business success. A satisfied customer who will talk you up to his or her friends and consider buying from you in the future can be one of your most valuable assets. On the other hand, a customer who is angry with you can easily scare away business—especially with tools such as the Internet and social media at his or her disposal. For these reasons, this chapter details several techniques for dealing with problem customers and complaints. We also provide our easily replicable suggestions for how to best interact with customers and exceed their customer service expectations.

1. Talk directly with your customers as much as you can.

EXECUTIVE SUMMARY: Talking with your customers is not a burden. Rather, it is a tremendous opportunity, so talk with your customers on the phone or in person as often as you can. Only by talking with them directly—and not through someone who is filtering their words—can you truly learn priceless information about what they like, what they dislike, what they want, and how much they are willing to pay for your products and/or services.

* * *

From time to time, Jim and I will greatly amuse ourselves by looking at how different the meaning of any given message can be, depending on who is delivering it (i.e., filtering it). A classic example of message distortion, of course, can be found in the news media. Back in 2006, I would turn on the news every night, and some nights I would watch CNN, while other nights I would watch Fox. When I watched CNN, I would see report after report about how we were losing the war in Iraq. If I flipped to Fox, however, I would see report after report on how we were *winning* the war. The difference was obvious—the message was being delivered by two different messengers. Really, the only way I could have truly gotten a sense of what was happening in Iraq was if I had gone over there myself and observed the situation firsthand—and I wasn't about to do that.

Just as second-hand information can be misleading in the news media, it can also cause confusion and misunderstandings when you acquire it from those who are filtering your customers' messages. As such, what we have learned over the years is that the best way to communicate with your customers is to talk with them directly. Don't rely exclusively on filters such as your employees, intermediaries, assistants, surveys, or written communications to converse with your customers. Instead, take as much time as you can to talk with your customers directly—and do so as often as you can, either in person or on the telephone. Jump into the trenches at every opportunity you get and talk with your customers.

We have found that there are four main advantages to talking with your customers directly. First, as discussed above, their message won't be filtered. You will be able to hear exactly what they are saying and can follow up with any questions you might have. In other words, the data is of the highest quality and accuracy. Second, you can get great feedback from them on your existing products and services. Third, you can get great ideas regarding additional products or services you should develop. Finally, you can build bonds and loyalty with your customers and buttress your brand because your customers will recognize that you are the face of your organization and, as such, are an integral part of your brand. If your customers have interacted with you and like you, they will be more likely to be loyal to your organization and its products and services. Always remember that customers who really like you, your products, and you services may act as your advocates, preaching to anyone who will listen about what they have discovered.

We make it a point to try to talk with our customers as much as possible. There are many ways that we do this. First, we give our direct telephone numbers to our clients and encourage them to call us for help or information. In addition, each e-mail we send out mentions our direct dial number, which is greatly appreciated by our customers. Yes, fielding phone calls eats up a lot of time, but we feel that it is well worth it. For example, oftentimes customers will call us to see how much we actually know about one of our products or services before they purchase it. These "kick the tires" calls enable us to demonstrate our knowledge, and they often result in additional sales. In addition, we view every customer that calls us with a problem as an invaluable and unfiltered source of market research. If they have a problem, others may be having the exact same problem, and we consider learning about these problems to be golden opportunities for new product development. For many years, for example, we had been receiving calls from customers who had been treated badly by their consulting clients, so we used these specific problems after we had been made aware of them to draft a model contract our clients could use to protect themselves. It was one of the most profitable products we ever produced, and its creation was made possible because we opened ourselves up to our customers.

Another thing we do is make it a point to take turns in the customer service trenches. As such, Jim and I will hand out nametags at our conferences. We'll answer the phones. We'll man the check-out area where our books are sold. Why do we do this? Because we strive to take advantage of every opportunity to learn what our customers like, what they don't like, how much they are willing to spend, and how we can serve them better. For example, one day Jim was manning the book table at one of our seminars, and he got to talking with one of our customers. Jim explained that we might not put on the seminar in question anymore, as we weren't making enough money. The customer looked up at Jim and pleaded with conviction, "Please raise your price! We'd pay much more; your courses are worth it. Please keep doing them." It was a memorable experience, to say the least. We followed the customer's advice, raised our prices 25 percent, and were able to turn a borderline product into a moneymaker that continues to run to this day. If Jim had not been working the table (which we could get someone else to do for $10 an hour), he would not have talked with the customer, we would have probably folded the course, and lost years of profits.

Another technique we have found to be helpful is to have lunch with our customers at our conferences. We have found that you can often find out more useful information by just sitting down for a meal with your customers than you ever could through surveys and quantitative analysis. When they are eating, your customers are relaxed and easy to engage. More important, they know that nothing is being written down, so they will give much a more frank opinion than if you asked them in writing. For example, recently I had lunch at our annual Workers' Compensation Conference with a group of seven nurse clients. We got to talking about what types of courses they would like us to put on for them in the future, and what I learned was eye-opening and extremely valuable. The nurses were tired of being talked down to by doctors and wanted courses taught on a high level. Because I had them there in person, I could ask follow-up questions. I also could see their passion, frustrations, and enthusiasm on a first-hand basis. By the end of the lunch, I asked if we should put on a series of high-level clinical courses that were focused on different injuries (back, arm, leg, etc.) and targeted to nurses. The nurses responded with a high level of enthusiasm, and we ended up successfully putting on these courses. The information I had obtained was unfiltered and thus more trustworthy. Equally important, because I was talking with our customers in person, I was able to expedite the process of information gathering by asking the right follow-up questions to my very captive audience.

Here's one final quick example. Many years ago, we had just started running our conferences at an ocean-front resort on Cape Cod. Jim and I were at the registration booth, and as we sat there, we watched client after client walk in late and frustrated. They had all gotten lost. Because we were manning the registration booth and interacting with our customers, we were able to learn about this problem and immediately act to eliminate it in the future by sending out more specific driving directions to the resort. It may seem as if we only fixed a small issue, but it really wasn't. The last thing we wanted was for our clients' first impression of our course to be associated with the frustration of getting lost. We ended up running many a successful program at this resort, and we never received any further complaints from our customers about getting lost.

2. Talk with unhappy customers on the phone or in person, and get back to them right away.

EXECUTIVE SUMMARY: Actually talking with your customers has become a lost art. Many companies purposefully refrain from listing a phone number on their webpage. This is unfortunate, because the best way to deal with unhappy customers is to actually talk with them. When you talk with your customers, you show them you care and are different than many other companies out there. You can also resolve miscommunication issues, problem solve, and often find out what is really happening.

* * *

We have found that the best way to communicate with unhappy customers is to do so orally, either in person or on the telephone. There are several reasons for this. First, by taking the time to talk with someone on the phone, you are making it clear that you are taking them and their situation seriously. Second, you can quickly get to the root of what the real problem is and what type of a person you are dealing with. Third, you can be sure your tone is supportive and helpful. Finally, people often tend to be less demanding and more restrained when talking with someone, as opposed to when writing to someone.

We have a great brand, but not all our customers are always happy. Every so often, we receive a complaint that can't be immediately resolved by our staff. One of these problems is "chargebacks," which occur when one of your customers calls their credit card company and tells them that your charge was unauthorized and should be reversed. Chargebacks are very serious matters, as they can escalate and lead to accusations of fraud. When a chargeback is requested, we typically receive written notice of the chargeback from the credit card company. Then we have to go back and forth with the credit card company and try to explain that we did nothing wrong and the charge was authorized. This wastes many hours and creates ill will with the customer when we eventually "win" the dispute. As such, chargebacks are almost always lose–lose situations.

We handle chargebacks quite differently than we used to, and now we actually call up the client who requested it. Recently, for example, a customer attended one of our conferences and paid $1,300 to us in tuition. After he got home, however, he called his credit card company and said that we were not authorized to charge his card. So, we called up the customer who had requested the chargeback and asked him why, after attending the three-day course, getting 21 hours of training, seven meals, and two course books, he called his credit card company and accused us of fraud. He informed me that we had promised him a free book with his registration that he never received. Now, keep in mind that this book is worth $15 and costs us around $8. I did not argue with him about why he charged back $1,300 for a $15 book. I apologized for the oversight, sent him the book again (the first time it came back refused), and he promptly e-mailed the credit card company, telling them to withdraw his chargeback request. I then instructed our staff to remove this person from our mailing lists—we didn't want to deal with him any further. The bottom line, of course, was that a quick phone call was able to amicably solve what appeared to be a Gordian knot-type situation.

Let me give you another example. Recently I received a strongly worded e-mail from a customer who wanted to complain about one of our conference speakers. It went something like this: "I tried to hire one of your speakers as a consultant to help me, and she never called me back. I was never so insulted in my life. How can you associate yourself with someone like this? What is wrong with you people? I spent all that money at your conference." When I received this e-mail, I was sorely tempted to shoot back an e-mail to the effect of, "If you want something, try asking nicely, and try letting people know what you want." Such an e-mail obviously would not have helped the situation, so I called up the customer within 15 minutes of receiving her e-mail. In a very friendly tone, I said that I was sorry this had happened to her and offered to refer her to some other people that could help her. She was very appreciative and said good-bye with a big thank you. Once again, this conversation proved to me that the best way to deal with unhappy customers is to promptly call them on the phone and work it out. Doing so can diffuse confrontations and allow you to quickly determine exactly what the customer really needs and how you can help them.

Here's another example. As previously mentioned, our consulting clients pay us a fee in exchange for listing them in a directory that we print, publish, and promote to tens of thousands of potential clients. To encourage consultants to purchase a listing in our directory, we offer and honor a money-back guarantee if they don't gain enough new work to justify their listing. A small percentage of consultants listed in the directory will request a refund. Typically, these requests arrive via e-mail and are worded like this: "Hi. I've been in your directory almost a month, and I haven't gotten any work. Please send me my money back. Please confirm receipt of this e-mail. Thank you." We used to respond to these e-mails with a return e-mail to the effect of: "Dear Dr. Smith: Thank you for the note. The directories have not been printed and mailed out yet. Your money-back guarantee does not expire for another eight months, so I suggest you give it some more time." The response back was almost always the same—something like, "Thanks for the heads up, but please send me my money back ASAP, per your written money-back guarantee policy. Please confirm in writing. Thank you."

Eventually we decided to try a different approach, and we began calling up the people who were requesting refunds before giving the directory adequate time to work for them. We would explain the same thing that we used to explain over e-mail; namely, we would suggest that they give it more time and remind them that their guarantee was good for many more months. The results, however were remarkably different. By actually talking with the customer, we were able to convince around half to refrain from cancelling. Maybe they believed us more when we talked with them in person? Maybe it was harder for them to say no to a live person? Maybe they trusted us more when they talked with us in person? We just don't know the reason. What we do know, however, is that the majority of the people that we called and talked out of cancelling did end up getting cases, never ended up cancelling their listing, and eventually actually *renewed* their listing. All in all, it was well worth our while to call up our angry customers, as opposed to sending them an e-mail.

3. Get rid of problem clients so you can focus on your good clients.

EXECUTIVE SUMMARY: We have found that a large percentage of your problems will be caused by a small percentage of your customers. Problem customers will cost you money. Once we identify a troublemaker, we try to make that person happy, and then we do everything we can to avoid doing business with him or her in the future. We need to concentrate on making money and the vast majority of our good customers, not on dealing with troublemakers.

* * *

About ten years ago, Jim was teaching a course on how physicians can protect themselves from medical malpractice lawsuits. The primary topic of the discussion was what to do with patients that you strongly suspect to be litigious, that is, patients who complain, bad-mouth other doctors, or bring up their lawyer in conversation. In other words, patients who are trouble waiting to happen. One of the people Jim was teaching with was a surgeon who had many years of experience in the medical field, and he gave the course attendees what we consider to be extremely good advice: "Make them love you if you can, discharge them, and don't accept them as a patient again." In a nutshell, get rid of them because it's just not worth the risk.

We love our clients, and most of them are great. Some of them, however, can be a royal pain. For example, we dealt with a client many years ago who would call us up whenever we sent out a flyer and tell us that, because he was such a good client (he wasn't), he should get the product we were advertising at a steep discount or for free. This ate up a lot of time and was a big distraction. Furthermore, we certainly couldn't agree to his requests because if word got out, we'd have to give *everyone* a discount or free goods. Also, we didn't feel it was worth our time to enter into prolonged negotiations every time we came out with a $60 product. The solution was to make him happy, and then get rid of him. After this game was played one time too many, we finally acquiesced to his request, sent him the product for free, and then removed him from all our mailing lists. He has never contacted us again, and we don't have to deal with him anymore. Instead, we are focusing on the 99.9% of our clients who are easy to deal with.

Another time, we were holding one of our seminars at a resort location when we were approached by the general manager of the resort. One of our clients was being very disruptive and complaining that the resort did not allow volleyball on their beach. We were trying to put on our program, but we were interrupted multiple times because of this customer's behavior. He was causing so much trouble, in fact, that the resort was getting ready to throw him out. The situation was distracting, to say the least, and there could have been a big, ugly scene—which is why, when the seminar was over, we immediately removed this customer from our mailing list. We didn't need the aggravation. We wanted to be able to focus on the 99.9% of our other customers who weren't disruptive.

If you know that a client is angry at you and is still not satisfied with the resolution of his dispute, by all means, do not try to sell that person something after the issue has been resolved. There's no profit in stirring up a hornet's nest. After one of our recent conferences, we received a lengthy and angry (and unjustified) note from an attendee who wanted a refund. We don't provide refunds for conferences after the fact, which made the customer even angrier. Unfortunately, we messed up and forgot to remove this malcontent from our mailing list. When, a few months later, we sent him an e-mail solicitation for another course that we were putting on, we received an almost violent diatribe in response. The customer was threatening to bad-mouth our business wherever possible (including online) and make sure that nobody he knew ever dealt with us again. This unfortunate result was our fault. We should have removed him from our mailing list, and we never, ever, should have stirred him up by trying to sell him something else. He was clearly never going to be won over.

Here's another example of how we purposefully dump bad clients. We work with a handful of companies that distribute (resell) the books we publish. Some of these distributors don't pan out and only sell three or four books per year. Unfortunately, the accounting and maintenance costs associated with working with underproducing distributors essentially nullify the few sales that they do end up making. Our solution? Close down their accounts and focus on distributors that can make us money. This is a similar approach to that which investment firms use when they refuse to take small accounts and require a significant minimum initial investment. Sure, it may seem unnatural to turn away business, but we need to be able to focus on clients that are or will likely become profitable. You don't want to keep customers that consistently cause you to lose money. If you have too many customers like that, you'll be out of business before you know it.

Here's one final distributor example. For many years, we worked with a book distributor that sold a moderate amount of our books per year. The volume this distributor was pushing wasn't huge, but it was large enough that it should have been worthwhile to continue working with them. The problem, however, was that this particular distributor was notoriously bad about paying for what they sold. Each order they fulfilled would result in multiple attempts on our part to collect the small amount of money we were owed. We would have to call, send certified letters, and so forth. In the end, the amount of time we were spending trying to collect our payments was more trouble than it was worth, and we dropped the account. Our calculation was simple: our time was better spent on people who are easy to deal with and who pay their bills.

4. Realize that you can never make EVERYONE happy.

EXECUTIVE SUMMARY: Just because someone is mad and complaining does not make them right. It is fact of life that the more people you deal with, the less likely it will be that you can make *everyone* happy. Listen to all the negative feedback you get. Where you are wrong, change your ways and make amends. If you are not wrong, however, and you can't meet a customer's request without taking an unacceptable cost, don't be afraid to stand by your beliefs. Trying to please everyone may mean you end up pleasing no one, and that's not the best way to run a business.

* * *

Many years ago, we were running one of our annual conferences, which usually is attended by 600 to 700 people. Jim had just started working for me, and he came up to me, fairly distressed, because he had just been chewed out by an attendee. As it turned out, this attendee was upset because we had substituted one of our scheduled speakers with another equally qualified speaker. Jim had explained to the client that the first speaker had had a family emergency, which was why he was unable to attend the conference. Jim also mentioned that he had listened to the substitute's talk and thought it was superb, but his efforts to mollify the customer were to no avail. The customer was extremely disappointed and irate.

I took Jim aside into a private area, looked him in the eye, and told him, "There are two things I want you to always remember. It's very important. First, you can't make everyone happy. We have 700 people here. This is the only person that has complained, and 699 people *didn't* complain. It's probably the customer, not us. Second, just because someone is mad at you and yelling at you doesn't mean that they are right." The point I was trying to make is this: just because someone is unhappy with you does not mean that you have done anything wrong. There could be all kinds of reasons why somebody is mad at you that do not involve your doing anything wrong. There could have been a misunderstanding. The person who is mad at you could just be having a bad day. The person could be a jerk. The important lesson here, of course, is that you should not run out and change everything you are doing just because one person (who might be an outlier) complained.

Here's another example. We were teaching one of our courses for expert witnesses a few years ago, and we were about ten minutes into the course when we saw a hand raised in the back of the room. We called on the attendee, and a man stood up, looking quite angry. He started going on and on about how our course was not helpful and did not meet his needs. Keep in mind that this was a two-day course, and we were only *ten minutes* into the first session. With the lesson I had taught Jim many years ago in the back of my mind, I listened to the man and took note of his accent. When he had finished, I paused about two seconds, looked straight at him, and asked, "Are you from New York or New Jersey?" The answer came back, "Long Island." The whole class laughed, and that was the last complaint we heard from this challenging customer over the course of the next two days. As you can see, I had used humor to diffuse a potentially problematic situation. I knew the person was being unreasonable, and I didn't want to get in a long debate with him or encourage more disruption. The goal, of course, was to focus on keeping the 49 normal people in the room happy, not to cater to an outlier that could ruin everyone's experience. To take on this one outlier would have been a mistake that jeopardized the experience of the 49 good customers we had.

Here's one final example of a similar occurrence. Very recently we were teaching another course for expert witnesses. As part of our teaching model, we perform mock cross-examinations on our attendees so that they can learn in a hands-on manner. In this particular course, a nurse came up to me before class with a request. She was going to be testifying in an important jury trial soon. Could I aggressively cross-examine her in front of the group so that she could be adequately prepared? I agreed and did.

The room was filled with 80 expert witnesses from across the country. You could hear a pin drop as I ripped the nurse up and down with the mock cross-examination. Then, about half-way through the 20-minute demonstration, an attendee stood up in the back and shouted out in an angry voice, "Don't you think she's had enough? Give it a break." On hearing this, I had to make a split-second decision. I thought the demo was highly instructive. In addition, the person I was cross-examining had asked for this, so she certainly wasn't going to complain. So I turned to the audience and asked in a low-key voice, "How many people are learning from this demo?" Seventy-nine hands shot up. Not only that, but a bunch of attendees started heckling the person that had interrupted me and were yelling, "Sit down and shut up!" What I had done was refuse to sacrifice the value and experience of the overwhelming majority of our clients for the sake of one outlier. Just because this person complained didn't make him right. I remembered that it is simply impossible to make everyone happy.

5. Don't say no. Focus on what you CAN do to help the unhappy customer.

EXECUTIVE SUMMARY: Oftentimes a customer will complain, and you will not be able to say "yes" to them. In these situations, try to avoid saying "no" and instead focus on what you *can* do to help them with their problem. You will probably find that a helpful attitude is much more effective than telling your customer "no."

* * *

One of the first things that I—and, later, Jim—learned about dealing with our toddlers was to be careful when using the word "no." There are two obvious problems with saying "no" to a two-year-old. First, they will start using the word on you. Second, because they are toddlers, they are likely to freak out when you tell them "no." As any seasoned parent can tell you, instead of telling your toddler "no," you are much better off using the art of distraction on them. As such, when your toddler tells you, "Daddy, I want to watch TV," you don't say "no" and cause a meltdown. Instead, you propose a counteroffer: "Alex, do you remember this toy that Grandpa bought you? See the sounds it makes?" The idea, of course, is to avoid saying "no," distract them, and tell them "yes"—but to a different question.

We use the exact same technique when dealing with customer complaints. The last thing in the world we ever want to tell a customer is "no." Instead, our philosophy is to focus on what we *can* do for the customer, not on what we can't. More than 90 percent of the time, using this approach resolves sticky situations in a mutually satisfactory manner and makes the customer feel good about the resolution you have offered them.

We see the results of our customer service strategy all the time. For example, we have a very liberal cancellation policy for the courses that we run. If an attendee cancels their registration for one of our courses anywhere up to two weeks or so before the course begins, we will refund 100% of their money. (Try that with an airline.) Unfortunately, however, sometimes conflicts arise and attendees need to cancel their registration at the last minute. As is often the case, the attendee will then request a refund from us. We cannot refund their money, but we don't focus on that. Instead, we immediately focus on what we can do. We change the subject and tell them that we can give them a credit for the full amount of the tuition they paid to use toward a future class. Focusing on what we can do has been very effective. Most people are audibly relieved and happy when you tell them that you can give them a credit. You can imagine why. Given the way that many companies do business nowadays, the answer they were expecting was probably, "Tough luck, those are the rules, no refunds."

Here's another good example. We put on the majority of our programs at hotels. The hotels are convenient locations for these events, as most attendees come from out of town, and they can stay right on site, where the courses are. Many of our courses are quite popular, and often the hotels we hold them at sell out of sleeping rooms. When that happens, we get complaints from attendees who want to stay at the site hotel. We don't control the hotel, and we most certainly can't create extra rooms. But whatever we can do, we do. For example, we will tell the attendee that we will call the hotel and place them on a waiting list. We will send the attendee a list and description of nearby hotels. We'll even call the general manager of the hotel to see if anything can be done and to determine whether the hotel really is sold out. In sum, we offer to do what we can and focus on what we can do, not on what we can't do. This "can do" attitude is generally well received and much appreciated by our customers.

Of course, one way to avoid saying "no" to your customers is to remain open minded and figure out a way to say "yes" to them. The companies that go above and beyond to find a way to say "yes" to their customers build loyalty and gain customers for life. Here is an example of what we mean. When a guest staying at Gaylord Opryland admired the clock radio in her room, she inquired about purchasing one. These radios had been made exclusively for the hotel, but the hotel did not blow her off by telling her "no." When she later returned to her room, she found that the hotel staff had placed a second clock radio in her room, along with a note: "We hope you enjoy these spa sounds at home."

Closer to home, we deal with a hotel in Florida that has impressed us by finding ways to say "yes" to us. Both Jim and I like to work out in the morning, and both of us are early risers. This hotel's gym doesn't open until 8:00 a.m., which is a nonstarter for us, because we start teaching as early as 6:30 a.m. We made the hotel aware of this situation, and their response was, "No problem. What time would you like us to open the gym for you?" Now they open the gym at 4:00 a.m. whenever we are on site. We've been doing business with this hotel for many years and expect to continue doing so for many years into the future because that's how we like to be treated.

It's a pleasure doing business with flexible, reasonable companies, and it sucks to do business with inflexible, unreasonable companies—such as airlines and telecoms. We suggest that you be flexible, be reasonable, say "yes" when you can, and always focus on what you can do for the customer.

6. Let your customers off the hook.

EXECUTIVE SUMMARY: Many times you may have the right to treat your customers in a certain manner, but just because you have this right does not mean that you should exercise it. If you and your business have not been severely damaged by a customer and his/her actions, consider waiving your right to respond in the way in which you are entitled to. What you give up might just come back to you many times over in the form of improved brand reputation, bolstered customer loyalty, and increased future business.

* * *

Nobody likes arbitrary rules and regulations. Who wouldn't be frustrated if they went to buy a special promotional item only to learn that the sale had ended the day before? What people do like and appreciate very much is your willingness to be flexible and fair with them. Being flexible with people is just another simple and easy way to build a great brand for yourself and create passionately loyal customers.

Let me give you some examples of how we are flexible with our customers. As part of many of the courses we put on, we agree to review a piece of our attendees' work—such as a sample consulting report they have drafted—if it is submitted to us by a certain date. What often happens, however, is that people miss the deadline and send in their work materials late. Even worse, some customers are unaware of this aspect of our courses until they show up. While we are at the course or even many weeks after it has concluded, we will receive work review requests from these people. How do we handle this situation? There's no question that they were late in submitting their work materials. There's no question that agreeing to do this work will eat up our time. There's also no question that we are not contractually obligated to review their materials after the deadline has passed. We do so anyhow. The reason is simple: we want to be different. We do not want to be petty with people. We want to build our brand, and we treat our customers the same way that we would want to be treated if we were in their shoes. In turn, our customers are thrilled when we agree to provide them with services that they technically are not entitled to receive. Extending little gestures such as these to your customers is just another simple way to go beyond their expectations and distinguish your brand.[1]

---

[1] See Chapter 1 on Build a Superb Brand.

As mentioned in Chapter 4, we set specific deadlines as to when the sales promotions we are running expire, but we also set deadlines as to when customers can return products or services they have purchased for a full refund. For example, we typically sell our books with a 30-day, money-back guarantee. Without any question, however, we'll refund books that come back anywhere in that ballpark: 35, 40, even 45 days after the date of purchase. Again, our attitude is to not be petty with our customers. Sure, we need to protect ourselves with deadlines, rules, and fine print, but we never actually invoke these protections unless we really have to. Our customers appreciate the courtesies we extend.

Here's one final example. A few years ago, we were hired to teach a course for a certain organization. We signed a contract to seal the deal, but then, about two months later, the group called us up to tell us they couldn't go through with the course. Under the terms of the contract we had signed, we could have sued them for breach and won. We didn't even consider suing, however. The course was still many months off, and we had not yet started working on it. Furthermore, we had not turned away any business on those dates to take the gig, so we simply told the client, "No problem, we'll take it off our calendars." When they asked about a cancellation fee, our response was, "Don't worry about it. We haven't sunk any work into the course yet." Our response was shocking to them. It was also very well received, and the client was extremely appreciative. In fact, a few years later they hired us to teach additional courses for them.

* * *

The better you interact with your customers, the better your business will perform. Listen to your customers, get back to them right away, get rid of problem clients, focus on what you can do for them, and let your customers off the hook when you can. Of course, everything in your business will be helped if you manage yourself optimally. How to manage yourself more effectively is the focus of our next chapter.

Manage Yourself

You and the people you work with are human beings. How you conduct, manage, and take care of yourselves will greatly influence the success of your business. This chapter contains some of the pointers we have learned over the years with regards to better managing yourself.

1. Take care of yourself.

EXECUTIVE SUMMARY: People who are not feeling well can and will make potentially costly decisions and statements that they may end up deeply regretting. To avoid this risk, you should prioritize taking care of yourself as a key business asset. Make sure that you get enough sleep, exercise, eat enough, and take the time to go to see your doctor when necessary.

* * *

Jim was doing some research for me recently when I gave him the name of someone who was slated to speak at one of our conferences and suggested that Jim contact him. When Jim called him up, the speaker started screaming at him into the phone, "What do you mean you need more information? I've done enough for you already! I never should have got the [expletive] involved with you."

Jim called me up after the call ended, and he was pretty upset. He felt bad that he had set the speaker off. I told Jim not to worry about and it and gave him this advice, "He was probably just having a bad day." The next day, we got an e-mail from the speaker, who apologized for his behavior on the phone. He explained that he hadn't been sleeping because he had been taking care of a sick child. We sent him a nice note back, thanking him for his apology and stating that we totally understood. We also made a point of saying that we hoped his child would get better quickly. The point of the story is this: you are a vital business asset, and you really have to take care of yourself—which means you need to get enough sleep, eat enough, and see the doctor when necessary. People are funny. They will have their car regularly serviced, check their computers daily for viruses, and maintain all of their office equipment. But these same people often go years without getting a medical checkup and generally operate on too little sleep, eat poorly, and fail to get regular exercise. Remember: your car and computer equipment can be replaced. The owners, partners, or key persons in your company, however, are significant business assets that need to be protected, nurtured, and taken care of. As Tony Robbins, the motivational speaker, said, "The higher your energy level, the more efficient your body. The more efficient your body, the better you feel and the more you will use your talent to produce outstanding results." We couldn't agree more.

How much will it cost you if one of your key employees is down for months or forced to retire due to poor health? Who will replace her, and how much institutional knowledge, foresight, imagination, and creativity will be lost? Sure, you might sound macho talking about the long hours you log, your lack of vacations, and the fact you are on call 24 hours a day, seven days a week. But when you approach your work in this manner, you are not protecting and nurturing one of the core assets of your business: your mental and physical health and well-being. Even if you're the nicest person in business today, you can easily turn into a bear when you're not feeling well. You can also say and do things that you will regret, neither of which is good for your business. Let us give you a couple of examples from our own experiences.

Many years ago, Jim and I were on our way to teach a course in New Orleans. We were scheduled to take the first flight out of Boston in the morning, and we arrived at the airport two hours prior to our departure time, as recommended. To get to the airport in time, I had to wake up at 3:00 a.m. While we were at the airport, we patiently made our way through security and waited at the gate for our plane to board. Fortunately, our plane boarded on time. Unfortunately, however, we sat on the plane at the gate for an hour because, as the pilot explained over the PA system, "There was a problem with the flight's paperwork." Finally we took off, but we arrived at our layover airport in Charlotte one hour late. Of course, our connecting flight was not held (we missed it by five minutes), and so we were now stuck in Charlotte. Given the situation that we found ourselves in, the good news was that flights were departing Charlotte en route to New Orleans every two hours. The bad news was that the airline refused to put us on any of those flights. Instead, they said that we could be seated on the last flight out to New Orleans that day, which left at 7:30 p.m. After about five hours of waiting, I decided that I just couldn't take it anymore. I demanded to talk to somebody in authority. What happened next was not a high point in my life.

STEVE: We missed our connecting flight because of your negligence in filling out paperwork. There's another flight going out to New Orleans at 3:30 p.m., and I want to be on it. We shouldn't have to wait here until 7:30 p.m.

REPRESENTATIVE: Well, sir, I'm sorry, but we just can't do that. That flight is full.

STEVE: It's not that you *can't* do it. It's that you *won't* do it. You do this all the time. You know how to get people off a plane.

REPRESENTATIVE: What do you mean?

STEVE: Offer somebody on the plane a free ticket if they agree to take a later flight.

REPRESENTATIVE: I'm sorry, sir, but we can't do that.

STEVE: Are you in customer service?

REPRESENTATIVE: Yes.

STEVE: Well I ain't getting any [expletive] service!

At this point, Jim grabbed and restrained me, and the representative turned his back on me and left. If Jim had not grabbed me, there's a chance that I might have done something I would have later regretted, but what had happened was clear. I was dog tired. I hadn't eaten. I was having a whopper of a bad day. And all of this almost cost me a lot. What I should have done was eaten lunch, taken a break, and then talked to the representative. Instead, I almost ended up in trouble—and not in New Orleans.

Here's one more quick story that can show the comically bad decisions that sleep-deprived people sometimes make. Jim and I were teaching a seminar in Las Vegas. Because of an impending blizzard back home on the East Coast, we decided to cancel our flight, which was scheduled to leave at 8:00 a.m. the next morning, and instead take an 11:45 p.m. red eye that night in an attempt to beat the storm. Now, keep in mind as you read through the rest of this story that Jim and I were still functioning on East Coast time during this debacle. We were jet-lagged and had gotten up that morning at 3:00 a.m. We had taught all day. We were exhausted. Nevertheless, around 10:00 p.m., Jim and I hopped into our rental car, with Jim behind the wheel, and headed out to the airport. When we neared the airport, we got lost trying to find the rental car return and ended up behind a line of about 100 cabs. We finally found our way out of this logjam and back into the airport, but unfortunately, because of the fog cloud Jim was in, we ended up right back behind the cabs. I was exhausted and could offer little help of any kind.

I looked over at Jim, who really didn't look so good. He looked as though he were about to collapse, and he asked me in all seriousness, "Can't we just leave the [expletive] car here with the keys in it and a note? I'm sure the rental car company will get it back." I spent the next five minutes debating with Jim, a lawyer and a summa cum laude college graduate, about why we couldn't just leave the rental car where it was sitting. Finally, I took over the driving and was able find the rental car return. The lesson here, of course, is this: don't try to go about your daily life when you are exhausted and not feeling well. Doing so could lead you to make foolish and costly mistakes that could impact you and your company.

Here is one final vignette. We were flying back to Boston from Florida late one night after a grueling four days of teaching. The plane was, as usual, late, and we were all dog tired. After we boarded and had settled in, a petite young woman stopped near our row and tried to get her luggage up into the overhead storage space, but she was having trouble. She looked at Jim and asked, "Would it be possible to give me some help?" Jim looked at her, frowned, and snarled back, "I'm already strapped in." He then took his cap and pulled it down on top of his face. I was flabbergasted and leapt up to assist the woman. Jim's unfortunate reaction was just another classic example of a normally pleasant, polite person acting regretfully when he wasn't feeling well.

2. Be persistent.

EXECUTIVE SUMMARY: The nice thing about persistence is that it is completely within your control. You may or may not be born with extraordinary talent, but everyone can be persistent. Often times, persistence is actually more important than talent when it comes to achieving success. You can be as persistent as your willpower allows you to be. For this reason, persistence is a key element of success and often pays huge rewards.

* * *

In the movie *Wall Street*, Bud Fox (played by Charlie Sheen) finally scores an appointment to meet with Gordon Gekko (played by Michael Douglas), a Wall Street big leaguer who is worth hundreds of millions of dollars and is not easily impressed. So, why did he agree to meet with Fox? What had impressed him? It was Fox's persistence. Said Gekko, "This is the kid, calls me fifty-nine days in a row, wants to be a player. There ought to be a picture of you in the dictionary under persistence, kid."

Gordon's reaction to Fox is understandable. After all, persistence is a rare and extremely valuable skill. In fact, some of the most successful people of all time have only been able to succeed because they were remarkably persistent. Take Thomas Edison, for example. The famed inventor said it well when he commented on his persistence: "Nearly every man who develops an idea works at it up to the point where it looks impossible, and then gets discouraged. That's not the place to become discouraged." Or look at J. K. Rowling, the author of the Harry Potter book series. Even though she was rejected by the first 12 publishing houses she approached, Rowling persisted and eventually amassed a fortune worth hundreds of millions of dollars. In a similar vein, John Grisham's first manuscript was initially rejected by numerous publishers. He persisted, however, and got his start selling his books out of the trunk of his car—and he later became one of the most successful novelists of all time.

As the preceding examples make clear, there are many things in business that are not within your control. You can't control the economy. You can't make people buy your products or services. You can't control governmental action that can negatively affect your business. You can, however, maintain total control over the persistence with which you approach your work. The only limitation to how persistent you are is your own stamina and will power. For our part, Jim and I pride ourselves on our persistence. Indeed, a number of our business successes only occurred because we were approached our work with persistence.

Here's an example. Many years ago, Jim and I decided to start a writing conference for physicians, and the only way we could see this conference succeeding was if we found a *New York Times* bestselling physician novelist to teach the course. This proposition was a bit problematic, however, as there were maybe five or six people in the world who fulfilled our teaching requirements. Luckily, one such person—we'll call him Doctor Jones—lived right here in Massachusetts. In fact, Doctor Jones actually had previously practiced medicine in the small, Cape Cod town where our company was based, so I figured he would be our best bet. Finding out how to contact Jones, however, wasn't easy. After all, bestselling authors don't just put their phone numbers in the white pages.

After researching the matter for a few weeks, I was finally able to track Doctor Jones down. I called him up but could not reach him. I left five different messages for him, but I never got a call back. Finally, I caught him when he inadvertently picked up the phone. I quickly began to explain that we wanted to put on a writing conference that featured him as the star trainer, that we would pay him handsomely, and that we would massively promote both him and his books. But before I could even finish my two-minute pitch, he hung up on me with a curt, "I'm sorry, I'm on deadline, I have no time." Now, most normal people would have stopped there. Not me. I called him a few days later, and he picked up again. This time he actually let me complete my sentence before saying, "Talk to my agent," and hanging up on me again.

I persisted. About a week later, I called him back and asked if I could meet with him for 15 minutes at his convenience. Once he met with me, I told him, I wouldn't bother him any further. Jones agreed, and when we met, he had just finished his latest blockbuster novel and was no longer on deadline. As such, he was in a much better mood and frame of mind than he had been when we had spoken over the phone. He was very gracious, agreed to teach the course, and gave us many ideas for improving it. Then he went on to teach the course annually for many years thereafter. The course, for its part, has been mutually beneficial for both Doctor Jones and me, and we have become good friends over the years. And to think! Our business relationship and friendship were only made possible because of the extraordinary amount of persistence that I exhibited.

Many young people today get a bad rap for being lazy slackers. The truth of the matter, however, is that some of our future leaders are remarkably persistent and anything but lazy. On March 16, 2010, for example, *The Wall Street Journal* featured a story about A. K. Barrett-Hart, a 22-year-old Harvard undergraduate who had approached her professor with the idea of writing about the subprime mortgage collapse and collateralized debt obligations. Her professor, however, discouraged her thesis choice and gave her reason after reason as to why it was not a feasible discussion topic. Nevertheless, Ms. Hart was persistent and would not take no for an answer. She utilized innovative research techniques and published her thesis—and the rest, as they say, is history. Her thesis was awarded summa cum laude honors and the Harvard Hoopes prize for outstanding scholarly work, and it is considered a seminal work on the mortgage crisis. Meanwhile, Ms. Hart is off and running in a stellar career in finance. The lesson here is clear: don't listen to the people who tell you that you can't do something when you know in your heart that you can.

Here's a final example. We only landed one of the most valuable distributors we have ever worked with because we were persistent. Even though I had called the organization dozens of times to ask them to meet with me, I did not receive one positive response. Finally, I decided to ask a friend that was connected to an executive at this organization if he could set up a brief meeting with me at their out-of-state headquarters. The meeting was a success, and we ended up doing a huge amount of mutually profitable business together—a result that, once again, was only made possible because of the persistence we had exhibited.

3. Don't wait until the last minute.

EXECUTIVE SUMMARY: Although it may sound pessimistic, you should always expect that something will go wrong in your business. Then, when something inevitably does go wrong, you will be in far better shape to deal with the problem than you would be if you had waited until the last minute to address it. Having extra time when you need it will make your life easier and your business more successful.

* * *

If we have learned one lesson over the years, it is the importance of proactively mitigating potential problems before they arise. Anybody who owns or manages their own business can tell you that, despite your best efforts, you will experience unexpected problems. As such, you must expect the unexpected and plan accordingly. If you do, you will have plenty of time to address problems in a suitable manner when they inevitably arise. If you don't, however, and you wait until the last minute to address problems as they arise, what once were small problems can quickly escalate into extremely harmful problems. For this reason, you should always account for the maxim that what can go wrong *will go* wrong—and it will usually do so at the worst possible time.

Here's a good example of what I mean. Recently, we asked a high-powered executive at a large international information technology company—we'll call him Jerry—to give a speech for us at one of our conferences. We asked Jerry to send us his PowerPoint presentation prior to the start of the conference so that we could ensure that it was compatible with our computing system and was all loaded up and ready to go. Jerry responded to our request by saying that he needed to use his own computer for the presentation, as his was better than ours. After attempting but failing to talk Jerry out of using his own computer for his presentation, we suggested that he meet us in the presentation room early in the morning to determine how his computer would work with our system. Jerry refused, as he was quite confident everything would work just fine, so no testing was needed. He also pointed out quite emphatically that he was a computer expert.

Jerry's talk was scheduled for 3:00 p.m., and he arrived ten minutes prior to his presentation and began to set up his computer. The room was filled with over 100 people, and as they sat and watched, Jerry tried and tried, but he just couldn't get his computer to work. (Keep in mind, Jerry is a computer executive.) Our entire staff was on hand to help him, but while we were trying to fix Jerry's computer woes, the audience was getting more and more anxious. After a few minutes had passed, a good number of them just gave up and left. Finally, around 3:20 p.m., we were able to get everything working, and Jerry was able to begin his talk.

In Jerry's case, what should have been a little computer problem turned into a big, embarrassing problem because he had waited until the last minute to try his computer out with our projection system. The situation was particularly frustrating because it was 100 percent avoidable. Had Jerry just come down early to test out his computer, as we had requested him to, we would have had plenty of time to work out the computing kinks while he was having breakfast, and the conference would have not suffered any interruption.

The situation with Jerry notwithstanding, one significant reason that we have been so successful in business is that we make it a point to *never* wait until the last minute to ensure that all of our work-related ducks are in a row. The payoff of our preparedness has been substantial. For example, we are often asked to speak at conferences and training sessions, and as a condition of these types of gigs, we are usually given a few weeks or months to send in our written speech outline. Despite the ample amount of time that we are generally given to complete the outline, however, we almost always send it in writing within a few days of booking the assignment. This way, we do not have to put the outline on a to-do list, nor do we have to worry about it. In addition, by sending in our materials so quickly, we demonstrate how easy we are to deal with, which results in more assignments. Contrast our behavior with that of others, who put the outline on their to-do list, procrastinate, miss the deadline, and then call up the conference organizers to ask what the drop-dead deadline is. Who would you be more likely to hire in the future?

Here are a couple of recent examples of how purposefully *not* waiting until the last minute has been a great help to us in our business. We are contractually bound by our publisher to submit annual updates to a legal text we coauthored by a certain date each year. This particular year, that date was February 15. To assist us in our research for this project, we hired a law clerk, and because the materials were due to our publisher on February 15 and it would take us about a week to compile them once the research phase of the project was completed, we gave our clerk a research due date—not of February 7 or 8—but of January 1. The reason for this was simple: we wanted to build in additional time in case something went wrong—and it's a good thing we did, because this particular year, something did go very wrong. Right after our law clerk delivered his research to us, his father fell ill and was in critical condition for many weeks before he eventually passed away. Our clerk was at his bedside throughout this painful ordeal. Because we had purposefully built extra time into our work schedule, however, we were able to deliver our manuscript well in advance of our deadline. Planning ahead and building extra time into our schedule made all the difference for us.

Here's one final example. We earned a contract a little while back to teach one of our courses on the West Coast. The contract was quite lucrative and would net us about $50,000 for one weekend's worth of teaching. About two weeks before the course, however, I blew my knee out while working out. I couldn't walk, couldn't travel, couldn't teach, and needed knee replacement surgery. Unfortunately, Jim was also unavailable to teach the course because he was scheduled to teach for another client over those dates, so I needed to find a substitute who would do a good job. Luckily, I had not waited until the last minute to prepare for the course. When I contacted a lawyer that used to work for me to see if he would teach for me, I was able to honestly tell him that all the prep work for the course had been completed and I could send him all the course materials that day. Fortunately, the lawyer agreed to teach in my place. After all, he would only be subject to a small learning curve, as I would be sending him everything he needed to teach the course on a silver platter. The bottom line here is that I was able to find a substitute easily because I had not waited until the last minute to prepare for the course. More important, the substitute was able to rapidly get up to speed and teach a good course because I had done much of the prep work for it already, and the client was saved because I had planned for the possibility that something would go wrong and did not wait until the last minute.

4. Sleep on important decisions.

EXECUTIVE SUMMARY: An excellent way to make better decisions is to sleep on them. Sleeping on your decisions can help minimize the emotion involved in your decision-making process and lead to decisions that are more likely to be in your best long-term interest. We have found that the most beneficial times to sleep on your decisions is when someone has made you angry, when you are emotionally involved in a course of action, or when you are searching for a solution and sense that the answer lies somewhere in your own subconscious.

* * *

Any good trial attorney or marketing professional will tell you that people ultimately base their decisions on their emotions. A juror may vote a particular way on a case because she feels sorry for one of the parties involved. A person may make a purchasing decision based on what he wants—and not what he needs. In short, it is common for human beings to make emotional decisions. The problem, of course, is that emotional decisions often turn out to be poorly considered and come with needlessly adverse consequences. As such, you often will find that you regret business decisions that were made not with your brain but with your heart. To ensure that your important decisions are well thought out and not overly clouded with emotion, we suggest that you sleep on them. The next day, you will find that you are refreshed and may have gained additional insight into the decision-making process. You also will be more analytical and removed from the heat of passion, which can cloud your judgment.

There are three main circumstances under which we suggest you sleep on your decisions. The first circumstance is when someone has made you angry. If you're in business long enough, plenty of people will tick you off, be they employees who were lazy, customers who are unreasonable, vendors who don't stand by their work, or inflexible bureaucrats who are making your life miserable. The list is almost endless. The key, however, is to not allow the negative emotions you feel towards these people to unduly influence your decision-making process.

The second common occurrence where we suggest you sleep on a decision is when there is a large or potentially large amount of money at stake. What is most dangerous is when you are emotionally invested in a potential course of action because you have worked hard to see it through or have been its major proponent. In such cases, allowing your emotional investments to blind you to rationality can easily contribute to poor decision making—which is why, in these types of situations, we make it a rule to sleep on our decisions. Only if the decision still looks great in the morning will we proceed. You have read many examples in this book of either Jim or me getting emotionally invested in one of our ideas. We will fight for our idea because it was ours, and we want it to succeed. Indeed, we have made an incredible number of bad decisions over the years by allowing ourselves to become emotionally caught up in a given course of action and only seeing its potential upside. Fortunately, however, we eventually learned that sleeping on important decisions can counter the clouding effects of our emotional investment in a course of action.

The third and final type of decision we often like to sleep on involves problem solving. Many times, when we are discussing a certain course of action, we will identify the presence of a significant problem, such as which pitch we should use when selling a product, who exactly to target in a direct marketing campaign, what to name a new product, how to resolve a conflict amongst our staff, and so on. During these types of discussions, we often cannot put our finger on the solution to the problem, but we really sense that it exists somewhere in our subconscious. When this happens, we often times sleep on the problem, and the answer will come to us in the middle of the night, while driving, or while we are working out.

Here is an example of what I mean. Jim and I were kicking around an idea for a new book for expert witnesses, and we thought about calling it *Writing Your Expert Witness Report*. The problem, however, was that we both knew something was missing. The topic was too narrow and boring. Furthermore, the book sounded like a grammatical tome on writing, which is not at all what we had in mind. We both slept on the problem, and the next day the solution leapt out: why not expand the concept to *Writing and Defending Your Expert Witness Report*? Doing so would make the book more expansive and increase its appeal to experts who are worried about defending their reports. We wrote the book with the new title, and it is now a perennial bestseller for us—all because we had the patience to sleep on it and let our subconscious solve the problem for us.

5. Have confidence in yourself.

EXECUTIVE SUMMARY: Having confidence in yourself has many benefits and is an extremely valuable business asset. If you appear to have confidence in yourself, others will follow you and believe what you say. Confidence can also help you get through crises and rough patches. Finally, confidence can open many doors for you, because when you have confidence in yourself, you will be more likely to try something new.

* * *

I did not do well in high school. I had a 72 average, and I would only do whatever homework I could finish in the 15 minutes I spent in home room. I cared much more about sports than academics. By my junior year, my good Jewish mother was becoming quite worried about the future of her child. In fact, she was so concerned that she set up a meeting with me, herself, my dad, and the high school guidance counselor. My mom and dad both took time off from work (without pay) for the big meeting.

Prior to the meeting, my mother was very upset about what she thought was going to happen to me on account of my mediocre grades. My father, for his part, was not at all happy that both he and my mother had had to take time off from work for this meeting. He also was quite upset that he had to put a tie on for the meeting, and his frustration was making my mother even more upset. The whole situation was quite tense for all concerned—except me. I thought it was all a big joke.

The guidance counselor began the meeting by explaining that he really couldn't put his finger on what was happening with me. The school had given me two

IQ tests, and I had scored very well on both of them. The meeting went on and on and reached no conclusions as to why I was underachieving. Meanwhile, my folks were becoming more and more upset. Finally, almost out of desperation, the guidance counselor turned to me and asked, "Steve, do you have any idea why you are not doing better in school?" All eyes turned to me. I paused for dramatic effect and responded, "Sure, I'm saving myself for graduate school." The guidance counselor paused a moment or two, shook his head a little bit, looked my parents right in the eye, and responded, "Mr. and Mrs. Babitsky, I wouldn't worry too much about Steve. He'll be just fine." Why did he respond in this manner? Because the guidance counselor clearly understood the incredible force and value of my confidence—the same confidence that is paying dividends in my business dealings today. You'd be amazed at what you can accomplish when you have confidence in yourself.

Jim learned the hard way how important it was for him to have confidence in himself. When Jim was working as the most junior lawyer at a certain Boston law firm, he was sent—as the sacrificial lamb—to argue every hopeless motion or case. If the judge had marked a case for no further continuances (delays), Jim would have to go in and ask for a continuance. When Jim's client had rear-ended someone else, Jim would have to go in and argue that the accident was the other driver's fault. You get the idea.

When Jim first approached these arguments, he would do so halfheartedly. He didn't believe in the cases and could barely push them with a straight face. The result was predictable— he always lost. However, Jim quickly recognized that he was never going to win any of these long-shot cases unless he appeared to believe in them, so he started arguing them as though he was confident in his opinion. Once he made this switch, an amazing thing started happening: he actually started winning these long-shot cases! The reason was simple: people were much more likely to believe what Jim was saying because he appeared to have confidence in his arguments.

Having confidence in yourself can be a huge asset for four main reasons. First, when you exhibit confidence in yourself, you will be better able to persuade others. For example, many years ago I helped form a nonprofit professional certification board for physicians, and I was on the organization's board of directors with ten high-powered doctors. We were trying to decide on an important course of action and spent a full day locked in a conference room. The discussion drifted back and forth without focus, and many of the doctors were talking over one another. I didn't say a word over the course of many hours. This was the longest I had sat still without saying anything since my Bar Mitzvah! Finally, late in the afternoon, one of the doctors turned to me and said, "Steve, we haven't heard from you yet today. What do you think?" I responded in a very calm but confident manner and told him exactly what I thought of the discussion and how I believed we should proceed. The room was dead silent as I spoke. I went to the white board and wrote a five-point plan of action. In short order, the board members agreed to everything I had proposed, and the drifting and bickering stopped. In effect, the confidence I had shown in myself and what I believed allowed me to lead a group of very intelligent and opinionated professionals.

Second, confidence immensely assists in your ability to solve problems. Consider the following example. A few years ago, when I was running one of our conferences, I began to introduce a speaker who was scheduled to give a one-hour talk. It was only at that moment, however, that I discovered that the speaker had not shown up. The room was filled with 200 people who were expecting a talk. Fortunately, I was familiar with the topic of the discussion, so I asked one of the attendees in the front row if I could borrow his seminar book, which contained the no-show speaker's outline. I then proceeded to, on the fly, wing a substitute talk that was very well received. I was only able to do so because I had the confidence to try and because the confidence I had exhibited while presenting gave me credibility with the audience.

Third, confidence will help get you through crises. Every business will face its fair share of crises. That's just a fact of life. When you are confident in yourself, your abilities, and your decision-making powers, however, you will quickly realize that you have faced many worse problems in the past. Once you recognize that you have gotten through difficult problems in the past, you will be able to get through the problem that you are currently facing.

Finally, confidence can open many doors for you. Consider this. I retired from a lucrative and very stressful law practice when I was only 44 years old. At the time, I was making a very large amount of money. I was also running my publishing and seminar business on a part-time basis, almost as a hobby. When I first left the practice of law, I got many, many calls from colleagues, and all of them contained the same general message: are you nuts? How could you just walk away? What are you going to do to provide for your family? The answer to each and every one of these questions was that I was confident that I could turn my hobby business into a lucrative, full-time business. The confidence I exhibited in my ability to reinvent myself as a businessperson has changed my life. It allowed me to get out from a career that was probably going to kill me with stress and switch to one that I love—running my family business. In sum, the confidence I showed in myself was a key to my success.

I still get phone calls from past colleagues. Now, however, they ask different questions: can you tell me how I can do what you did? I am miserable practicing law, how can I get out? How much fun is it working with your children?

6. Don't be afraid to fail.

EXECUTIVE SUMMARY: Do not be afraid to fail. If you are afraid to fail, you will become paralyzed, and that paralysis will destroy your business. Understand that many things in business will not work out as you had hoped—and don't take it personally when they don't. That's just a part of being in business. If you learn from your failures and keep plugging away, you will find that the sum of your successes will far outweigh the sum of your failures.

***

Jim used to serve as a liquor commissioner in the city where he grew up. One day, while he was at his law office, he received a call from someone who identified himself as an official of the Massachusetts State Lottery Commission. Jim lit up when he heard this and excitedly asked, "Did I win? Did I win?" The official quickly replied, "Did you play?" The answer to this question was no, Jim hadn't played. Therefore, there was no chance that he could have won. As it turned out, the reason for the official's call had to do with a bar's Keno machine, but the point of this story is that in business, you can't win if you don't try.

Not every endeavor you undertake in business will be a success. Many, if not most of your ventures, products, campaigns, and ideas will fail. The key to success in business, however, is realizing that, even though you will experience failures from time to time, you should continue to attempt new undertakings. In sum, you should not be afraid to fail. Contrary to popular opinion, failure is not necessarily bad for a company. As long as you don't bet the farm, controlled, intelligent failures are a crucial part of innovation and product development at many companies. Scott Anthony, the managing director of the consulting firm Innosight, expressed his thoughts about failure well: "Figuring out how to master this process of failing fast and failing cheap and fumbling toward success is probably the most important thing companies have to get good at."

Creating a culture at your company in which innovation and controlled, intelligent failures are accepted is a crucial part of any business's success. The old saying that we learn more from our mistakes than we do from our successes is a true and valuable lesson to remember. Let me give you a simple example. We mail over one million pieces of direct marketing materials annually at our company. In one of our many mailings, we needed to know if our teaser copy (a few words printed on the outside of the envelope) actually helped sales or made them worse, so we ran a test and sent out a 10,000-piece mailing using envelopes without teaser copy. The response to our test was dismal. The response rate (sales per thousand) was about 25 percent of what we received when we sent out envelopes that included teaser copy. Although we were certainly a bit disappointed with the results, we had conducted a controlled, valuable, intelligent failure. We also learned a valuable lesson that confirmed what we had suspected. We can now work on tweaking our teaser copy to generate even more sales.

Keep in mind that some of the largest and most well-known companies have survived and thrived after even colossal "failures". Coca Cola had its "New Coke"; Ford Motor Company had its "Edsel"; Sony had "Betamax"; and McDonalds had its "Arch Deluxe". All of these companies have survived and thrived after their failures.

Defining what is a failure and what is a success may not be as simple as it looks. Take one of the greatest baseball players of all time, Babe Ruth, for example. He is famous for starting his baseball career as a highly successful pitcher before switching to batting and hitting 714 home runs (without steroids). Ruth was phenomenally successful at bat and achieved one of the highest lifetime batting averages in history at .342, but he also holds the record for the most strikeouts. When asked about his 1,330 strikeouts, Ruth famously said, "Every strikeout brings me closer to a home run." In the end, Babe Ruth is not remembered for his strikeouts or failed at bats; instead, he is revered as one of the most successful sluggers of all time.

In a similar vein, there is a great and successful trial lawyer in Boston who I interviewed with for a job many years ago. During the interview, the lawyer proudly told me that he had lost more trials than any other lawyer in Boston. Of course, he had also won more trials than anyone else and was wildly successful. Unquestionably, a large part of the reason this lawyer was so successful was that he wasn't afraid to fail. Like Babe Ruth, this lawyer was not known for his losses; he was known for his wins.

Contrast this successful lawyer with another lawyer—we'll call him Ted—that Jim and I know. After practicing law for about 15 years, Ted brought to trial what he thought was a very good personal injury case—and he lost. This experience severely shook Ted's confidence, and he became so gun shy that in the 20 years since, Ted has never again tried another case. His fear of failure has caused him to settle cases for lesser amounts so that he can avoid the risk of losing at trial. The problem, of course, is that Ted's confidence should not have been so shaken by his loss. When you try cases, sometimes you win, sometimes you lose. There are many reasons why lawyers lose at trial, including bad facts, an unattractive client, difficult judges, and so on. Unfortunately, however, because he let the fear of loss take over, Ted's law practice has been severely damaged.

Being overly afraid to fail is toxic to any business. If you are afraid to fail, you will refrain from trying anything new, and if you refrain from trying anything new, your business will underperform. Sooner or later, you may even go out of business. The key to success, then, is to undertake new endeavors in a way that gives them the best chance to succeed—not in a way that forces you to bet the farm. In other words, expect that your new venture might not work out as planned and prepare your business to handle the resultant fallout. Expect that you might fail, build a certain amount of failure into your equation for success, and don't take it personally when you do fail. To win a war, you don't need to win every battle. When Thomas Edison was perfecting the light bulb, he said, "I have not failed. Not once. I've just discovered 10,000 ways that didn't work." Likewise, to be successful in business, you don't need to win every battle you undertake. Instead, you must learn from your mistakes and never let the fear of failure inhibit you from trying a new product, venture, or sales or management technique.

* * *

The better you manage yourself, the more successful your business will be. Take care of yourself. Be persistent. Don't wait until the last minute. Sleep on important decisions. Have confidence in yourself, and don't be afraid to fail. A further personal skill that will greatly help your business succeed is your ability to effectively negotiate. How to be a better negotiator is the focus of our final chapter.

Become a Better Negotiator

Every penny you save as a result of negotiating directly benefits your bottom line. This chapter contains advice for becoming a better negotiator.

1. In a win–win relationship, you win.

EXECUTIVE SUMMARY: In many instances, you are better off negotiating a win–win solution rather than forcing the party you are negotiating with into a marginal deal. You win in win–win deals because they allow you to build long-term, stable, and mutually beneficial relationships. You lose in win–lose deals because they cause you to leave a sour taste in the other party's mouth and potentially poison the well, thus preventing you from engaging in future business deals with them.

* * *

We have been on both sides of win–lose negotiations, and we have learned that it is rarely in your best interests to negotiate a deal whereby you win and the other party loses. In fact, we can say with confidence that, where possible, you will be better off negotiating a win–win arrangement. Why? Because win–win agreements can lead to the very same type of long-term relationships that have been so helpful to our business.[1] Think about the relationship you have

---

[1] See Chapter 5 for more on the benefits of long-term business relationships.

with your employees, for example. There is no question that, when hiring a team member, you can often get them to agree to take less pay than they want, do a job they don't want to do, and work under conditions that they don't want to work under. This is especially true when jobs are painfully scarce. Employers hold the cards and can play them freely if they so choose, but we don't subscribe to this short-sighted philosophy. We have found that when we make our employees happy, they win, but we also win because we are able to retain a loyal, hard-working staff with deep institutional knowledge. Making your employees miserable because you have the negotiating leverage to do so is not a strategy that we have found to be helpful. Doing so increases the likelihood that your employees will be less-than-well motivated and will spend all of their time looking for a better job. Then, as soon as the first new job opportunity presents itself, they will bolt, leaving you with instability and a less experienced workforce.

Let me give you an example. For many years, we worked with a graphic design company that was owned and operated by a man we'll call Simon. Simon was a talented designer, but his business ultimately failed after he developed a substance abuse problem and was divorced by his spouse. We kept in touch with Simon and tried to support him through his hard times, and a few years later he was back on his feet and working in someone else's marketing department. We needed his graphic design services, so we called Simon up to see if he would consider doing some freelance design work for us. He said that he would, but he also stated that he wanted to talk to us about his fee, so we started to negotiate with Simon. It was rather a strange negotiation, however. Simon started by explaining that because he no longer was running a big company with overhead, he could do the same work as before for a much lower hourly rate. We told him, no, we'd pay him the same as before, which is what he was worth. Simon again stated that he thought that his old fee was too much, but we told him he was worth it. We shouldn't get a windfall just because his company went under, we explained. Eventually, Simon agreed.

Simon has been doing graphic design work for us under this arrangement for a number of years now. He's happy, as he's being well paid, and we're happy because we're getting good work, stability, institutional knowledge, and the same price we received from Simon when he ran his own company. For us, the many benefits associated with maintaining this long-term relationship more than justified our insisting on a win–win deal.

Here's another, somewhat counterintuitive example that demonstrates how beneficial win–win arrangements can be for both parties involved in a given negotiation. We work with distributors to sell our products, but instead of negotiating to pay them as little as possible for their services, we pay them as much as possible, that is, fifty percent. Why would we do this? The more we pay them, the more incentive they have to push our products as hard as they can.

We have seen time and time again that we're better off trying to find win–win arrangements when we are involved in negotiations. After all, when you negotiate a win–win solution and refrain from taking advantage of your counterparty, you lay the groundwork for both a long-term relationship and positive word of mouth. Here's another example that illustrates this point. Many years ago, we were asked to present a course for a professional society, so we negotiated a fee that amounted to 50 percent of tuition receipts. The course was extremely well attended, and as a result, our fee turned out to be much higher that anyone had really anticipated. The course also was well received, and everybody agreed that we did a good job. As such, we were invited back to repeat the course the next year, but the society insisted that we take less money. They felt that they had gotten a raw deal on the first course. In their opinion, we had been overpaid and they had been underpaid. In the end, we refused to take less than we had received the first time the conference was held, and the society never hired us to put on the course again. That was over 15 years ago, and it's hard to speculate how much business and money we ended up losing because we "won" that first negotiation. Had we arrived at a win–win payment schedule, we probably would have been invited back many times and made much more money over the long haul.

2. Build negotiating power by emphasizing the possibility of long-term business.

EXECUTIVE SUMMARY: A simple but remarkably effective way to obtain better terms in a negotiation is to emphasize that you have additional business that you would like to bring to the vendor in the future—*if* you are provided with superior terms and service. Emphasizing this point can, in effect, turn you into a very important client who commands premium pricing and treatment. Be wary of requests that lock you into long-term contracts, however. It is difficult to predict your needs many years out. Furthermore, once you are contractually locked in to an agreement, the quality of service you receive might nosedive, and prices may go down in the future.

* * *

As we have stated throughout this book, we have learned the substantial advantages of building long-term, win–win relationships with our employees, customers, and vendors. Long-term, win–win relationships result in our receiving superior service, stability, and quality and help us save time. Furthermore, because we have developed a reputation for forming long-term business relationships with others, we have gained extra leverage that has helped us obtain better terms and saved us a lot of money in our negotiations.

Here's an example. As part of our business, we put on continuing education conferences, and these events are almost always held at hotels. To gain access to the hotel's facilities, secure rooms for our staff and speakers, receive audiovisual support, and be supplied food and beverages, we must contract with and pay the hotel an agreed on amount of money. Now, these conferences are boons for the hotels we deal with, as they can result in anywhere from a low of $10,000 to as much as $200,000 or more in revenue for the hotel. As such, our philosophy has always been to find a hotel that we like, make sure that we get a good deal and good service, and then loyally use that hotel over and over again. For example, there is one hotel in Cape Cod that we have been working with for over 30 years, and we have used other hotels year after year for over ten years. We then use our demonstrable history of loyalty to obtain better terms whenever we expand to new areas and negotiate with new hotels.

Typically, we tell the hotel that we are negotiating with that our business model is to find a long-term partner that we can work with over and over again. We invite them to visit our website, which lists the programs we have put on for the last ten years and shows that we use the same hotels over and over again. We even encourage them to call the other hotels we work with to check up on us. We tell them explicitly that we need a superb but fair win–win deal and that, when we get it, our intention is to use that hotel repeatedly in the future. We have found that emphasizing the possibility of long-term business is an extremely effective negotiating technique when we are in search of new hotel sites for our conferences. Because we state over and over again our hope to come back and work with the hotel year after year, we are in effect greatly multiplying the hotel's potential upside of landing us as a client. As such, instead of looking at us as a one-time, $200,000 client, they look at us as a potential $2,000,000 client over ten years. As you can see, by emphasizing the long-term nature of our business, we effectively turn ourselves from a little client into a potentially big and important one.

We have used this technique effectively with our printers as well. Because we send out over 1,000,000 pieces of business mail each year, we do a lot of printing. As such, whenever we negotiate with a printer, we explain that we have a lot of printing needs and are looking for a long-term partner who will learn our needs and to whom we can give additional business. In turn, we have found that the printers we deal with and spend hundreds of thousands of dollars on each year are receptive and reactive to this argument.

Now, just because lasting relationships can be beneficial for your business does not mean you should allow yourself to become locked in to long-term contractual agreements. Examples of long-term, locked-in deals that have gone south are numerous. In the field of sports, quarterback JaMarcus Russell was signed to a six-year, $68 million contract by the Oakland Raiders. He then ate himself up to 300 pounds and was later cut by the team after it had lost millions on the deal. When Time Warner agreed to merge (a merger being the ultimate long-term arrangement) with America Online, AOL's inflated stock price was valued at twice that of Time Warner, even though the company had less than half the cash flow of Time Warner at the time. AOL has now lost most of its value, the companies have split, and the combined value of the companies is less than one-seventh of their worth on the day of the merger. Airlines also get into trouble after they enter into long-term fuel contracts. For example, Delta Airlines recently reported a $155 million quarterly loss when the price of crude oil went down after it had entered into a long-term fuel contract. These examples all show why we stay away from getting locked into long-term contracts.

3. You are best off dealing with the decision maker, not an underling.

EXECUTIVE SUMMARY: You will obtain more advantageous negotiating results when you deal with the decision maker as opposed to an underling. Underlings want to look good in front of their superiors and may be reluctant to offer you fair terms because they are afraid that they will be perceived as giving away the store. In addition, underlings may not have the authority to give you what you are looking for and may be lazy, unresponsive, and/or uninformed.

* * *

Negotiating theory contains a concept known as trickle-down loss that can be explained as follows: let's say that you are trying to buy a particular item, and the company that is selling this item can do so profitably at a price of $1,000. To see the sale through to completion, you must deal with the assistant sales manager—not the boss. The assistant sales manager, however, may not make any commission if he sells you the item for the $1,000 price. In addition, he would certainly not look good to his boss if he made the sale at the absolute lowest possible price. What are the chances, then, that you can actually buy the item in question for $1,000? They are pretty slim, and trickle-down loss is to blame.

Here is another example of trickle-down loss in action. Let's say you invent and want to sell a simple device that removes splinters. Because you are a savvy businessperson, you want to sell the device to Johnson & Johnson in exchange for a royalty on all sales. The person in charge of licensing devices for Johnson & Johnson instructs a manager to try to license your invention for a 4 percent royalty. This manager, however, wants to be recognized for his work, so he directs a supervisor to try to license the device for a 3 percent royalty. The supervisor also wants to be a hero, so he offers you a 2 percent royalty on all sales. In this situation, trickle-down loss is working against you, so you must negotiate as high up the chain of command as possible to obtain the royalty rate you want.

Trickle-down loss is one of the many reasons you should always, always try to deal with the final decision maker on the other side of a negotiation. Dealing with lower-level employees will almost always cost you money, as these individuals generally are afraid of the consequences of giving away too much in a negotiation and want to look good in front of their superiors. They also may simply not have the authority to give you what you are looking for. Now, we deal with lower-level employees in negotiations all the time. Sometimes we are the buyers, sometimes we are the sellers. A recent negotiation in which we were the sellers is instructive of the difference.

An important part of our business involves selling customized, onsite continuing education courses to other businesses. In other words, we are paid to visit a company's facility, usually for a day or two, and train its staff. When a company contacts us to explore the possibility of hiring us to train its staff, the person on the other end of the line usually want to negotiate with us on the price of our services. The way in which these types of negotiations typically evolve is, first, we are contacted by a training coordinator or another lower-level employee with an inquiry of cost. We then spec out the job and provide the company with a written quote, after which one of many things typically happens. Most common, nothing happens. We never again hear back from the person with whom we were in contact, despite following up with him or her numerous times. It is also common for the individual on the other side of the negotiation to give us some pushback. When this latter situation occurs, the negotiation process is usually lengthy and can sometimes go on for more than a year. Recently, however, we were contacted by the CEO of a huge national engineering firm who wanted us to come in and train his people. We took the CEO's phone call at 11:30 a.m., and by 1:30 p.m., we had a firm training contract in hand. It was the fastest finalization of a training assignment we had ever experienced, and the reason the negotiation had progressed so quickly was that we were dealing with the decision maker. He didn't need to run anything up the flagpole, nor did he have to worry about looking bad in front of his boss. This experience taught us that dealing with decision makers is completely different than dealing with underlings. It also saved us time and made us money.

Another thing that we have learned about underlings is that they can be lazy, unresponsive, and ignorant. Many years ago, when I was practicing lawyer, one of my clients had badly injured his leg. The injury eventually led to an amputation at the knee. I tried over and over again to settle the case with the adjuster that had been assigned to it, but my efforts were in vain, as he was being unresponsive and taking what I considered to be an unreasonably hard line. As such, I decided to go around the underling and try to deal with the decision maker. I took some color photos of my client's oozing stump. I then had these photos blown up into eight-by-ten, glossy images and mailed them to the president of the insurance company, along with a demand for settlement. A few days later, I received a call from the president of the insurance company. He had three things to tell me. First, he had received the photos. Second, he would be meeting my demands forthwith. Third, under no circumstances was I to mail him any photographs again—ever. Dealing directly with the decision maker had clearly paid off.

4. Information is power, so do your homework.

EXECUTIVE SUMMARY: The more information you have, the better the deals you will be able to negotiate. Finding out essential information, such as how much you can buy a given service for elsewhere or how much the potential buyer is willing to spend, is invaluable information.

* * *

Success in negotiating is often the result of how much information you have access to. The more information you have, the better the results of your negotiation will be. As such, doing your homework and unearthing vital information prior to negotiating will help you get better deals. The most basic implementation of this concept, of course, involves shopping around.[2] The typical way in which we shop around is by obtaining competing bids from various vendors. We then use the low bid of a vendor that we *don't* want to do business with to convince the vendor that we do want to do business with

---

[2] See Chapter 5 on the benefits of shopping around.

to lower their price. This is a very basic yet effective technique for obtaining better deals.

A few years ago, for example, I asked one of our employees to get a better deal from one of our main printers. He asked how he could do that, so I told him to obtain lower competing bids and then tell our printer that if they couldn't match those bids, we were going to stop doing business with them. My employee reminded me that he obtains three bids each year from competing printers, and our printer is always the best priced. I then looked my employee straight in the eye and told him, "We are spending hundreds of thousands of dollars a year on printing costs. We need to save money. There are thousands of printers in this country. I don't care if you have to call every printer in North America, or if it takes you the next two months to do so. I want you to make 1,000 percent sure we are getting the best pricing."

After this frank discussion, my employee agreed to dedicate an ample amount of his time to researching competitive bids, and—lo and behold—he found printers that were *significantly* less expensive than the printer we were using. We confronted our current printer with these prices, and he came down a bit on his price, but he said he couldn't match them. As a result, we gave our business to the competition. Then, in a relatively unsurprising turn of events, the next time we contacted our original printer for a competing bid, he was able to beat the lowest prices we could obtain elsewhere. The savings of our new printing prices added up to over one hundred thousand dollars over the course of five years, and this money contributed directly to our bottom line. We were only able to bolster our business and save (i.e., make) money because we were extremely careful about doing our homework and gathering relevant information prior to negotiating.

Here's another example that shows the sheer power of information. A few years back, a governmental agency contacted us and asked us to provide them with our training services. When we asked them what their training budget was, they told us—and even better, they stated that they had to spend the money they had budgeted for training expenses by month's end or else they would lose it. We gave them a price that matched their budget because we knew that's how much they were willing to spend, and *the figure was four times greater than what we would have and could have charged for the training.* The agency accepted our price, and we held the training session for them. In this case, finding out how much the other party was willing to spend helped us negotiate the most favorable terms possible.

5. Develop an alternative to improve your bargaining position.

EXECUTIVE SUMMARY: When you are negotiating with a buyer, seller, or vendor, you will be much more effective and successful if you have alternatives in hand—especially if you can share these alternatives with the person with whom you are negotiating.

* * *

When you actively seek out alternatives, you automatically improve your negotiation power. Let me give you a few examples. When we are looking to hire a printer or secure a hotel for one of our conferences, we always obtain one or more quotes or contracts before we start negotiating with the vendor with whom we most want to do business. Then, after getting that vendor's "best offer," we break out the quotes or contracts that we have previously acquired and simply e-mail them to the party with whom we are negotiating. Doing so proves to the other party that we are doing more than just *talking* about alternatives; it demonstrates that we have hard, readily available alternatives in hand. The effectiveness of this strategy is obvious: when we proceed with negotiations in this manner, we almost always get a better deal from our preferred vendor than their previously extended "best offer."

Here's another example that demonstrates how powerful it can be to have alternatives in hand before you enter into negotiations with another party. When we ask a high-powered professional to serve as a trainer for us, we always enter the inevitable negotiations regarding their fee with a backup or alternative. If the price becomes a sticking point during the negotiation process, we do not fail to mention alternative trainers who will do the work within our budget. This strategy usually convinces our first-choice trainer to accept the fee we are offering.

We use this technique in our personal lives as well. Recently, I discovered that my neighbor was paying $35 to his landscaper each time his lawn was cut. I had been paying my landscaper $45 per cutting for a similar-sized lawn, so I called up my neighbor's landscaper, who told me that he could cut my lawn for $35 as well. Then I called up my landscaper and asked for a better deal. She told me that I was already getting a great deal and that I was lucky she hadn't raised my price in several years. I politely told her that I thought she was overpriced and that I had a quote in hand for $35. I then proceeded to ask her to meet this competing quote. She did because she correctly suspected that I would use my alternative if she didn't agree. If I didn't have an alternative lined up, however, I don't think I would have been able to obtain better pricing.

6. Beware of weak links in your negotiating team.

EXECUTIVE SUMMARY: When negotiating as a team, it is critical that every team member is on the same page. Furthermore, one team member—and one team member alone—should be in charge of the negotiations. Anyone who has loose lips, is not a team player, or is a poor negotiator (in other words, a weak link) needs to be kept off the negotiating team and left at home.

* * *

Team negotiations, in which more than one representative from your company negotiates with parties from the other side, require special care. In particular, when more than one of your team members attends a negotiation discussion, it is extremely important that only one person does the talking and that everybody is on the same page. Failure to follow these all-important rules can lead to disaster.

Recall that in *The Godfather*, the Corleone family is approached by a rival family, who offers them the opportunity to get into the narcotics business. At the meeting, however, Sonny Corleone expresses disagreement with his father, the Don. Because Sonny is not on the same page as his father, the Don suffers an assassination attempt and a costly and bloody war breaks out. All of these consequences could have been avoided if Sonny had just kept his mouth shut and let one person do all of the talking. Now, let's be honest: Our business is unlikely to confront the same challenges face by the Corleone family in *The Godfather*. Regardless, whenever more than one of us are involved in a negotiation; we have learned to adhere to the following four rules. First, we agree on what our goals are. Second, we agree on the limits of the negotiation. Third, we agree on who the negotiator will be and appoint that person to do all of the talking during the negotiation. Fourth, we make sure we keep any weak links as far away as possible from the negotiation.

What do we mean by a weak link? A weak link is a person who is unsuited for negotiating—especially team negotiating. As such, weak links can include employees who like to hear themselves talk, like to feel important, are not team players, have loose lips, or are just poor negotiators. In *The Godfather* example above, Sonny was clearly the weak link in his family's negotiations. He should have been left at home and not brought to the conversation.

We have had countless experiences over the years that have demonstrated the perils of allowing a weak link anywhere near a negotiation conversation. For example, I was part of a three-person team that was tasked with negotiating with a large insurance company for a training contract. I sat next to our team's weak link during the negotiation proceedings, and though I did my best to control his contributions to the negotiation, I lost sight of him during a break, when one of the team members from the insurance company asked if he would help carry a few boxes of materials into the conference room. We lost the contract, and I later found out that the reason the insurance company had hired another trainer was because of how our weak link had responded to a question he had been asked during the time that he was out of my sight:

Q: Do we really need to hire all three of you and your partners to do this training?

A: No, not really. I could probably do it myself for less than half the price.

The moral to the story is as follows: always leave your weak link at home.

7. Be prepared to walk away.

EXECUTIVE SUMMARY: Make sure that the person with whom you are negotiating understands that you are prepared to walk away from the deal at any time. When the other party in a negotiation realizes that you can take or leave a deal, you will gain leverage over him or her, as it will appear as though you do not need the deal. This technique works effectively with both vendors and sales prospects.

* * *

To succeed as a negotiator, you need to make the person with whom you are negotiating believe that you are prepared to walk away from the deal at any time. When you give off such an impression, you are communicating to the other party that although you may be interested in the deal, you certainly don't need the deal. This, in turn, gives you power and leverage, as the person with whom you are negotiating will fear that you just might walk away from the deal.

We have learned that this negotiation technique can be quite effective, especially if you leverage it against long-term vendors, who you will need to negotiate with regarding disputes from time to time. The nature of the disputes you might have with your long-term vendors could range from a charge that you contest or your displeasure at the level and quality of the service that you have been provided. For example, recently we received shoddy service from and were over billed by a hotel that we had been using for a number of years. One of their employees had treated us rudely and unfairly and had tried to rip us off, so we called the hotel to receive an adjustment on our bill and express our displeasure. At first, the answer we received was unsatisfactory: "Well, I am sorry you feel this way, but those are our prices, and the services were delivered." We then pointedly reminded the sales manager that hotels in his area are constantly contacting us to get our business. Second, we noted that although we would like to continue doing business with them for the next 20 years, we can only do so if we get great service and aren't taken advantage of. Finally, we asked if he wanted our continued business or if he wanted us to go somewhere else. We then casually mentioned a few of the hotel's competitors.

After we pushed back with these talking points, the dynamic of the conversation completely changed. The hotel immediately agreed to drop the disputed charge and apologized for the behavior of its employee. Because we reminded the hotel that we were ready, willing, and able to walk away from the negotiation, we motivated their action. In sum, we had successfully communicated to the hotel that if it failed to be reasonable, they might win the bill dispute, but they would lose many times more than the cost of the bill in future lost business.

It may seem counterintuitive, but you can even use your willingness to walk away from a negotiation to your advantage when you are trying to sell your products or services to a prospective client. We do this all the time. For example, typically we quote out projects, and then our client will need to run it up the flagpole or think it over. As anyone in sales knows, convincing a prospective client to close the deal is often an enormous challenge. Some salespeople will spend weeks, months, even years wining and dining prospective clients in an attempt to close the sale. We take a somewhat different approach, however. Quite simply, we demonstrate to the prospective client that we don't need his or her business and are prepared to walk away from the deal. We typically do so by sending a very short e-mail that contains the simple question, "Should I close my file?" This question communicates negotiation power and helps prod the prospect into making a decision. We can't tell you how many prospects have been successfully prodded to take favorable action by our asking this simple question, which communicates that we don't need to make the deal.

Another effective way to communicate that you are ready, willing, and able to walk away from a deal is to offer the prospective client a cheaper (but not as good) alternative. Here is how this conversation usually goes:

CLIENT: We would like you to do a full marketing consultation and plan for our company.

AUTHORS: We would be happy to assist. We have done dozens of these successfully. The all-inclusive price is $7,500.

CLIENT: We heard about the quality of your work, but the price is too high. Can you lower the price?

AUTHORS: I'm sorry, but no. We do not sacrifice the quality of our work. I can recommend Mr. Jones if you want a lower price. Do you have a pen?

CLIENT: No—we need the services you provide. We will bite the bullet and pay the $7,500.

8. Nothing should be agreed to until everything is agreed to.

EXECUTIVE SUMMARY: Do not agree to any given term in a negotiation unless you know exactly what you are getting yourself into. Often times, you may need to negotiate many crucially important contractual details *besides* the price. Nothing should be agreed to until everything is agreed to.

* * *

During contentious negotiations, U.S. House Speaker John Boehner often responds to rumors pertaining to Congress's progress by saying, "Nothing is agreed to until everything is agreed to." Boehner's negotiating philosophy is one that we agree with wholeheartedly. Unfortunately, however, we've seen far too many people get themselves into trouble by not focusing on all the terms of a deal.

Here's an example. One of the niches in which we operate involves assisting physicians who want to stop practicing clinical medicine. There are many reasons that doctors may want to leave the field of medicine. Some are frustrated that they aren't making enough money while others detest the paperwork and bureaucracy of dealing with the government and insurance companies. One of the most common reasons doctors want to stop practicing medicine, however, is that they want a change in lifestyle. You see, many doctors work very long hours. Even worse, they are on call frequently, which means that they can and do get emergency calls at all hours of the day and night. Living the lifestyle of a doctor is very challenging. It takes a toll on the doctors, their health, and their family life.

What we have found when we work with client physicians is that many of them tell similar stories about their backgrounds. First, most of them were great students. Second, they generally always wanted to be doctors or family members pushed them into becoming doctors. Third, they ran up huge debts getting through medical school. Finally, and most important, *they negotiated terrible employment contracts because they focused only on their salaries.* Here's what we mean: when you are thinking about accepting a job offer, it is absolutely critical that you find out everything you can about the position and the company in question before you agree to anything. There are all kinds of details related to the offer that may be as much or more important than your salary. For example, a doctor should also be asking: what kind of hours will I need to work? How often do I need to take calls? When and how can I buy into the practice? Am I allowed to make money on the side? If so, how much? How much time off will I be provided with? Unfortunately, however, many doctors typically make the critical and avoidable mistake of agreeing to take a job before they know all of the relevant details about the position. Then, as soon as they agree to a salary that sounds decent, their new employer hits them with all kinds of unfavorable twists, such as requiring them to be on call for four nights every week, all year long.

We are very careful to avoid making a similar mistake. The mantra that we, like Boehner, follow all of the time is that nothing is agreed to until everything is agreed to. For example, we have been approached many times by businesses that are looking to acquire our business. Each time we enter into these types of negotiations, the selling price is only one of the many issues that we are concerned about. We also need to know when the selling price would be paid, how it would be paid (cash or stock), what types of employment agreements would be involved, what languages would be included in the noncompete clause, how long the noncompete clause would stay in effect, and so on. This issue also comes up when we are quoting jobs to prospective clients. We never quote a price until we have had a chance to talk to the prospect on the phone. Why? Because we need to understand exactly what types of services they are looking for before we can offer them a price. In other words, we need to know everything; otherwise, we can offer nothing.

* * *

Every penny saved or made through better negotiating directly contributes to your business's bottom line. By stating that you are looking for long-term, win–win relationships, dealing with the decision maker, doing your homework, and making sure to agree to nothing until everything is agreed to you, will become a better negotiator. We truly hope you have found the lessons we have provided in this book to be helpful. It is our earnest hope that you will learn from our successes and mistakes and that your business will prosper over both the near and long term.

Index

P, Q, R

S

T, U

V

W, X, Y, Z

CPSIA information can be obtained at www.ICGtesting.com
Printed in the USA
LVOW121732211212

312807LV00002B/219/P

9 781430 247678